Beethoven Essays

Beethoven Essays

*Studies in Honor
of Elliot Forbes*

Edited by
Lewis Lockwood and Phyllis Benjamin

Harvard University Department of Music

Distributed by Harvard University Press
Cambridge, Massachusetts
1984

Library of Congress Cataloging in Publication Data
Main entry under title:

Beethoven essays.

    Includes indexes.
    1. Beethoven, Ludwig van, 1770–1827. 2. Forbes,
Elliot. I. Forbes, Elliot. II. Lockwood, Lewis.
III. Benjamin, Phyllis.
ML410.B4B2814   1984   780'.92'4   84–10834
ISBN 0–674–06378–3

The editors wish to acknowledge the assistance of Warren Blumenfeld in the preparation
of this volume.

Contents

Plates

Preface

To those familiar with Beethoven scholarship over the past twenty-five years, the name of Elliot Forbes needs no introduction. For them "Forbes" represents the modern half of the celebrated pair of authors whose product, known in the trade simply as "Thayer-Forbes," denotes the standard modern revised edition of the great 19th-century classic of Beethoven biography: Thayer's *Life of Beethoven*. Long before Elliot Forbes set to work in the 1950s to complete his revised version of Thayer's monumental book, it had at various times been edited, augmented, and translated by others. Its publishing history is among the most complex of any major biography in any field. But in Forbes's edition of 1964, Thayer's text was provided for the first time to modern readers in the form that is closest to Thayer's original intentions. The result is that "Thayer-Forbes" is one of the canonic pairings in musicology. It takes its place in an honorable line of musicological *Doppelmeister* that includes Jahn and Abert, Kinsky and Halm, and—closer to home—David and Mendel, Apel and Davison.

Yet "Thayer-Forbes" is only the most conspicuous of Forbes's contributions to Beethoven scholarship. His articles and editions, especially the Norton Critical Score of the Fifth Symphony—along with his work as choral conductor and as teacher on the undergradute and graduate levels at two great universities—are all facets of a deep-seated interest in, and love for, the music of Beethoven that has been widely communicated to generations of students, to colleagues and friends, to the musicological fraternity, and to the broad musical public.

This volume is intended essentially as a tribute to El Forbes as a Beethoven scholar. It has for that reason a special focus upon this aspect of his professional work. It does not attempt even partially to reflect, or to acknowledge formally, the breadth of his other activities as teacher and conductor, especially of choral music, or his work in early years as conductor of the Princeton Freshman Glee Club (1947–50) and his much longer association with the Harvard Glee Club (1945–47 and 1958–70). Only indirectly can it provide an echo of what he accomplished during his eleven years on the Princeton faculty (1947–58), and thereafter for twenty-six years on the Harvard faculty (1958–84), where he has been Fanny Peabody Professor of Music since 1961. What he has contributed in the classroom, in tutorials, in the give-and-take of friendly contact with generations of students and colleagues—all this remains to be acknowledged, as it certainly will be, in other ways. Nevertheless, if I may write as one of his former graduate students at Princeton, who took his first graduate seminar on Beethoven there under El Forbes, in the mid-1950s, I can hardly refrain from at least this brief mention of these important aspects of his career.

It was, in fact, in that seminar, devoted to the problem of revising Thayer's *Life*, that I first glimpsed some of the complexities of biographical research on Beethoven. Thayer, like Forbes, was a Harvard man. Born in 1817 in Natick, Massachusetts, he had attended Harvard College and graduated in 1843; he had first conceived the idea of working on Beethoven's biography as early as 1845. Despite the complex circumstances of his later career, which saw him at first shuttling back and forth between the United States and Germany, then from 1865 onward serving as United States Consul in Trieste, Thayer persevered in his work until his death in 1897. Not only was he able to take advantage of important Beethoven documents in Bonn and Cologne, plus others that were gradually becoming available through bequests to the Berlin Library, but he was able to make personal contact with a number of older contemporaries who had known Beethoven in his later years.

In the rigorous spirit of fact-finding historiography that dominated the mid-19th century, Thayer worked assiduously to establish the historical record and to correct legends that had sprung up in the wake of Beethoven's emergence as a Romantic artist of gigantic stature. Against a hero-worshiping trend, Thayer strove to maintain a firmly rational and objective approach to the gathering and sifting of biographical data, with a cool avoidance of rhetoric and flourish. In the spirit of the enterprise as he saw it, he intended in the final version to forgo extended critical discussion of the stylistic aspects of Beethoven's works. Not that this was truly outside his interests, as his other writings show; but he believed the long-range value of his biography to lie not in analytical commentary but rather in the ordering and presentation of the vast array of documents that were being supplied to the public for the first time.

The later and remarkable history of Thayer's *Life*—first in the hands of his earliest editor and translator, Hermann Deiters; still later in the greatly expanded version brought out by Hugo Riemann; and then in the first English version, by Henry E. Krehbiel—has been told in great detail by Elliot Forbes in the preface to his own Thayer and need not be recounted here. But what must be stressed, again, is that in Thayer-Forbes, Forbes's main accomplishment lay in restoring the book to the form in which Thayer would have wanted it, and also in bringing it up to date in the light of modern Beethoven scholarship by means of copious annotations. He did so despite the loss of Thayer's personal papers and notes, which unfortunately disappeared after Krehbiel had made use of them sometime before 1914.

Yet if we are not able to present El Forbes with those old and yellowing Thayer papers, which he did so ably without, we are delighted instead to present him now with what I shall call instead the "Forbes papers." This volume contains new studies on a wide range of Beethovenian topics by both American and European scholars, all dealing with current historical or critical problems. The first group is made up of biographical studies, arranged in chronological order by subject. For Beethoven's early years, James Webster provides an important new study of the known documentation that records the personal relationship between the young Beethoven and the aging Haydn, a topic that has long been controversial in the biographies of both men. Martin Staehelin, in recent years Director of the Beethoven Archiv in Bonn, offers a new document that seems to convey a judgment on the young Beethoven by the learned composer and teacher Johann Georg Albrechtsberger, who became Beethoven's tutor in counterpoint after Haydn's departure for England in 1794. From the later years of Beethoven's career comes a newly found price list of 1822, published here for the first time by Alan Tyson. And from the later world of Thayeriana, Maynard Solomon gives us an essay on contacts between Oscar Sonneck, one of the founding figures in American musicology, and Henry Edward Krehbiel, which sheds light on the relationship between the two at the time of Krehbiel's work on his edition of Thayer's *Life*. Finally in this section Michael Ochs contributes a valuable list of Thayer's writings in that venerable 19th-century Boston music periodical, *Dwight's Journal of Music*.

The other set of essays deals with important individual works. Two concern early concertos. Edward T. Cone brings his deep experience as composer and critic to bear on the problem of completing an unfinished cadenza for the First Piano Concerto. Geoffrey Block, who wrote his doctoral dissertation at Harvard under Elliot Forbes's direction, discusses aspects of the background material for the Second Concerto. Christopher Reynolds writes on the second of Beethoven's finales for the Violin Sonata in A Major, Op. 30, no. 1, while Sieghard Brandenburg, recently appointed Director of the Beethoven-Archiv, offers a major study of the entire body of extant source material for the third movement of the Fifth Symphony. This offers solid new light on the problem, recently much discussed, of whether this movement should or should not be performed with repeats. Finally, J. Merrill Knapp and Robert Winter supply valuable essays on the two Beethoven Masses: Knapp on the C Major Mass, Op. 86, and Winter on the source material for the *Missa solemnis,* Op. 123. Thus, appropriately, the volume ends with studies of what are, by common consent, the greatest of Beethoven's purely choral compositions (omitting the Ninth Symphony from that category) and closes with a Forbesian ring after all.

This cross-section of current Beethoven research is the collective gift of Beethovenians who owe much to Thayer-Forbes and also to El Forbes for his other basic contributions to Beethoven scholarship over the past thirty years. Yet at the same time I feel certain that it mirrors only a small part of the respect, warmth, and affection that so many of El Forbes's Beethovenian colleagues feel for him.

—Lewis Lockwood

List of Benefactors

The persons listed below have made a contribution to the Department's Publication Fund in honor of Elliot Forbes. On behalf of the Department of Music, I wish to express my gratitude to them for making it possible to present this volume as a tribute to a beloved teacher, scholar, colleague, and friend.

Christoph Wolff, Chairman
June 15, 1984

Guilliaem Aertsen III
H. Peter Aitken
Henry F. Allen
Edward Phelps Allis IV
James B. Ames
William & Elizabeth Austin
G. d'Andelot Belin
John Louis Bremer II
Peter C. Brooks
Robert Manton Burnett
Daniel Sargent Cheever
Hoima Forbes Cherau
Francis Douglas Cochrane
Charles C. & Amy Lee Colt
Loring, Jr. & Louise Conant
John & Melba Coolidge
William Crout
Rodney G. Dennis
Charles W. Dunn

William Edgar, Jr.
William & Lois Edgerly
Mason Fernald
John Mansfield Ferry
John H. Finley
John Wyman Flint
A. Irving Forbes
Anne Forbes
Charles Forbes
David C. Forbes
John M. & Wendy Forbes
Stephen H. Forbes
Richard F. French
Paul Fromm
Janet F. Frothingham
John L. & Susan K. Gardner
Rodman Gilder
Rollin Van N. Hadley
Mason Hammond

Abbreviations

Anderson	Emily Anderson, ed., *The Letters of Beethoven*, 3 vols. (London, 1961)
DSB	Deutsche Staatsbibliothek, Berlin
GdM	Gesellschaft der Musikfreunde, Vienna
Hess	Willy Hess, *Verzeichnis der nicht in der Gesamtausgabe veröffentlichten Werke Ludwig van Beethovens* (Wiesbaden, 1957)
Kinsky-Halm	Georg Kinsky, *Das Werk Beethovens: thematisch-bibliographisches Verzeichnis seiner sämtlichen vollendeten Kompositionen*, completed and ed. Hans Halm (Munich and Duisburg, 1955)
N I	Gustav Nottebohm, *Beethoveniana* (Leipzig and Winterthur, 1872)
N II	Gustav Nottebohm, *Zweite Beethoveniana: nachgelassene Aufsätze* (Leipzig, 1887)
N 1865	Gustav Nottebohm, *Ein Skizzenbuch von Beethoven* (Leipzig, 1865); Eng. trans. in *Two Beethoven Sketchbooks* (London, 1979), pp. 3–43
New Grove	*The New Grove Dictionary of Music and Musicians*, ed. Stanley Sadie, 20 vols. (London, 1980)
PrStB	former Preussische Staatsbibliothek, Berlin
Schindler (1840)	Anton Schindler, *Biographie von Ludwig van Beethoven* (Münster, 1840); Eng. trans. as *The Life of Beethoven*, ed. I. Moscheles, 2 vols. (London, 1841)

Schindler (1860)	Anton Schindler, *Biographie von Ludwig van Beethoven*, 2 vols. (3rd ed. Münster, 1860); Eng. trans. as *Beethoven As I Knew Him*, ed. Donald W. MacArdle (London, 1966)
SBH	Hans Schmidt, "Die Beethoven Handschriften des Beethovenhauses in Bonn," *Beethoven-Jahrbuch*, VII (1971), vii-xxiv, 1–443
SPK	Staatsbibliothek Preussischer Kulturbesitz, Berlin
SV	Hans Schmidt, "Verzeichnis der Skizzen Beethovens," *Beethoven-Jahrbuch*, VI (1969), 7–128
Thayer I (1866) II (1872) III (1879)	Alexander Wheelock Thayer, *Ludwig van Beethoven's Leben*, 3 vols. (Berlin, 1866, 1872, 1879)
Thayer-Deiters-Riemann I-V	Alexander Wheelock Thayer, *Ludwig van Beethovens Leben*, continued Hermann Deiters, rev. Vol. I (Berlin, 1901); completed Hugo Riemann, Vols. IV-V (Leipzig, 1907, 1908), rev. Vols. II-III (Leipzig, 1910, 1911), rev. Deiters's 1901 ed. of Vol. I (Leipzig, 1917); Vols. II-V Reissued (Leipzig, 1922–23)
Thayer-Forbes	*Thayer's Life of Beethoven*, rev. and ed. Elliot Forbes, 2 vols. (Princeton, 1964)
Thayer-Krehbiel	Alexander Wheelock Thayer, *The Life of Ludwig van Beethoven*, Eng. trans. ed. Henry Edward Krehbiel, 3 vols. (New York, 1921)
Wegeler-Ries	Franz Gerhard Wegeler and Ferdinand Ries, *Biographische Notizen über Ludwig van Beethoven* (Coblenz, 1838), suppl. by Wegeler (Coblenz, 1845); Eng. trans. ed. Alan Tyson (in preparation)
WoO	Werk(e) ohne Opuszahl (work(s) without an opus number) in the listing of Kinsky-Halm

Beethoven:

Biography and Biographers

The Falling-out Between Haydn and Beethoven: The Evidence of the Sources

James Webster

Several recent much-admired biographies offer provocative psychological interpretations of what are said to have been the difficult and prob-
lematical relations between Haydn and Beethoven. Maynard Solomon
writes of a relationship that "took on a complex and tangled character
from the very start," and states that around 1800 in particular Beethoven
"felt the weight of Haydn's influence . . . as an impediment to the
growth of his own musical individuality." Conversely, Haydn was "unable to follow Beethoven beyond the limits of the high-Classic style
which he himself had perfected . . . [unable] to comprehend
Beethoven's greater achievements." Alan Tyson states, "Temperamen-
tally . . . they were set for conflict. . . . [Beethoven] was bound to feel
the genius of 'Papa' Haydn standing in his way, one more father to be
defied or circumvented." H. C. Robbins Landon writes of their "mutual
distrust which was to take on extremely nasty overtones," and of "direct
confrontations," not only in composition but even in the daily rounds of
Viennese musical life.[1] And without directly addressing the question of

This study has materially benefited from comments by Sieghard Brandenburg,
Douglas Johnson, Richard Kramer, Maynard Solomon, Alan Tyson, and Horst Walter.
For this reason, and because some aspects of my treatment may be found controversial, I
must emphasize even more strongly than is customary that these authorities cannot be
presumed to agree with my arguments, and that none of them is responsible for any
errors of fact or interpretation that may remain.

[1]Maynard Solomon, *Beethoven* (New York, 1977), pp. 68, 74–75, 77. Alan Tyson and
Joseph Kerman, "Beethoven," *New Grove* II, 357; cf. 360; the revised version of this essay
published in book form (London and New York, 1983) makes it clear that the biographical sections are by Tyson, the analytical ones by Kerman. H. C. Robbins Landon, *Haydn:
Chronicle and Works*, 5 vols. (London and Bloomington, 1976–80), III, 224; IV, 502–8; V,
256–59. An important survey that eschews psychological interpretation is Horst Walter,
"Die biographischen Beziehungen zwischen Haydn und Beethoven," in Carl Dahlhaus
et al., ed., *Bericht über den Internationalen musikwissenschaftlichen Kongress Bonn 1970* (Kassel [1973]), pp. 79–83. A recent lecture on this subject by Brandenburg will appear in the
report of the symposium "Joseph Haydn in seiner Zeit" (Eisenstadt, 1982), scheduled to
appear in 1984 as Vol. 13 of *Jahrbuch für österreichische Kulturgeschichte*, ed. Gerda Mraz.

their personal relations, Joseph Kerman and Douglas Johnson similarly stress Beethoven's need to assert compositional independence from Haydn in the 1790s.[2] In Haydn's case, too, we are beginning to become dimly aware of the necessity of moving away from the "Papa Haydn" myth and of interpreting his complex personality more accurately and sensitively.[3]

I do not quarrel with these interpretive tendencies. Our desires in this direction comprise part of today's general intellectual orientation, and their appearance in the biographies of the great composers, as a corrective to the witless mythologizing of yesteryear, comes none too soon. But they have, so far, largely glossed over the question of the accuracy and reliability of the *sources* for this tradition of a falling-out between the aging champion and his impatient challenger. The present study therefore seeks to establish the degree of reliability and independence of these sources. They are listed in Table 1, along with the dates of the authors' personal contact with the principals, the events reported on, and some details of their dissemination.[4] The Appendix quotes the relevant passages. To give the results in brief: No direct word or action of Haydn's or Beethoven's, and few reliable contemporary observers, document any falling-out or feeling of artistic incompatibility between the two. The tradition to this effect depends chiefly on anecdotal accounts, of which almost all originated after Beethoven's death, and many seem marked by special pleading.

*   *   *   *   *

The elementary prerequisites for credibility in a witness are that one be testifying without bias to events personally experienced, within a reasonable period of time after their occurrence. The majority of the authors listed in Table 1 lack persuasiveness in this regard. Of the thirteen persons listed, only Georg August Griesinger, probably Giuseppe Carpani

[2]Joseph Kerman, *The Beethoven Quartets* (New York, 1966), esp. Chapter 1; Douglas Johnson, "1794–1795: Decisive Years in Beethoven's Early Development," in Tyson, ed., *Beethoven Studies 3* (Cambridge, 1982), pp. 1–28; here, 16 ff. A recent influential work of literary criticism based on similar assumptions is Harold Bloom, *The Anxiety of Influence* (New York, 1973). For a comprehensive survey of Haydn's and Beethoven's stylistic relations¹(not treating the kinds of structural and psychological issues raised by Kerman, Johnson, and Solomon), see Georg Feder, "Stilelemente Haydns in Beethovens Werken," *Bericht über den . . . Kongress Bonn 1970* (cf. n. 1), pp. 65–70.

[3]See Feder, "Joseph Haydn als Mensch und Musiker," in Mraz, ed., *Joseph Haydn und seine Zeit (= Jahrbuch für österreichische Kulturgeschichte*, I/2 [1972]), pp. 57–68; James Webster, "Prospects for Haydn Biography After Landon," *The Musical Quarterly*, LXVIII (1982), 476–95.

[4]Works cited in Table 1 and its notes appear in the notes to the main text only in short-title form. In Table 1, material in square brackets represents conjecture (as to authors and dates) or editorial additions.

Table 1

Sources Reporting on Ill-feeling or Conflict between Haydn and Beethoven

Name	Dates of Contact	Dates of Events Described	Dates of Writing	Nature of Source; Original Dissemination	Modern Editions[a]
1 Carpani	H: ?c. 1796—[b] B: 1808 (1806?)[b]	After 1800?	"25 Sept. 1811"	(1) *Le Haydine* (Milan, 1812; 2nd ed. Padua, 1823) [(2) Bertini, *Dizionario*[c]	Facs. of 2nd ed.: Bologna, 1969 Solomon, 77]
2 Czerny	H: ? B: c. 1801—	c. 1795–1805	1842	Autobiography (MS); publ. (in part) *Jahresbericht der Ges. d. Mfr. in Wien*, 1870, 4-10	Kerst, I, 39 ff.
3 Czerny			1852?	Orally to Otto Jahn (Jahn's notes left to PrStB)	Kerst, I, 47 ff.
4 Doležalek	B: c. 1800—	c. 1799[1795?]–1808	1852	Orally to Jahn	Kerst, II, 191 ff.
5 Drouet	B: ? (1816? 1822?)[d]	c. 1793–95	?	J. F. Kayser, *Ztg. f. Gesangvereine u. Liedertafeln*, II (1858), 67 f.	Thayer-Deiters-Riemann II, 197 ff.
6 Fuchs	——		—1846	Vienna AMZ, 1846, No. 39	Kerst, I, 108 f.
7 Griesinger	H: 1799— B: 1800—	1800–08	1799—	Letters to Härtel	W. Hitzig, *Der Bär*, 1927, 23-24; G. Thomas, *Haydn-Studien*, I (1965-68), 49-114

Table 1 (Continued)

Sources Reporting on Ill-feeling or Conflict between Haydn and Beethoven

Name	Dates of Contact	Dates of Events Described	Dates of Writing	Nature of Source; Original Dissemination	Modern Editions[a]
8 Griesinger		(a) 1814— (b) ?	1816 Apr. 1827	Letters to Böttger	H. Volkmann (cf. Thomas, 50 n.), quoted Thomas, 113 f.
9 Marx	——	[1801]	—1859	*Ludwig van Beethoven*, 2 v. (Berlin, 1859; 2nd ed. 1863)	Kalischer, *Beethoven u. seine Zeitgenossen*, IV,7 [from 2nd ed.]
10 Moscheles	B: c. 1808—	[c. 1799–1801]	?	Diary; publ. *Aus Moscheles' Leben* (1872), tr. *Life of Moscheles by his Wife* (London, 1873)	Solomon, p. 340, n. 47
11 Ries	H: ?1802—[e] B: Winter 1801-02—	c. 1803 [in (b) and (d) reporting from c. 1795]	1836–37 (cf. n. 10)	Wegeler-Ries (1838)	Kerst, I, 90 ff.
12a Schenk	H: ?[f] B: 1793-94; 1824?	1793	1830	(1) Autobiog. (MS) (1830)[g]	*SMw*, XI (1924), 75 ff.

12b [Schenk?]				(2) Jahn, copy of same; publ. Thayer I, Vol. 2, p. 411 ff.	Kerst, I, 25 ff.
				Condensed, altered version of (12a), anonymous, in *Der Freischütz* (Vienna), Vol. 13, No. 4, Jan. 28, 1837, p. 58 f.[h]	Thayer I, Vol. 1, p. 380 ff.
13 Schenk				Luib, reporting on Schenk's oral account (reported by Jahn)	Kerst, I, 29 f.
14 Schindler	B: 1814; c. 1820—	(a) 1793 (b) 1824	—1839	Schindler (1840)	
15 Seyfried	H: ?[j] B: ?c.1797—; 1803—	1793	After 1830	"Schenk," in Schilling, *Encyc. musik. Wissenschaften*, 6 v. (Stuttgart, 1835–38)	Thayer-Deiters-Riemann I, 353 f.
16 Seyfried		c. 1801—	—1832	*Beethoven's Studien* (Vienna, 1832), *Anhang*	Kerst, I, 77 ff.
17 F. Lorenz		[1790s?]	—1863	*Recensionen und Mittheilungen über Theater und Musik* (Vienna), Vol. 9, No. 33, August 16, 1863, pp. 513 ff.	—

[a]In the case of oft-reprinted material, only a single modern source is given, usually Friedrich Kerst, ed., *Die Erinnerungen an Beethoven*, 2 vols. (Stuttgart, 1913; repr. 1925). In the Appendix I have of course quoted the original whenever possible; the source is cited there for each entry. References to widely available English translations are given following each passage; where none exists, an original translation is appended. An exception is made for Passages 12b and 13, which are not translated here despite the absence of English translations, because of their dependence on (12a).

[b]Carpani's personal acquaintance with Haydn seems to be documented only by his own accounts of it, and perhaps also by his having made the Italian translation of the libretto of the *Creation*, "at the express order of the Empress," as Griesinger wrote to Härtel (Thomas, p. 71). The dates of his sojourn(s) in Vienna are uncertain; cf. the partially conflicting statements in Vernon Gotwals, "The Earliest Biographies of Haydn," *The Musical Quarterly*, XLV (1959), 439–59; Richard N. Coe, foreword to his translations of Stendhal, *Haydn, Mozart and Metastasio* (New York, 1972), pp. xviii-xx; Landon, *Haydn*, IV, 126. He must have arrived there late in 1796, if not earlier, and must have been there in the spring of 1798 for the premiere of the *Creation* (to judge by his description of it in *Le Haydine*) and c. 1800–04 (to judge by the appearance of his translation of the *Creation* in Artaria's piano-vocal score [Hoboken, II, 39], and by the premieres of Weigl's opera *L'uniforme* and oratorio *La passione di Gesù*, both on his texts [see Rudolf Angermüller, "Weigl," *New Grove*, XX, 297]). The only known indications of an acquaintance with Beethoven are the latter's setting of his verses (WoO 133) in 1806–07 (not 1808, as suggested by Anderson's date for the sole surviving letter, no. 171; cf. Tyson, " 'In questa tomba oscura,' " in Harry Goldschmidt et al., ed., *Bericht über den Internationalen Beethoven-Kongress Berlin 1977* [Leipzig, 1978], pp. 239–45); and the undocumented anecdote of Carpani's introduction of Rossini to Beethoven in 1822.

[c]The passage from Giuseppe Bertini, *Dizionario storio-critico degli scrittori di musica*, I (Palermo, 1814), 96, quoted in translation by Solomon, is an almost exact duplicate of Carpani and must have been copied from him.

[d]There seems to be no direct evidence other than Drouet's own statement for any personal contact between Drouet and Beethoven. Landon (IV, 63) asserts that he was in Vienna in 1816, without documentation; Thayer-Deiters-Riemann and, by implication, Philip Bate in *New Grove*, V, 638, assume 1822.

[e]I know of no evidence for a personal acquaintance between Ries and Haydn save Ries's own statements in (11). But he did study with Albrechtsberger, presumably in 1801–02, according to the biographical sketch in the *Harmonicon* (1824; information kindly supplied by Alan Tyson).

[f]It seems highly likely that Schenk knew Haydn from general conditions of Viennese musical life, and perhaps well before 1790. Passage 17, if accurate, must prove that unpleasant personal contact had taken place.

[g]Thought by Thayer, Deiters, Riemann, Kerst, etc., to be lost, Schenk's manuscript autobiography was located by Rosenfeld-Römer (cf. n. 11) in Göttweig, where it had come from Fuchs's estate.

[h]The first published version (information generously supplied by Horst Walter).

[i]Seyfried's account in Passage 16 implies that he heard Haydn ask after Beethoven. He and Haydn must have been acquainted in the normal course of Viennese musical life from c. 1797 on; cf., for example, J. F. Berwald's report of their attendance at a soirée *chez* Fries in 1799 (Mörner, p. 7). Seyfried claimed in 1841 that Haydn had written him thanking him for a successful *Singspiel* in 1799 (cf. Pohl-Botstiber, p. 115; *Haydn Briefe*, No. 237). There is no independent corroboration that they should have been as friendly as the tone and content of (16) imply.

and Johann Baptist Schenk, and perhaps Ferdinand Ries and Ignaz von Seyfried had personal contact with Haydn (see the notes to Table 1). Nine had personal contact with Beethoven; Adolf Bernhard Marx certainly had none, and Aloys Fuchs and Franz Lorenz almost certainly did not; the case for Louis Drouet is conjectural at best.

More to the point is that only a modest proportion of the incidents could have been witnessed by those reporting on them. Carpani and Marx expressly designate their reports as hearsay or "tradition"; the same is true of Ries's account of Haydn's never having written a string quintet (beginning with the second sentence of Passage 11c). Drouet, Fuchs, Marx, Moscheles, Ries (regarding Beethoven's Op. 1, no. 3 and Haydn's request that Beethoven acknowledge that he was a "pupil of Haydn"), Anton Schindler (Passage 14a), and Seyfried in (15) could not have been present at the events they describe. An equally damaging point is that, except for Carpani and Griesinger, the accounts originated not merely long after the events, but after Beethoven's death. An account from a man in late middle or old age, written or (worse) told at thirty to fifty years' remove, about a figure who in the meantime had become a culture-hero and whose friendship had therefore become one of the greatest events in the storyteller's life, must be treated with great skepticism—even if its author is Czerny or Ries. The more circumstantial the detail, the greater the extent of "quoted" dialogue, the more suspect it must be.

Internal evidence suggests the extent of such unreliability. Czerny (Passage 2) portrays the contemporary opposition to Beethoven in lurid, highly exaggerated terms; there is no evidence of such widespread, passionate opposition.[5] Johann Emanuel Doleželek's naughty one-liners in (4) hardly give the impression of accurate reportage. Perhaps Koželuch really disliked Op. 1, no. 3 (see 4b), but it seems more likely that Doleželek was elaborating on Ries, whose anecdote focusing on this work (11b) he would have read between its appearance in 1838 and his interview by Jahn in 1852. Koželuch was disliked by all three Classical masters,[6] and it seems unlikely that Haydn would have confided in him about Beethoven, as Doleželek describes in (4c). Hence the concluding sentence, that Haydn failed in general to appreciate Beethoven's merits, is also suspect. In view of the hearty correspondence between Beethoven

---

[5]Thayer-Deiters-Riemann III, 61; Thayer-Forbes, pp. 444–45; cf. Solomon, p. 75. Czerny himself elsewhere says the opposite (Kerst, I, 48–49).

[6]See the anecdotes and references in Hermann Abert, *W. A. Mozart*, 7th ed. (Leipzig, 1956), II, 43–44. Ordinary folk disliked Koželuch too, for example, Griesinger (Thomas, p. 54) and Alexander Straton, Thomson's agent in Vienna (C. F. Pohl, *Joseph Haydn*, III, written from his notes by Hugo Botstiber [Leipzig, 1927], p. 159; Landon, IV, 493–96).

and Albrechtsberger in 1796–97,[7] Passage 4a is equally implausible. (As far as I can see, even the notion that Gyrowetz disliked Beethoven's music derives chiefly from Doležalek's one-liner [4d]. I find no indication to this effect in Gyrowetz's autobiography; perhaps it too should be revised.) Drouet, whose account belongs in any case to the realm of fantasy, has Haydn uttering completely implausible, Romantic and self-conscious sentiments such as: "The style of the composer is always that of the man himself," or "I juxtapose serious and comic ideas, as in Shakespeare's tragedies" (5.2); and the notion (5.5) that Beethoven destroyed autographs of juvenile versions of Opp. 1 and 2—Drouet can have had no other works in mind—is refuted by their chronology.[8]

The question of Ries's credibility is crucial. As has often been noted, he mixes up the chronology even of events at which he was present, or which took place during his contact with Beethoven, such as the *Akademie* of 1803 or the composition of the *Eroica* (Passage 11a). As has also been noted, the chronology of his story (11b) of Haydn's advising Beethoven not to publish Op. 1, no. 3 is impossible.[9] At best, Ries would have heard some version of this from Beethoven six or more years after the event, and have written it down thirty-five years later still; at worst, the entire story might be groundless (so far, only Landon, III, 61–62, has risked this suggestion). Of course, it does not follow from such errors in detail that the point of an anecdote must be false. Perhaps Haydn did make one or another remark about Beethoven's boldness in publishing such an overwrought work, or about not having expected it to do so well; and maybe Beethoven, in his paranoid way, took offense. Ries does seem to be relatively free from the sort of animus we find in Doležalek or Schenk, and he often seems to capture the "atmosphere" of Beethoven's personality and daily affairs. And he enhances his credibility here by claiming to have been skeptical of Beethoven's story, and to have accepted it only after Haydn himself verified one part of it.[10]

Johann Baptist Schenk's story about correcting Beethoven's counterpoint exercises for Haydn, it has long been clear, is also couched in terms

[7]First published in 1921 by Andreas Weissenbäck (I have not seen this); paraphrased in translation by Landon, IV, 115 and n. 2.

[8]Beethoven wrote Op. 1, nos. 2–3 and Op. 2, nos. 2–3 in 1794–95; the dates of no. 1 in each opus are obscure, but it seems unlikely that either reached any even temporarily complete status in Bonn. (It seems inconceivable that Drouet could have known of the 1785 piano quartets.) See Johnson, *Beethoven's Early Sketches in the 'Fischhof Miscellany,'* 2 vols. (Ann Arbor, 1980), I, 304 ff., 318 ff.; "1794–1795," pp. 24–26.

[9]See Thayer-Forbes, pp. 164–65; Johnson, *loc. cit.*; Landon, IV, 61–63.

[10]These views in favor of Ries's credibility paraphrase those expressed privately to me by Tyson and Johnson. A study by Tyson of the origins and credibility of Wegeler-Ries, particularly as regards Ries's contributions, is scheduled for publication in *19th-Century Music* in the spring of 1984.

of an impossible chronology, August, 1792 to May-June, 1793.[11] But its main contents, which have always been taken for granted, also require scrutiny. There is essentially only the original autograph version (Passage 12a). The anonymous first publication in *Der Freischütz* (12b), Luib's account (13), and Seyfried's influential version (15) all derive directly and, it appears, independently from (12a).[12] The structure and contents of all four are essentially the same; all except (12b) include the false date August, 1792 and agree on May, 1793; all include such details from (12a) as Gelinek's appealing to Mozart as the standard for improvisation, Schenk's hearing Beethoven perform in Gelinek's quarters, the oath of silence, and Beethoven's rewriting the corrected exercises before submitting them to Haydn. Seyfried's language leaves no doubt of his source: "wissbegierige" (12a.1, 12a.3) becomes "lernbegierige" (15.1); "bis zu Ende Mai 1793 ununterbrochen fortgesetzt" (12a.4) recurs as "währte bis Ende Mai [1793] ununterbrochen fort" (15.1); "das feste Band der Freundschaft, das bis an [Beethovens] Tod noch unverwelkt geblieben" (12a.9) lives on as "in jenem Freundschaftsbund, das unverwelkt auch noch fortblühte" (15.3). To clinch matters, Seyfried quotes verbatim Beethoven's note to Schenk informing him of his impending departure for Eisenstadt (12a.7 vs. 15.2); so does *Der Freischütz* (12b.4), with the interesting variant "I didn't know that I was to go to Eisenstadt today" in place of "I wish I weren't. . . ." Therefore Schenk must have shown his manuscript to Seyfried (and perhaps discussed it with him) between writing it down for Fuchs in 1830 and Seyfried's publication in 1838; and likewise with the editor of *Der Freischütz*.

But it all beggars reason. Given the course of study as a whole, Beethoven could hardly have remained stuck in first species, let alone first species in two parts, after "more than six months" of study.[13] He

---

[11]See Thayer-Forbes, pp. 142–43; Landon, III, 217–18. The dissertation of Ernst Rosenfeld-Römer, "Johann Baptist Schenk als Opernkomponist" (Univ. of Vienna [1921]), is said by the institution no longer to be available and could not be consulted for this study.

[12]I am most grateful to Horst Walter for supplying a text of (12b).

[13]Beethoven was presumably not "stuck" in the first *exercise* (as Schenk's "erste Übung" [12.3] has been translated), but in first *species*, or somewhere in two-part counterpoint. Both Schenk ("gewahrte ich bei jeder Tonart . . . etwelche Fehler"; 12a.3) and Schindler ("Schenk . . . fand in den frühesten Elaboraten die gröbsten Fehler"; 14a.2) specify that numerous exercises were involved. The plan of study began with two-part exercises in all species; even so, Beethoven produced fourteen two-part exercises in first species. See Alfred Mann, "Beethoven's Contrapuntal Studies with Haydn," *The Musical Quarterly*, LXI (1970), 722. If Schenk's story should after all be true, this detail appears to provide support for Thayer-Forbes's interpretation of the chronology (pp. 140, 142), which has Schenk meeting Beethoven after only a few weeks' work with Haydn. I am grateful to Richard Kramer for clarifying certain aspects of Beethoven's studies with Haydn and Albrechtsberger.

would have had a digest of Fuxian principles similar to the one Haydn gave F. C. Magnus,[14] whereas Schenk speaks of his "ignorance" of these rules and of Fux's *Gradus*—a near impossibility. Like Seyfried (15.3), Schenk (12a.5) juxtaposes Beethoven's study of dramatic Italian vocal style under Salieri (which both authors generalize into "free style") directly with the Haydn-Albrechtsberger period, whereas the Salieri studies did not take place until c. 1801–02.[15] These are mere inconsistencies, but Schenk also trips up over "facts." (His entire biography has been characterized as "interesting, but factually unreliable.")[16] According to an anecdote attributed by Jahn to Grillparzer, Schenk claimed that Beethoven was inexperienced at thoroughbass; in view of Neefe's statements and Beethoven's keyboard positions at the Electoral court, this cannot have been true.[17] Schenk did not know, and did not want to believe, that Beethoven had studied with Albrechtsberger (12a.4–5). He states that Beethoven's study with Haydn proceeded through completion of double counterpoint at the octave (12a.4), whereas in fact this stage was reached only after many months with Albrechtsberger.[18] Most incredibly, Beethoven's exercises contain numerous errors; but this utterly refutes Schenk's assertions that he corrected them *and that Beethoven submitted fair copies of the corrected versions to Haydn.*[19] Schenk thus hangs himself on his own circumstantial details. Like all Viennese musicians, he would have heard stories of Beethoven's having complained about Haydn's teaching. In 1830, after Beethoven's death, he (and Seyfried? and Fuchs?) doubtless saw no harm in puffing up his (their) relationship with the great man into something more rewarding personally and, in its dupe-like role for Haydn, more titillating. The story of Schenk's having corrected Beethoven's counterpoint exercises for Haydn is most likely a pure fabrication.

If this interpretation is correct, the "letter" from Beethoven to Schenk announcing his impending departure for Eisenstadt may also be a fabrication. (Schenk's manuscript is the only source.) Its orthography is im-

---

[14]Mann, *op. cit.*, pp. 719–21; idem, "Haydn's Elementarbuch: A Document of Classic Counterpoint Instruction," *The Music Forum*, III (1973), 197–238. Gustav Nottebohm, *Beethoven's Studien* (Leipzig and Winterthur, 1873), p. [21], asserts that Beethoven himself possessed such an extract; no basis for this assertion was given, and it cannot now be verified.

[15]Richard Kramer, "The Sketches for Beethoven's Violin Sonatas, Op. 30" (Diss. Princeton Univ., 1973), pp. 145–59, esp. 156; Johnson, 'Fischhof,' I, 169, 389, 397; Brandenburg, in *Ludwig van Beethoven: Kesslerisches Skizzenbuch: Übertragung . . .* (Bonn, 1978), I, 31–32. Note that Ries [11d] gets this right.

[16]Peter Branscombe, "Schenk," *New Grove*, XVI, 625.

[17]Thayer I (1866), p. 413; cf. Nottebohm, *Beethoven's Studien.*

[18]Nottebohm, *Beethoven's Studien*, p. 43.

[19]This devastating contradiction seems never to have been noted in the literature.

possibly error-free. Its tone seems more formal than we would expect from Beethoven, scrawling in haste to a firm friend; phrases such as "rechnen Sie auf meine Dankbarkeit," "Ich werde mich bestreben," and especially "das Vergnügen Ihres Umganges geniessen zu können" have a stiff, stylized, un-Beethovenian air about them.[20] On the other hand, the fact of Beethoven's journey to Eisenstadt seems recently to have been confirmed by the discovery of a note, still unpublished, from Beethoven to Zmeskall of June 18, 1793.[21]

By his own account, Schenk's role was the modest one of correcting exercises in species counterpoint. But his language gives him away here too, in its (doubtless unconscious) aggrandizement of this role into that of responsible, loving teacher: "my pupil" (12a.3), "[der] Wissbegierige" (12a.1, 12a.3), "honorable office" (12a.4), and having become "Beethoven's guide in musical composition" (12a.8). One deeper motive—that of augmenting, in old age, the meaning and luster of a life that evidently had enjoyed relatively little of either—emerges clearly from the final emphasis on Beethoven's "lasting friendship" (12a.9), the touching repeated apostrophizations "my good Louis" (12a.4,6,9), and the protestation that Beethoven himself, "honest and forthright," would have informed him of a shift to Albrechtsberger (12a.5). It was an attractive footnote for Seyfried (15.3) to interpret Beethoven's friendship as Schenk's "reward" for having provided his services free of charge. Schenk himself nowhere mentions this, unless by implication in the passage (12a.9): "For my efforts (if they should be thought worthy of the name) I received a precious gift from my good faithful Louis [!], namely a firm bond of friendship." But for one who, like Schenk, often depended on lesson fees for his primary income, such an arrangement seems in fact highly unlikely.

A second possible motive for Schenk's fabrication (if that is what it was), overlooked until brought into the picture recently by Horst Walter, is that Schenk seems to have hated Haydn! This is the thrust of an anecdotal account by the Viennese music journalist Franz Lorenz, describing encounters with Schenk in the 1820s (Passage 17):[22] "He continually found fault not only with Haydn's works, but also his character. . . . 'Mozart was a good soul, but Haydn was false through and through.' "

[20]Marx (2nd ed., I, 20) noted the false tone, but interpreted it as implying "between the lines" that Beethoven was using his "need" to depart for Eisenstadt as a pretext for *breaking off* his relations with Schenk.

[21]Catalogued in SBH, p. 364. A paraphrase in translation appeared in Sotheby's auction catalogue, May 12, 1970, No. 435. (I am indebted to Maynard Solomon for referring me to the *Beethoven-Jahrbuch* entry and to Lenore F. Coral for providing a copy of the Sotheby entry.)

[22]Once again I am indebted to Dr. Walter for the reference to and a copy of this item.

Lorenz attributes these feelings to the envy and bitterness with which many third-rate artists confront a genius. Some particular event or events, about which we know nothing, must have been the proximate cause of Schenk's hatred. (Not unnaturally, Lorenz wondered at the notion that "Papa" Haydn could ever in his life have aroused anyone's ire. The modern reader may measure the extent to which he has rid himself of this clichéd attitude according to the ease with which he can accept such a situation as a realistic possibility.) To be sure, this anecdote appeared long after the events described; it is still more remote from the 1780s and 1790s, when Schenk's difficulties with Haydn (if there were any) must have originated; and it utterly lacks corroboration. It must therefore be treated with the utmost caution. But if it should be accurate, it would go some distance toward explaining the animus that could have led Schenk to fabricate his story about Haydn and Beethoven.

An obvious difficulty with this interpretation of Schenk's story is its apparent confirmation in the first edition (1840) of Schindler's biography (Passage 14). But this too is suspect. In the later editions Schindler felt constrained to buttress the "strange, almost incredible fact" of Schenk's role. To do so he adduced, first, having heard it from Schenk himself; and second, Seyfried's published account (15)—not any word or deed of Beethoven's. (Just how extensively Schindler resorted to fabrications even in this context may be judged from his false statement that Haydn had given up systematic teaching long before 1792.)[23] But he could have received Schenk's own version only before that worthy's death in 1836, and it seems highly unlikely that he would not have known Seyfried's 1838 account when writing around 1839. If this is true, then Schindler too depends ultimately only on (12).

Schindler states falsely that Haydn and Beethoven never got along after 1793, and that Schenk continued to help Beethoven after he had moved on to Albrechtsberger. The latter claim is refuted not only by Schenk's own account, but by Beethoven's papers for Albrechtsberger, which also exhibit errors and whose contents preclude any possibility of third-party intervention.[24] Of course, Schindler "confirms" Schenk's story by his anecdote (14b) about Schenk and Beethoven meeting in 1824 and laughing about having duped Haydn. Given Schindler's general lack of reliability, however, we can hardly accept this as sole support for Schenk's story as a whole.

The perhaps somewhat surprising result of this analysis of the sources

---

[23]Schindler (1860), I, 28 (Schenk and Seyfried), 26 (Haydn's teaching); on the latter point, see n. 30 below. It seems hardly necessary any longer to emphasize Schindler's general untrustworthiness.

[24]Information kindly supplied by Richard Kramer.

is that the only one that entirely satisfies the criteria for credibility noted above are the letters from Georg August Griesinger to Härtel in Leipzig. Griesinger's credibility is further confirmed by his status as generally the most reliable among Haydn's early biographers. To be sure, Griesinger, born in 1769, was of Beethoven's generation rather than Haydn's, and his literary, philosophical, and (eventually) musical tastes were more in tune with those of the younger composer. He was contemptuous of Van Swieten, whose "puritanical" literary pedantry and incessant word-painting, both of considerable influence on Haydn, were painful to him.[25] He somewhat deprecated Haydn's literary taste: "Haydn seems to have been predestined to poor texts; in this he actually reaps the harvest of his ordinary [*unwissenschaftliche*] education"; this was more than a little unfair.[26] When in 1802 Griesinger asked Haydn whom he would prefer as librettist for a possible last oratorio, and Haydn promptly named his own contemporary Wieland (born 1733), he was apparently slightly taken aback, but dutifully urged Härtel to try to win this "veteran" for the project.[27] Still, apart from his own overemphasis on the "Papa"-like aspects of Haydn's character, there seems to be little trace of bias in his letters, and none of invention or fabrication. And, alone among our authors, he reports events the very day they occurred, or very shortly thereafter; by exception, therefore, even the circumstantial details and quotations in his letters have some claim to credibility.

Of course, it does not follow that only the events reported on by Griesinger can be true. Czerny (2,3), Doležalek (4a,b,d), Ries (11a, b[first two and last two sentences], c[first sentence], d[second sentence on]), Schenk, Schindler (14b), and Seyfried (16) also claim to reproduce eyewitness encounters. To evaluate this point further, however, we must now turn to the contents of the tradition of the falling-out between Haydn and Beethoven.

*   *   *   *   *

The elements of the tradition are listed in Table 2, along with the sources that testify to each. (Material in brackets in Table 2 has no foundation in contemporary Viennese sources, but either comes from elsewhere [e.g., Bruening and Neefe] or is an exclusively modern interpretation.) Putting aside until later the question of Beethoven's deception, and turning instead to the issue of Haydn's teaching, the verdict for the counterpoint training is clear: Haydn's correction of Beethoven's counter-

---

[25] See Thomas, pp. 69–70, 83, 91, *et passim*.

[26] Thomas, p. 93. A similar remark appears at the end of (7f). But cf. Feder, "Mensch und Musiker," pp. 46–48.

[27] Thomas, p. 88.

Table 2
The Elements of the Tradition

Elements	Sources
Beethoven deceived Haydn in 1793	Schenk (12a-b, 13), Schindler (14), Seyfried (15)
Used Schenk as secret corrector	[Elector's reply to Haydn's letter (cf. pp. 20–21)]
[Regarding compositions and salary?]	
Beethoven's attitudes towards Haydn	
Haydn's teaching inadequate	Griesinger (8b), Ries (11d), Schenk etc. (as above)
Counterpoint	[Ries? (11d)]
[Free composition?]	
Haydn's musical orientation limited	Griesinger (7f, 7g, [8a]), Ries (11a)
Simple, trivial; word-painting	Griesinger (7a), Moscheles (10), Ries (11b)
Not on my high level	[Ries (11b; a modern misinterpretation)], Seyfried (16)
Did not understand my music	[Not transmitted as Beethoven's attitude, but a common
Could not write quintets	one; cf. pp. 19–20]
Haydn's personal behavior inappropriate	
Envious of me	Ries (11b)
Not upright in his dealings	Griesinger (7c)
The independence "complex"	
General ["Papa" too fatherly?]	Seyfried (16) [modern extension; cf. pp. 20, 23]
With respect to Haydn's *Creation*	Doleżalek (4e), Fuchs (6), Marx (9), Moscheles (10)
Haydn's attitudes towards Beethoven	
[Altered plans to take Beethoven to London?]	[Breuning; Neefe; cf. p. 22]
Beethoven ungrateful and excessively proud	
Refused to print "Pupil of Haydn"	Ries (11d)
Arrogant	Fuchs (6), Griesinger (7g), Moscheles (10), Seyfried (16)
Lack of understanding for Beethoven's music	Carpani (1), Doleżalek (4c), Drouet (5.1-2), Marx (9),
	Seyfried (16)
Insecurity regarding Beethoven	Griesinger (7f)

point exercises was materially lacking in comprehensiveness and somewhat so in consistency. This is evident not only from the testimony of several witnesses but also from the surviving sources; Alfred Mann's persuasive defense of Haydn against Nottebohm's censure of his methods does not alter this point.[28] Of course, Beethoven was a difficult student under the best of circumstances, as emphasized by Ries (11d) and confirmed by Julius Streicher.[29] It is also noteworthy that Ries omits Haydn from his final criticisms of Albrechtsberger's "dry" rules and Salieri's "less important" ones. But Schenk himself, in referring to Haydn's own intense compositional activity as a reason for his lack of interest in correcting exercises (12a.3), calls attention to a more interesting question: the extent to which Haydn instructed Beethoven in free composition.

The anecdotal tradition never mentions this point, if one assumes (as seems likely) that Ries's report (11d) that Beethoven said he never learned anything from Haydn refers only to the counterpoint training. But, as especially Solomon and Johnson have emphasized, Beethoven's primary interest in studying with Haydn must have been to perfect himself in the newly triumphant Viennese modern style (that which we today misleadingly call "Classical"). It was probably Haydn's primary interest too; recent research, especially by Walter, has shown that he not only had many more pupils than is generally recognized, but that he actively preferred instruction in free composition and informal "shop talk."[30] Haydn's letter of November, 1793 to the Elector in Bonn not only shows that he cherished and admired his pupil, but implies that he had looked through, approved, and perhaps counseled Beethoven with respect to the five works enclosed or, more precisely, the revisions he had made to them in Vienna: The octet Op. 103 was revised, and the oboe concerto Hess 12 and the wind quintet Hess 19 were sketched (i.e., revised?) in 1793. The former was certainly and the latter two probably were among the works sent to Bonn.[31] (This letter is discussed further below.)

Beethoven's believing in and making fun of limitations in Haydn's compositional powers and aesthetic orientation enjoy a certain indirect

---

[28]Mann, "Beethoven's Contrapuntal Studies."

[29]Vincent and Mary Novello, *A Mozart Pilgrimage*, ed. Rosemary Hughes (London, 1955), p. 194.

[30]Walter, "Beziehungen," pp. 80–81; idem, "On Haydn's Pupils," in Jens Peter Larsen et al., ed., *Haydn Studies: Proceedings of the International Haydn Conference, Washington, D. C., 1975* (New York, 1981), pp. 60–63; idem, "Kalkbrenners Lehrjahre und sein Unterricht bei Haydn," *Haydn-Studien*, V/1 (March, 1982), 23–41. Cf. Fredrik Samuel Silverstolpe's account of Haydn's criticism of a student's composition, in C. G. Stellan Mörner, "Haydniana aus Schweden um 1800," *Haydn-Studien*, II (1969–70), 27.

[31]Johnson, 'Fischhof,' I, 98–99, 104–5, 404–6.

legitimacy from Haydn's own vigorous defense against the charge of excessive and inappropriate word-painting in the *Seasons*—on the grounds that Van Swieten had forced them on him.[32] The issue of word-painting was becoming central to musical aesthetics around 1800. Griesinger himself, for example, reveals divergences of attitude among (a) his defenses of Haydn's setting of the *Seasons* to Härtel—"He has a Midas touch, and turns dross [*Drek*] into gold"—and in the *Allgemeine Musikalische Zeitung*, and his unstinting praise of the effect—"No preacher is capable of portraying the glory of the Creator with [such] penetrating power";[33] (b) his unfair comment (end of 7f) about Haydn's predilection for trivial texts; and (c) his later equation (8a) of Beethoven's defense of *Wellington's Victory* with Haydn's earlier defenses of the *Creation*. (Possibly this was a slight lapse of memory; in contemporary notices of the *Creation*, the occasional criticisms of word-painting are directed almost exclusively at the libretto, whereas by the time of the *Seasons* Haydn himself was drawn into the line of fire.)[34] This all lends Ries's report (11a) a certain credibility, in that Beethoven's reported attitude was widely shared; ironically, Beethoven himself was to suffer from the same prejudice not only for *Wellington* (8a) but for the *Pastoral Symphony*.

Aside from the "independence complex," discussed below, the notion that Beethoven felt superior to Haydn as a composer is documented only by Griesinger (7a). Because of its limitation to piano works—a genre which had never constituted one of Haydn's greatest public successes—at a time (c. 1801–02) when Beethoven was in fact breaking new ground, Beethoven's opinion seems reasonable and need not have been motivated by animus. Ries's comment (11b), nicely rendered by Sonneck as "Haydn seldom escaped without a few digs in the ribs," serves as a transition to the more familiar story about Op. 1, no. 3. As noted above, the latter narrative constitutes, at most, evidence of Beethoven's resentment of Haydn's possible advice regarding publication. (It is inconceivable

---

[32]Haydn's letter to A. E. Müller, December 11, 1801, in Dénes Bartha, ed., *Joseph Haydn: Gesammelte Briefe und Aufzeichnungen* (Kassel, 1965), no. 292; Griesinger, *Biographische Notizen über Joseph Haydn* (Leipzig, 1810; modern ed. by Horst Seeger [Berlin, 1959]), pp. 69–72; Albert Christoph Dies, *Biographische Nachrichten von Joseph Haydn* (Vienna, 1810), pp. 180–81; a passage in Sigismund Neukomm's manuscript comments on Dies, repr. Horst Seeger, "Zur musikhistorischen Bedeutung der Haydn-Biographie von . . . Dies," *Beiträge zur Musikwissenschaft*, I/3 (1959), p. 31. Cf. Thomas, pp. 82–83.

[33]Thomas, p. 73; Landon, V, 43 ff.; Thomas, p. 82.

[34]See Landon, IV, 572 ff.; V, 42 ff., 88 ff., 182 ff. Possibly the origin of this confusion was an erroneous report, in the same issue of the *Zeitung für die elegante Welt* in which Haydn's remark to Müller about "französische Quark" was leaked, that Haydn had deprecated his own *Creation*.

that the powerful and original genius of Haydn at the height of his powers should have had any difficulty with this work.)[35] Since Ries makes no
claim that Beethoven believed that Haydn failed to understand his music, the only independent testimony is Seyfried (16); this will be discussed below.

A related, if peripheral, notion also adumbrated by Ries (11c) was that
Haydn was unable to compose string quintets. (Perhaps this canard was
an unconscious by-product of the growing Mozart cult, or was related to
the decline of Haydn's reputation following his death.) Ries carefully
states only that it was said that Haydn "couldn't find the fifth part," leav-
ing open the question whether he or Beethoven accepted this proposi-
tion. If Haydn really responded to Ries's query with a remark that four
parts had always sufficed, we still cannot tell whether he was uttering a
simple truth, or aggressively enunciating an aesthetic doctrine to the effect that a string quintet was likely to be too full in texture,[36] or curtly and
ironically dismissing an impertinent question on the part of an eighteen-
year-old pianist (although in fact he seems to have enjoyed the company
of young musicians in his later years).[37] In any case the topic was widely
current. A different anecdote transmits his reply as simply that nobody
had ever commissioned a quintet from him;[38] this is also plausible, insofar as he hardly ever composed in the absence of a definite obligation or
financial opportunity. Yet another, apocryphal anecdote has one of the
Princes Lobkowitz putting the question; Haydn replies that Mozart's example was too formidable; Lobkowitz insists on paying for a quintet any-
how; Haydn delivers but, alas, the completed manuscript leaves the fifth
staff blank![39] Even Griesinger reports, one must presume falsely, that
Haydn had been commissioned to write quintets for Count Fries—the
eventual dedicatee not only of his Op. 103 but of Beethoven's quintet Op.
29.[40] (Or could Fries have actually wanted quintets from Haydn between

---

[35]Cf. Johnson, "1794–1795," p. 26: "Ironically, the old man's models are lean and
taut, while the young man's copies are overweight and long-winded." I agree entirely;
but why "ironically"? Less unlikely would have been a temperamental distaste for the
"callow and stagey . . . insistent gestures of pathos and high drama" that characterize
Beethoven's early music (New Grove, II, 379).

[36]Haydn disliked any excess in texture, elaboration, or the like; cf. Feder, "Mensch
und Musiker" and "Haydns Korrekturen zum Klavierauszug der 'Jahreszeiten,' " in
Thomas Kohlhase and Volker Scherliess, eds., Festschrift Georg van Dadelsen zum 60. Ge-
burtstag (Neuhausen-Stuttgart, 1978), pp. 101–12.

[37]Walter, as in n. 30.

[38]I have not located the original (said to be Rochlitz, reporting Haydn's remarks to the
Romberg brothers); reported in Pohl-Botstiber, p. 314; Landon, IV, 112, n. 1.

[39]G. G. Ferrari, as reported in Landon, III, 154–55.

[40]Thomas, pp. 58, 76.

1799 and 1801, eventually turning to Beethoven when Haydn was unable to produce; and Beethoven, resenting this preference on Fries's part, have encouraged or tolerated the canard?) A *Schönheitsfehler* for all concerned is that Haydn *did* compose one quintet, the early Hob. II:2; this of course does not affect the meaning of the anecdotes after 1800.

Accounts of Beethoven's belief that Haydn was envious of or ill-disposed towards him arise chiefly with respect to the counterpoint instruction, secondarily to Ries's account of Op. 1, no. 3; both have already been found wanting. The only independent anecdote to this effect is Griesinger's report (7c) of Beethoven's censure of Haydn's practice of pocketing two or more fees for the same work. But this report arose out of Beethoven's dispute with Breitkopf & Härtel regarding Artaria's unauthorized publication of Op. 29, and it therefore seems to have been a classic case, on Beethoven's part, of the pot calling the kettle black; his own dealings with publishers offer ample evidence of how much he learned from Haydn in this respect, as well as in composition. Also, Griesinger's role as middleman required him to portray Beethoven's actions and motives in such a way as not to offend or alarm Härtel unduly. A censure of Haydn's well-known sharp practice laid in Beethoven's mouth would have served this purpose.

But most fascinating for us today is the issue of Beethoven's "complex," his ambivalence toward Haydn during the period of his striving for compositional independence and self-sufficiency. Solomon states forthrightly (p. 70): "He learned too much from Haydn—more than he could acknowledge," and interprets his striking lack of productivity in the year 1793 as reflecting (among other things) the "deep ambivalence towards Haydn [which] blocked his creativity. . . . Perhaps it was this creative impasse which led Beethoven to pretend that some Bonn works . . . were new compositions" (p. 71). Tyson, Kerman, Landon, and Johnson, who do not explicitly discuss the issue of Beethoven's 1793 output in this context, make similar observations about his rapid, if uneven, assimilation of Haydn's style in the 1790s (see notes 1–2).

But no direct evidence implies that Beethoven harbored such feelings in the early or middle 1790s. The impression that he did depends entirely on his supposed turn to Schenk and on Haydn's letter to the Elector in Bonn of November, 1793; only the latter need concern us further. The Elector's draft reply, asserting that four of the five compositions enclosed "as evidence of [Beethoven's] diligence beyond his studies proper" were familiar Bonn works and that Beethoven already had additional funds at his disposal, have led Solomon, Tyson, and Landon to the conclusion that (in Tyson's words) "Beethoven had misled Haydn in respect both of his total income and of the music that he had written in Vienna, and thus exposed Haydn to the Elector's withering reply."[41] Concerning the money, we have no way of telling whether he had in fact been deceiving Haydn; if so, it would be almost the only time on record that Haydn, who was both clever and avaricious, had been so deceived. But with respect to the compositions, it seems highly unlikely that Haydn did not know the facts. For of the four works in question, Beethoven had worked extensively on at least three in 1793 (see page 17). It is of course possible that he showed Haydn only coherent new drafts on Viennese paper, claiming that the works were current. But it seems more likely that Haydn saw the earlier versions, pointing out areas for improvement as we know he did on other occasions; indeed, he could well have *assigned* these revisions of recent works as first, appropriate studies in free composition during a period of (supposed) intensive study of counterpoint.

In this case, the only thing that would have surprised Haydn about the Elector's reply would have been its ungenerous and peremptory tone. Similarly, Beethoven's plea for continued favor, enclosed with Haydn's letter, while acknowledging that this output for the year 1793 was a disappointing harvest, is much more clearly worried about losing financial support. (Beethoven's having given this note to Haydn to enclose with the latter's letter also seems to argue strongly against deception in the affair.) In any case, the interpretation that Beethoven's lack of production of finished new compositions in 1793 is to be equated with "lack of productivity" seems premature, and ignores the considerable activity that did take place; and that it should be in any way related to ambivalence regarding Haydn remains wholly within the realm of conjecture.[42] Similarly, we have no evidence of Haydn's reaction to the Elector's reply—if indeed it was actually sent, or if, drafted December 23, 1793, it succeeded in reaching him in Vienna before his departure for London about January 19, 1794.[43]

If this interpretation should be correct, it would follow that corollaries such as that Beethoven's and Haydn's relationship was [merely] "outwardly cordial" and "not badly strained," that Beethoven tried to "patch it up" with Haydn, that Haydn "appears to have forgiven" Beethoven,

[41]*New Grove*, II, 358; cf. Solomon, pp. 70–72; Landon, III, 224. The originals were published in Fritz von Reinöhl, "Neues zu Beethovens Lehrjahr bei Haydn," *Neue Beethoven Jahrbuch*, VI (1935), 36–47; Haydn's letter and the Elector's draft reply are reprinted throughout the subsequent literature, Beethoven's note however only in Thayer-Forbes, pp. 145 and *A* 8.

[42]Cf. similar caveats in Lewis Lockwood's review of Solomon, *19th-Century Music*, III (1979–80), 81–82.

[43]The date of Haydn's departure follows Dies, p. 148. Max Franz himself traveled to Vienna in this month (*New Grove*, II, 358).

and so forth[44] may rest on a false premise. The same is true of the supposed corollary that this "worsening relationship, however masked"[45] may "explain" why Beethoven did not accompany Haydn to England in 1794. For not only is no "worsening relationship" to be assumed, but the entire notion of a "plan" regarding England seems highly questionable. Only two insecure indications that such a plan was ever conceived are known. One is a cryptic poem entered by Christoph (?) von Breuning into Beethoven's *Stammbuch* on his departure from Bonn in November 1792: "Es winket . . . lange dir Albion . . . Eile denn ungesäumet ueber die flutende See, wo . . . dir so freundlich die Hand reichet ein Barde dar, der von unsren Gefilden floh' auch in Albions Schutz." This would appear to refer to an invitation from Salomon (the "bard" who earlier fled the Rhine for England) to Beethoven, which in turn implies Haydn's knowledge of and participation in such an enterprise.[46] The other is Neefe's communication published in the *Berliner musikalische Zeitung* of October 26, 1793, including an ostensible letter from Beethoven in Vienna (*A* 6) thanking him for his earlier training and support; Neefe includes a sentence that is rarely quoted: "Haydn intended taking [Beethoven] on his second trip to London; but nothing has come of this trip so far."[47] But the question is complicated by Landon's recent hypothesis (consistent with Neefe's remark) that Haydn's original intention had been to return to London as early as January of 1793, not 1794.[48] If this should have been so, then Haydn's plans had changed fundamentally long before November, 1793—as Beethoven's could equally well have done—and his eventual departure for England without Beethoven need have had nothing whatever to do with any deceit or ill-feeling on either man's part.

By the same token, Beethoven's and Haydn's actions upon the latter's return in the fall of 1795 give little reason to posit ill-feeling or rivalry. The question of Op. 1, no. 3 aside, this was the period of Beethoven's dedication of the sonatas Op. 2 to Haydn (published spring 1796), of his performing a concerto (presumably a version of Op. 19) at Haydn's benefit

---

[44]*New Grove*, II, 357, 359; Solomon, pp. 72, 73.

[45]*New Grove*, II, 358.

[46]Beethoven's *Stammbuch* has often been published; the text is conveniently available in Thayer-Deiters-Riemann I, p. 501. The interpretation that the "bard" is Salomon and that Beethoven might have been destined for England was made by Nottebohm in N I, p. 143n.; this line of reasoning then disappeared, as far as I can see, until Landon (without, however, acknowledging Nottebohm) revived it (III, 192).

[47]Likewise paraphrased in N I, p. 143n. and given in translation by Landon, III, 193; it seems to be ignored in the standard literature.

[48]This hypothesis of Landon's, which depends on much circumstantial evidence (by no means all included in *Haydn*, III, 192–94, 213–14), seems not unlikely; full consideration must await another occasion.

concert on December 18, 1795, of their joint participation in Mme. Bolla's benefit concert on January 8, 1796, and so forth. None of this proves much in the way of closeness or intimacy, or even mutual understanding in artistic or professional matters; but it tends to belie the notion of positively bad relations.

The situation seems to have been quite different from about 1800 (or even 1798?) to 1804. These years were obviously critical for Beethoven, in fundamental ways that not only put his entire career as performer and composer in jeopardy, but threatened (he believed) to subject him to the scorn and contempt of his rivals and enemies.[49] It is perhaps not entirely coincidental that this was precisely the period of Haydn's greatest public triumph; the potential of the *Creation*, premiered in 1798, as a new (and, I would add, unexpected) "hurdle" for Beethoven at this time has not been overlooked.[50] Indeed, the anecdotal tradition is rich in stories attesting to an ambivalence toward Haydn on Beethoven's part around this time. The most plausible is Seyfried's (16). His attribution of sensitivity (*Scheu*) is both flattering to Beethoven and psychologically credible. Seyfried is also the only source to state explicitly that Beethoven believed that Haydn did not understand or approve of his "new way," as Beethoven himself called it, just after 1800 (the tradition for Haydn's own beliefs will be discussed below). Haydn is also portrayed sympathetically, and the not unfriendly ambivalence implied by his epithets for Beethoven—"Telemachus" and "Grand Mogul"—is quite attractive.

Finally, Seyfried alone, in his first sentence, suggests a convincing reason for Haydn's "role" in Beethoven's ambivalence at this time: *It was a consequence of his mental and physical decline*, which, as we know from Haydn's letters and from Griesinger, began as early as the middle of 1799. The *Seasons* (1799–1801) and the last three masses (1800–02) were composed under increasing physical and psychological duress; and following the *Harmoniemesse* (premiered September, 1802) Haydn—not without painful, failed attempts to continue—completed no further large-scale works.[51] It is difficult to imagine Beethoven, desperately concerned for his own health and the future of his career, wishing to see

[49]Tyson, "Beethoven's Heroic Phase," *The Musical Times*, CX (1969), 139–41. In a private communication, Johnson emphasized Beethoven's fears of his rivals' taking advantage of him.

[50]*New Grove*, II, 360.

[51]The first letter is from Haydn to Härtel, June 12, 1799 (*Haydn Briefe*, pp. 319–20); the most poignant, to none other than Pleyel, December 6, 1802 (p. 415); cf. also pp. 345–46, 378, 396, 410–11, 412, 419, *et passim*. See also Thomas, pp. 63–64, 65, 78, 96, 99, 100, 101, *et passim*. Landon (IV, 325; V, 282) goes so far as to speculate that the beginning of the decline in Haydn's public reputation, which he dates to the somewhat qualified success of the *Seasons* (premiered 1801), compared to the *Creation*, was a necessary precondition for Beethoven's triumph after 1803.

Haydn under these circumstances. (To be sure, Seyfried's account originated late, and it stands in a work which as a whole is the opposite of trustworthy.[52] But perhaps the anecdotes in his supplement need not be compromised thereby.)

Related to this issue is an entire series of anecdotal comparisons between Beethoven's music and the *Creation*. Doležalek (4e), Marx (9) in his first edition, and Moscheles have Beethoven (or, in Moscheles's case, Haydn) draw the comparison with the septet Op. 20; Fuchs (6) with *Prometheus*, a variant taken over by Marx in his second edition (1863). Each work is plausible chronologically; the latter carries the additional "virtues" of a possible play on words ("Schöpfung" vs. "Geschöpfe") and a vague similarity of subject matter. Strikingly, each is utterly unworthy as a rival to the *Creation*. In fact, if this anecdote really did circulate around 1800, that must have been its point: Beethoven's pride and lack of self-control (we would say his ambivalence) led him not only to insult Haydn, but to do so under terms impossible to justify on their merits. This motive is explicit, however, only in Fuchs. Moscheles attributes to Haydn a response, "The septet is splendid," that if actually uttered in this context could only have been meant ironically. By the 1830s, however, Beethoven votaries would perhaps have stated without irony that the *Creation* was the inferior work; by Marx's time this attitude was all too common. But this point only throws into relief the undistinguished pedigree of the anecdote: All four sources are among the latest and most unreliable of the entire tradition. Furthermore, the issue of word-painting aside, Beethoven's comments about the *Creation* were flattering; see Griesinger (7g) and Ries (11a), as well as Czerny's account in relation to the *Messiah* (3), all reporting incidents from the period 1803–05. The anecdote was therefore most likely a later one, widespread among Viennese musicians in the 1830s, but without authentic basis for Beethoven himself around 1800.

A feature of Beethoven's remarks in this period is that his criticism of Haydn took the form of deprecatory half-truths, or minor truths, while fundamental ones were omitted or glossed over. Thus the *Creation* became the butt of jokes about word-painting, while its essential merits were only mentioned afterwards, as a kind of footnote. Beethoven's remarks about never having learned anything from Haydn, which must have been relatively widely disseminated, apparently referred mainly to the counterpoint training, while his real debt to Haydn, as Solomon says, was so profound that he could not acknowledge it. For this period in these ways, the interpretation that Beethoven's attitude was essentially ambivalent seems incontrovertible.

---

[52]See Nottebohm's analysis of *Beethoven's Studien* (1863–64), N I, 154–203.

*   *   *   *   *

Far less evidence survives regarding Haydn's feelings about Beethoven. The familiar statement that he wanted Beethoven to place the phrase "Pupil of Haydn" on the title pages of his first works, and its necessary (if unstated!) corollary, that Beethoven refused, is found only in Ries (11d), and thus transmits at best only Beethoven's statement to him. But Haydn does seem to have been sensitive on this score. An anecdote about Pleyel, installed in London in 1792 as the star of a rival concert series to Haydn's, has Haydn insisting, "But I hope it will be remembered that he was my pupil."[53] His letters to Marianne von Genzinger from this period are full of the difficulties created by this rivalry; both in those letters and in others—though not when writing to Pleyel himself!—Haydn referred to Pleyel as his pupil. And several of his pupils, including Pleyel (in his string quartets Op. 2, 1784), the cellist Anton Kraft (in his cello sonatas Op. 2, 1790s), Paul Struck, and M. A. Wranitzky, did include such phrases on title pages.[54] Mozart himself implied an acknowledgment of Haydn as his involuntary teacher in quartet-writing in his dedicatory letter of September, 1785.[55] (Whether Haydn had anything to do with these professions of pupillage cannot be determined.) In Beethoven's case, the issue might be said to be moot, in view of his dedication of the Op. 2 sonatas to Haydn, an act of homage

[53]This anecdote appears in John Taylor, *Records of my Life*, 2 vols. (London, 1832), I, 275–76. It is transmitted in the literature only in paraphrase and without citing the source (e.g., Karl Geiringer, *Haydn: A Creative Life in Music* [Berkeley, 1968], p. 130; Solomon, p. 68), and so I quote it here: "Mr. Salomon invited [Haydn], Dr. Wolcot, and myself, to dine. . . . At length the name of Pleyel was mentioned, and Dr. Wolcot, who was apt to blunder, burst into a rapturous eulogium on the admired concertante of that composer, and on his taste and genius as a musician. The doctor carried his zeal to such an extent, forgetting that there was so great a musical genius in the room, that Haydn at last, readily admitting the merit of Pley[el], could not help adding a little warmly, 'But I hope it will be remembered that he was my pupil.' The doctor felt this remark as a rebuke, and attempted a confused apology." (Geiringer escalates "a little warmly" into "with considerable warmth," and Solomon raises the temperature further.) This anecdote, like so many of those relating to Beethoven, appeared forty years after the fact, and on internal evidence it appears that Taylor too did not fail to give fancy its due.

[54]Rita Benton, *Ignace Pleyel: A Thematic Catalogue of his Compositions* (New York, 1977), No. 3091; for Kraft, see Wolfgang Matthäus, "Das Werk Joseph Haydns im Spiegel der Geschichte des Verlags Jean André," *Haydn Yearbook*, III (1965), 84; for Struck, see RISM, Series A1, *Einzeldrücke vor 1800*, S6996; for Wranitzky, see Alexander Weinmann, *Die Wiener Verlagswerke von Franz Anton Hoffmeister* (Vienna, 1964), pp. 114–15.

[55]Mozart's implication of pupillage was confirmed anecdotally by Rochlitz in the *Allgemeine Musikalische Zeitung*, I (1798–99), 53 and by Niemetschek, *Mozart* (Prague, 1798), p. 60.

for which Mozart's quartets should have been ample legitimizing precedent for either man.

Haydn seems to have been offended by Beethoven's arrogance (or what he interpreted as such) just after 1800. Not only is this the burden of Fuchs's version of the *Creation* anecdote, and indirectly of Seyfried (16), but it appears explicitly in Griesinger's report (7g) of January, 1804 that Haydn "was delighted that Beethoven judged [his oratorios] so favorably, for he has been guilty of great arrogance *[eines grossen Stolzes]* against him." The stimulus for this violent expression of ill-feeling is unknown. It must have been of a part with Haydn's deferential agreement the preceding month that Griesinger should seek Beethoven's opinion on the suitability of the "Polyhymnia" oratorio text (7f). But, once again, the unexpected vehemence in the one case, the touching humility in the other, only reinforce the obvious chronological point that these utterances date from that period when Haydn was no longer able to summon up the strength and concentration to complete musical compositions, but was still attempting to do so; when he had not yet fully admitted to himself that his career had come to an end. Griesinger and Seyfried reinforce each other's reports that Haydn's ambivalence towards Beethoven was more a function of this frustration than of any fundamental personal or artistic incompatibility. The legend of ill-feeling thus forms part of the generally unsatisfactory tradition regarding Haydn's character, in which the chief literary accounts originated precisely during this atypical period of decline and hence give a one-sided and in many respects inaccurate portrait of his personality.[56]

The same point must be made regarding the issue of Haydn's not having understood or approved of Beethoven's music. The idea as applied to Beethoven's works from around 1795 is absurd in any case (see note 35). Even for the critical period around 1800, Haydn's difficulties can hardly be attributed to any inherent limitations of personality or musical outlook. As long as he remained healthy, the composer of fantasy-like, non-sonata works like the string quartet Op. 76, no. 6 in E♭ and the "Chaos" will hardly have failed to understand or have been shocked by anything Beethoven produced through 1802, not even the "Malinconia" from Op. 18, no. 6 or the "Quasi una fantasia" sonatas Op. 27. A general comparison of Opp. 76 and 77 (1797–99) with Op. 18 (1798–1800) would demonstrate, *pace* Josephine von Deym, Lobkowitz *le jeune,* and others in Beethoven's camp, that at the end of the decade Haydn had still not laid down the scepter.[57] (Much discussion of these points even today seems

---

[56]Cf. n. 3; also Larsen, "Haydn," *New Grove,* VII, 349.

[57]Cf. Landon's overwrought interpretation (IV, 503-5, 508). Even as a speculation, his conjecture that Haydn "withdrew" from implied competition with Beethoven upon

to assume that something like "mature Classical style" existed in the minds of composers and audiences in the 1790s, and that Haydn not only would have identified with such a thing, but would have been concerned to defend "it" against Beethoven's incursions—ignoring the absence of such concepts before the musicologists came along, and ignoring Haydn's non-Classical irregularity, experimentation, eccentricity, and unceasing progressivism.)

Regarding his lack of understanding of Beethoven, the anecdotal tradition comprises statements by Carpani (1), Doležalek (4c), Drouet (5), Marx (9), and Seyfried (16); only the first and last of these need be taken seriously. In general, however, Carpani is not trustworthy;[58] furthermore, his statement that Haydn found Beethoven's "most recent" works more and more "fantastic" or "fantasy-like" is expressly designated as hearsay. Conceivably, this transmits an opinion of Salieri.[59] Seyfried remains an attractive and plausible but uncorroborated story. The tradition of Haydn's having failed to understand Beethoven's music, at least through 1802, thus rests on a highly insecure foundation.

Although hardly our proper subject, the role of Romantic musical aesthetics in the rise of this anecdotal tradition must at least be noted. By the 1830s, when the mainstream of this tradition originated (at least in written form), Haydn's reputation was already well on its way toward the now debased myth of "Papa Haydn" from whose debilitating influence we still have not entirely freed ourselves. Schumann's notorious epithet for Haydn, "gewohnter Hausfreund," dates from 1841;[60] Marx's 1859 biography of Beethoven (I, 21–24) offers an appalling example of the contempt for and misunderstanding of Haydn that could arise in this atmosphere. The other side of the coin was the veneration of Beethoven as a revolutionary and of his works as the evolutionary goal of Western music. Under such conditions, it must have been all too easy to portray Haydn as the unwitting dupe of the impatient Beethoven and the good-hearted Schenk; as the old-school composer bamboozled by Op. 1, no. 3 (not to mention later works); as the princely servant who identified with the *ancien regime* and who was flustered and outraged by the revolutionary's declarations of independence. Such an attitude would have corre-

---

hearing Op. 18, evidenced by the failure to write more than two works in Op. 77, seems implausible: His declining productivity and the press to compose the *Seasons* and three large masses seem an adequate, documented explanation.

[58]See Vernon Gotwals, "The Earliest Biographies of Haydn," *The Musical Quarterly,* XLV (1959), 439–59.

[59]Landon, in another context (IV, 130), speculates that Carpani's musical statements may reflect the opinions of Salieri.

[60]*Gesammelte Schriften*, 4th ed. F. Gustav Jansen, 2 vols. (Leipzig, 1891), II, 303.

spondingly exaggerated the opposition that Beethoven stimulated among his contemporaries, and ignored his profound respect for good musical training and sound part-writing. In its cultural-historical origins and prejudices, the tradition tells us more about the beliefs of the 1830s and 1850s than about Haydn or Beethoven around 1800.

*   *   *   *   *

This study of the sources confirms the tradition that Haydn's and Beethoven's relationship was marred by mutual distrust and feelings of ambivalence, but only for the approximate period between 1800 and 1804. Along with many others, Beethoven made fun of Haydn's word-painting in the oratorios (but he qualified such comments with praise of the choruses and hence, by implication, of the grandeur of Haydn's conception and the nobility of its execution). He may have deprecated Haydn's piano music compared with his own, and he may have developed a kind of complex about the *Creation*. If so, this complex was associated with his own confused and contradictory fears about his health and career on the one hand, and with his need for compositional independence from Haydn on the other. (It would seem likely that Beethoven was at least as envious of Haydn's overwhelming public triumph as he was insecure about his ability to surpass it as a musical achievement.) But his ambivalence doubtless stemmed from having "learned too much" from Haydn as well. Conversely, during these years of declining powers, Haydn resented not only Beethoven's "arrogance" and lack of gratitude, but perhaps also his success in continuing to push forward into new domains of music—domains that he believed would have lain open to him if only his health had not failed.

Further than this the record does not go. There is no sufficient reason to believe that Beethoven much resented Haydn's methods of correcting his counterpoint exercises; no clear grounds for believing that the letters to the Elector involved deception on Beethoven's part regarding his 1793 compositions or had anything to do with Beethoven's not going to London; no great importance to be attached to any misunderstandings about Op. 1, no. 3 or public protestations of pupillage; no reason whatever to suppose that Haydn disliked Op. 1, no. 3, or indeed any of Beethoven's music of the 1790s, unless for reasons that reflect on Beethoven's limitations rather than his own; or that he was envious of Beethoven. Against all this must also be placed the clear evidence of productive professional association and positive feelings on both sides.

Of course, documents and anecdotes can never tell the whole story. Haydn was strong-minded, jealous of his stature as the greatest living composer, and proud of his pupils (doubtless increasingly so as he got older); Beethoven was not only strong-willed but paranoid, disrespectful of authority, eager to supplant Haydn as greatest living composer and perhaps frustrated by Haydn's continual forestalling of this event through the production of new masterworks. But the nineteenth century made more of this than was warranted; and some modern interpretations have not distinguished with sufficient care between credible and dubious sources, and have extrapolated the relatively limited well-documented difficulties described above into a generalized portrait of conflict and ambiguity that is not supported in the record. The recent tradition of scholarly interpretation is too valuable to justify compromising it by such exaggerations.

Appendix

1   Carpani [*Le Haydine*, p. 253 (= 2nd ed., p. 257)]: Fu chiesto una volta ad *Haydn* da un mio amico, che gli sembrasse di questo giovine compositore [Beethoven]. Rispose il vecchio con tutta la sincerità: "Le prime sue cose mi piacquero assai; ma le ultime confesso che non le capisco. Mi pare sempre che scriva delle *fantasie.*" [Translation: Vernon Gotwals, *Joseph Haydn: Eighteenth-Century Gentleman and Genius* (Madison, 1963), p. 264, n. 136. Cf. Solomon, p. 77.]

2   Czerny [quoted from Kerst, I, 41]: . . . so war [Beethoven] doch über die Anhänglichkeit gerührt, mit welcher Krumpholz selbst die bittersten Feindschaften nicht scheute, um gegen die damals so zahlreichen Gegner seine Sache zu verfechten. Denn in jener Zeit wurden Beethovens Kompositionen vom grösseren Publikum gänzlich verkannt und von allen Anhängern der ältern Mozart-Haydnschen Schule mit der grössten Bitterkeit bekämpft. [Translation: O. G. Sonneck, ed., *Beethoven: Impressions by his Contemporaries* (New York, 1926), p. 25.]

3   Czerny [quoted from Kerst, I, 57]: [After analyzing Graun's *Der Tod Jesu* in unflattering terms] Drauf nahm [Beethoven] mit den Worten: "Das ist ein andrer Kerl!" Händels "Messias" und spielte die interessantesten Nummern, machte uns dann auf mehrere Ähnlichkeiten mit Haydns "Schöpfung" aufmerksam usw. (um 1805). [Translation: Thayer-Forbes, p. 367.]

4a   Doležalek [quoted from Kerst, II, 191–92]: Die Komponisten waren damals gegen Beethoven, den sie nicht verstanden. . . . Doležalek brachte Albrechtsberger eine Arbeit über ein Beethovensches Quartett. Albrechtsberger: "Von wem ist denn das Zeug?" "Von Beethoven." "Ach gehen Sie mir mit dem, der hat nichts gelernt und wird nie etwas Ordentliches machen."

4b   Kotzeluch warf ihm [Doležalek] das C-Moll-Trio [Op. 1, no. 3] vor die Füsse, als er es ihm vorspielte. . . . [Translation of (4a) and (4b): Landon, ed., *Beethoven: A Documentary Study* (New York, 1970), p. 60.]

4c   Zu Haydn sagte [Koželuch] über Beethoven: "Nicht wahr, Papa, wir hätten das anders gemacht." Haydn antwortete lächelnd: "Ja, wir hätten das anders gemacht." Auch Haydn konnte sich nicht recht in Beethoven finden.

4d   Als Doležalek sich die Rasumowskyschen Quartette kaufte, sagte Gyrowetz: "Schade um das Geld." [Translation of (4c) and (4d): Thayer-Forbes, p. 409.]

4e   Das Septett wurde beim Fürsten Schwarzenberg zuerst gespielt und sehr bewundert. "Das ist meine 'Schöpfung.' " [The Septet was premiered at Prince Schwarzenberg's and much admired. "That is my *Creation*."]

5.1   Drouet [quoted from Thayer-Deiters-Riemann II, 198–200]: "Haydn," sagt Drouet, "war gewiss ein grosser Musikus, . . . und doch hat er sich in Bezug auf Beethoven . . . geirrt. Als er dessen erste Trios ansah, über welche man ihn nach seiner Meinung fragte, sagte er: 'Aus diesem jungen Manne wird nie etwas werden.' "

5.2   "Ganz und gar nicht," antwortete die Dame, "man schreibt diese Worte Haydn zu, aber er hat sie nicht gesagt. . . . Als Beethoven, noch sehr jung, . . . seine ersten Arbeiten Haydn zeigte, und diesen um seine Meinung befragte, sagte ihm Haydn: 'Sie haben sehr viel Talent. . . . Ihre Einbildungskraft ist eine unerschöpfliche Quelle von Gedanken. . . . Sie werden mehr leisten, als man bis jetzt geleistet hat, . . . Sie werden nie (und sie tun recht daran) einer tyrannischen Regel einen schönen Gedanken opfern, aber Ihren Launen werden Sie die Regeln zum Opfer bringen; denn Sie machen mir den Eindruck eines Mannes, der mehrere Köpfe, mehrere Herzen, mehrere Seele hat. . . . Ich . . . sage, das . . . immer etwas—um nicht zu sagen: Verschrobenes—doch: Ungewöhnliches in Ihren Werken sein wird: man wird schöne Dinge darin finden, sogar bewunderungswürdige Stellen, aber hier und da etwas Sonderbares, Dunkles, weil Sie selbst ein wenig finster und sonderbar sind, und der Styl des Musikers ist immer der Mensch selbst. Sehen Sie meine Compositionen an. Sie werden darin oft etwas Joviales finden, weil ich es selbst bin; neben einem ernsten Gedanken werden Sie einen heiteren finden, wie in Shakespeares Tragödien. In einem meiner Quartette fängt ein Satz in einer Tonart an und endigt in einer andern. . . . Muss man nicht heiter sein, um solche Dinge zu erfinden? . . .' In den ersten Compositionen Beethovens war alles Ueberfluss. Welch schöner Fehler ist aber der . . . eines übergrossen schöpferischen Reichtums. . . ."

5.3   Drouet: "Aber in den ersten Werken Beethovens sehe ich nicht jenen ungeheuren Ueberfluss von Gedanken . . . es sind nicht mehr Gedanken darin als nöthig, sie sind gut verarbeitet; es ist gute musikalische Rhetorik."

5.4   Die Dame: "Sie finden die ersten Compositionen Beethovens sehr gut, weil Sie sie kennen wie sie gedruckt worden sind, aber nicht wie er sie Haydn zeigte."

5.5   Drouet: "Diese Bemerkung ist sehr richtig . . . ich entsinne mich jetzt ganz genau, dass Beethoven mir sagte, '[Meine ersten Arbeiten] sind nicht so gedruckt, wie ich sie zuerst geschrieben hatte; als ich meine ersten Manuscripte, einige Jahre nachdem ich sie geschrieben, ansah, habe ich mich gefragt, ob ich nicht toll war, in ein einziges Stück zu bringen, was dazu hinreichte, zwanzig Stücke zu componieren. Ich habe diese Manuscripte verbrannt, damit man sie niemals sehe, und ich würde bei meinen ersten Auftreten als Componist viele Thorheiten begangen haben ohne die guten Rathschläge von Papa Haydn und von Albrechtsberger.' " [Translation of (5.1–5): Landon, *Haydn*, IV, 63–64.]

6   Fuchs [quoted from Thayer I, Vol. 1, p. 126 f.]: [mir] von achtbarer Hand eines Zeitgenossen mitgetheilt. Als Beethoven im Jahre 1801 die Musik zu dem Ballet "die Geschöpfe des Prometheus" geschrieben hatte, begegnete ihm sein ehemaliger Lehrer, der grosse Joseph Haydn, welcher ihn alsogleich festhielt und sagte: "Nun! gestern habe ich Ihr Ballet gehört, es hat mir sehr gefallen!" Beethoven erwiederte hierauf: "O lieber Papa! Sie sind sehr gütig, aber es ist doch noch lange keine 'Schopfung'!" Haydn, durch diese Antwort überrascht und beinahe verletzt, sagte nach einer kurzen Pause: "Das ist wahr, es ist noch keine 'Schöpfung,' glaube auch schwerlich, dass es dieselbe je erreichen wird!"—worauf sich beide—etwas verblüfft—gegenseitig empfahlen. [Translation: Thayer-Forbes, pp. 272–73.]

7a   Griesinger, letter to Härtel, April 3, 1802 [quoted from Thomas, p. 88]: Er [Beethoven] wünscht die hiesigen Verleger los zu sein; mehr als 31 Ducaten ist ihm bis jetzt für keine Klaviersonate bezahlt worden, und doch sollen seine Klaviersachen besser als die Haydn'schen sein. [Beethoven wants to be rid of the publishers here; up till now he has never been paid more than 31 ducats for a piano sonata, and yet his piano works are supposed to be [?he thinks that his piano works are] better than Haydn's.]

7b   April 7, 1802 [quoted from Hitzig, p. 24]: Haydn hat dem

Beethoven Ihre gute und richtige Bezahlung schon gerühmt. Beethoven will in Zukunft nur wenig fürs Klavier, aber desto mehr vielstimmig schreiben. [Haydn has already praised your generous and worthy honoraria to Beethoven. In the future, Beethoven intends to write but little for the piano, all the more, however, for larger ensembles.]

7c   December 8, 1802 [Hitzig, p. 27; Thomas, p. 92]: Er [Beethoven] habe, hiess es, nicht die gemeine Erziehung wie viele seiner Kollegen genossen und sei unfähig, ein Manuskript, das ihm einmal bezahlt worden sei, zum zweiten mal zu verkaufen. Papa Haydn habe sich dadurch genug prostituiert usw. [Beethoven said that he had not shared the vulgar upbringing of many of his colleagues, and that he was incapable of reselling elsewhere a manuscript [work] for which he had already been paid. Papa Haydn has prostituted himself more than enough in this respect, etc., etc.]

7d   September 17, 1803 [Hitzig, p. 28]: Beethoven hat jetzt den Auftrag erhalten, Schottische Lieder zu arrangieren. . . . [Beethoven has now received a commission to arrange Scottish songs.]

7e   November 12, 1803 [Hitzig, p. 28; Thomas, p. 99]: Auf Haydn rechne ich wegen der Komposition der Polymnia nicht mehr, ungeachtet er es nocht nicht geradezu abgewiesen hat. Wollen Sie, dass ich mit Beethoven darüber spreche? [As far as the composition of *Polymnia* is concerned, I've given up counting on Haydn, although he hasn't yet precisely turned it down. Do you want me to speak to Beethoven about it?]

7f   December 14, 1803 [Thomas, pp. 99–100]: Haydn war so gut gestimmt, dass ich den Augenblick ihm wegen der Polymnie zu Leibe zu gehen, nicht vernachlässigen könnte. . . . Er müsse aber noch das Gedicht einigemahle durchlesen, ehe er einen Entschluss fassen könnte. Das war nun die Sache wieder auf die lange Bank geschoben; ich erzählte ihm also, dass Beethoven gute Gedichte suche, und dass er vielleicht froh wäre, die Polymnia bearbeiten zu können. Diese Nachricht machte so viel Eindruck, dass mir der Papa auftrug, (doch ohne ihn dabei zu nennen) das Gedicht dem Beethoven zu zeigen, und von ihm zu erforschen, ob er es für eine musikalische Bearbeitung passend finde und glaube, dass man dadurch eine Ehre einlegen könne. Diese Condescenz des Papa wird Sie nicht weniger wundern als mich; allein dem ist einmahl so! Ich lief, wie Sie leicht glauben können, gleich mit der Polymnia zu Beethoven. . . . Nach Beethovens Äusserung wird sich also Haydn vermuthlich bestimmen. Sein Urtheil ist gewis competenter als das von Swieten. . . . So viel ich Haydn kenne, ist das Gedicht vielleicht zu hoch

für ihn geschrieben, denn ihm ist das triviale "süsse Liebe, reine Triebe"
u.s.w. geläufiger. . . . [Translation: Landon, *Haydn*, V, 271.]

7g   January 4, 1804 [Hitzig, p. 29–30; Thomas, p.
100–101]:
[Beethovens] Urtheil über die Polymnia ist folgendes: Das Gedicht sey
gut geschrieben, aber es sey nicht genug Aktion darinn; der Anfang erin-
nere ganz an die Schöpfung von Swieten, es sey zu reich an Mahlereyen
und dadurch etwas einförmig. In der Art von Lehrgedichten habe
Haydn durch d. Schöpfung u. d. Jahreszeiten Meisterstücke aufgestellt,
und er kenne in diesem Fache keinen glücklicheren Compositeur als
Haydn. Ihm scheinen die dramatischen Oratorien, dergleichen Händel
bearbeitete, besser zu musicalischen Compositionen geeignet; er wenig-
stens glaube in solchen besser zu reussiren. . . . Ich brachte nun meinen
Rapport . . . dem H[aydn]. Es freute ihn sehr, dass Beethoven so günstig von ihm urtheile, denn er beschuldigt diesen eines grossen Stolzes
gegen ihn; dass Beethoven dem Gedicht mehr Aktion wünsche, schien
ihm sonderbar, denn es soll ja nur ein Oratorium sein und kein Drama.
[Translation: Landon, *Haydn*, V, 281–82.]

8a   Griesinger to Böttger, October 10, 1818 [Thomas, p. 114, from
Volkmann]: Griesinger kommt auf die realistische Nachahmung von Na-
turlauten durch die Musik zu sprechen und erzählt, wie sich Haydn gegen die Vorwürfe, die ihm solche in der "Schöpfung" angebrachte Nach-
ahmungen eingetragen hatten, verteidigte. "Etwas ähnliches," fährt
Griesinger fort, "hörte ich von Beethoven bei Gelegenheit seiner
Schlachtmusik." Beethoven hatte die Vorwürfe zurückgewiesen, die
ihm wegen der Verwendung von Ratschen und Kanonenschlägen in der
"Schlacht von Vittoria" gemacht worden waren. [Griesinger turns to the
subject of the realistic imitation of sounds of nature in music, and relates
how Haydn defended himself against the criticisms that had been made
against him on account of such imitations in the *Creation*. "I heard something similar," continues Griesinger, "from Beethoven with respect to
his Battle Symphony." Beethoven had rejected the criticisms made
against him for using ratchets and cannons in the *Battle of Victoria*.]

8b   April 25, 1827 [*ibid.*]: Sein [Beethovens] gewaltiger Genius trieb
ihn! Dieser Naturgabe hatte er fast alles zu verdanken, nicht dem Unterricht bei Haydn, von dem er zuweilen lächelnd erzählte. [Beethoven was
driven by his overpowering genius! He owed almost everything to this
force of nature, not to his studies with Haydn, which he would occasionally describe condescendingly.]

9   Marx [*Beethoven*, I, 23 f.]: [Paraphrases Ries (11d) regarding

Beethoven's refusal to state "Pupil of Haydn," and continues:] Ja, als um 1801 Haydn das damals erschienene Septuor von Beethoven höchlich und gewiss aufrichtig belobte, erwiederte der Komponist halb artig, halb spöttisch: das Septuor sei noch lange keine Schöpfung; worauf denn doch Haydn bei aller Anspruchlosigkeit etwas gereizt bemerkte: "Die hätten Sie auch nicht schreiben können, denn Sie sind ein A t h e i s t." [More than that: When in 1801 Haydn warmly and doubtless sincerely praised Beethoven's Septet, which had just appeared, the composer replied half respectfully and half mockingly, "The Septet is a long way from the *Creation*"; whereupon Haydn, somewhat nettled despite his modesty, could not help replying, "You could never have written that, because you are an *Atheist*."]

10   Moscheles [*Life*, I, 34 f.]: I must note a proof of Haydn's love of justice. Haydn heard that Beethoven had spoken in a tone of depreciation of his oratorio the "Creation." "That is wrong of him," said Haydn; "what has he written then? His Septet? Certainly that is beautiful, nay, splendid!" he added, in tones of earnest admiration, completely forgetting the bitterness of the censure directed against himself.

11a   Ries [Wegeler-Ries, p. 77 f.]: Im Jahre 1802 [*sic*] componirte Beethoven . . . seine dritte Symphonie. . . . Beethoven dachte sich bei seinen Compositionen oft einen bestimmten Gegenstand, obschon er über musikalische Malereien häufig lachte und schalt, besonders über kleinliche der Art. Hiebei mussten die Schöpfung und die Jahreszeiten von Haydn manchmal herhalten, ohne dass Beethoven jedoch Haydns höhere Verdienste verkannte, wie er denn namentlich bei vielen Chören und anderen Sachen Haydn die verdientesten Lobsprüche ertheilte. [Translation: Sonneck, p. 53.]

11b   [p. 84 f.]: Von allen Componisten schätzte Beethoven Mozart und Händel am meisten, dann S. Bach. . . . Haydn kam selten ohne einige Seitenhiebe weg, welcher Groll bei Beethoven wohl noch aus frühern Zeiten herstammte. E i n e Ursache desselben möchte wohl folgende gewesen sein: Die drei Trio's von Beethoven (Opus 1) sollten zum erstenmale der Kunst-Welt in einer Soirée beim Fürsten Lichnowsky vorgetragen werden. Die meisten Künstler und Liebhaber waren eingeladen, besonders Haydn, auf dessen Urtheil Alles gespannt war. Die Trio's wurden gespielt und machten gleich ausserordentliches Aufsehen. Auch Haydn sagte viel Schönes darüber, rieth aber Beethoven, das dritte in C moll nicht herauszugeben. Dieses fiel Beethoven sehr auf, indem er es für das Beste hielt, so wie es denn auch noch Heute immer am meisten gefällt und die grösste Wirkung hervorbringt. Daher machte diese Aeusserung Haydn's auf Beethoven einen bösen Eindruck und liess bei ihm die Idee zurück: Haydn sei neidisch, eifersüchtig und meine es mit ihm nicht gut. Ich muss gestehen, dass, als Beethoven mir dieses erzählte, ich ihm wenig Glauben schenkte. Ich nahm daher Veranlassung, Haydn selbst darüber zu fragen. Seine Antwort bestätigte aber Beethoven's Aeusserung, indem er sagte, er habe nicht geglaubt, dass dieses Trio so schnell und leicht verstanden und vom Publikum so günstig aufgenommen werden würde. [Translation: Sonneck, pp. 48–49.]

11c   [p. 85 f.]: Bei der nämlichen Gelegenheit, fragte ich Haydn, warum er nie ein Violin-Quintett geschrieben habe und erhielt die lakonische Antwort: er habe immer mit vier Stimmen genug gehabt. Man hatte mir nämlich gesagt, es seien drei Quintette von Haydn begehrt worden, die er aber nie hätte componiren können, weil er sich in den Quartett-Stil so hinein geschrieben habe, dass er die fünfte Stimme nicht finden könne. Er habe angefangen, es sei aber aus einem Versuche am Ende ein Quartett, aus dem andern eine Sonate geworden. [I asked Haydn on the same occasion why he had never written a string quintet, and received the laconic reply that four parts had always sufficed for him. For I had been told that three quintets had been commissioned from Haydn, but that he had never been able to compose them, because he had written himself into quartet style so deeply that he couldn't find the fifth part. He had even begun, but one attempt had ended up as a quartet, the other as a sonata.]

11d   [p. 86]: Haydn hatte gewünscht, dass Beethoven auf den Titel seiner ersten Werke setzen möchte: "Schüler von Haydn." Beethoven wollte dieses nicht, weil er zwar, wie er sagte, einigen Unterricht bei Haydn genommen, aber nie etwas von ihm gelernt habe. . . . Auch bei Albrechtsberger hatte Beethoven im Contrapuncte und bei Salieri über dramatische Musik Unterricht genommen. Ich habe sie alle gut gekannt; alle drei schätzten Beethoven sehr, waren aber auch einer Meinung über sein Lernen. . . . Beethoven sei immer . . . eigensinnig und selbstwollend gewesen. . . . Besonders waren Albrechtsberger und Salieri dieser Meinung; die trockenen Regeln des Erstern und die unwichtigeren des Letzteren über dramatische Compositionen . . . konnten Beethoven nicht ansprechen. [Translation: Sonneck, p. 49.]

11e   [Ries follows directly with the familiar anecdote of Beethoven's supposed contempt for the traditional prohibition against parallel fifths:] "Und s o erlaube i c h sie!" war seine Antwort. [Translation: Sonneck, pp. 49–50.]

12a.1   Schenk [Autobiography; quoted from *SMw*, XI (1924), 80–83]:[1] 1792, geruheten Sr. k. Hoheit Erzherzog Maximilian, Churfürst von Cölln, seinen Schützling Louis van Beethoven, nach Wien zu geben, [und] [um] bei Josef Haydn die musikalische Komposition zu lernen. Gegen Ende Juli gab mir Abbé Gellinek Kenntnis, das er mit einem jungen Menschen in Bekanntschaft getreten seye, der auf dem Pianoforte eine seltene Virtuosität bewährt, [wie er sie] [und] seit Mozart nicht wieder gehört habe. Inmittelst erklärte er sich, dass Beethoven schon vor mehr als 6 Monaten von Haydn die Lehre des Contrapunktes hat angefangen und noch immer bei der ersten Übung sich verweile: und dass auch Se. Excellenz Baron van Svieten ihm das Studium des Contrapunktes ernstlich empfehle und öfter in Frage gestellt, wie weit er schon in seiner Lehre fortgeschritten seye? Zufolge dessen mehrmalendem Anregen und so auch noch immer auf der ersten Stufe seines Unterrichtes zu sein, erzeugte in dem wissbegierigen Lehrling ein Missbehagen, das er an seinem Freund oft laut werden liess. Gellinek, dem diese leidige Gemütsstimmung nah zu Herzen ging, stellte mich in Frage: ob ich wohl geneigt wäre, seinen Freund im Studium des Contrapunktes behülflich [zu] [wolle] sein. Nach besagter Erklärung verlangte es mich, mit selbigem bald in nähere Bekanntschaft zu treten. Nun war ein Tag bestimmt, an welchem ich Beethoven in der Wohnung Gellineks sehen und auf dem [Pianoforte] [P.F.] hören [sollte] [werde].

12a.2   [Schenk describes hearing Beethoven improvise.]

12a.3   Den darauffolgenden Tag war es mein erstes, diesem noch unbekannten Künstler, der seine Meisterschaft so hoch bewährte, meinen ersten Besuch zu machen. Auf seinem Schreibpulte fand ich einige Sätze von [den ersten Übungen] [der ersten Uebung] des Contrapunktes vor mir liegen. Nach kurzer Übersicht gewahrte ich bei jeder Tonart (so kurzen Inhaltes sie auch war) etwelche Fehler. In Rücksicht [darauf] [dessen] haben sich die oben erwähnten Äusserungen Gellineks wahrhaft befunden. Da ich nun gewiss war, dass mein Lehrling mit den

---

[1]The versions of Schenk's autobiographical statement appearing in Thayer I, Vol. 1 (from Jahn's copy of the original) and in *SMw* both lay claim to "diplomatic" status, the latter explicitly (p. 75), the former by virtue of Jahn's usual standards of accuracy and from internal evidence. Yet they differ not only substantially in orthographic detail but occasionally in the sense. Despite what appears to be a greater proportion of implausible readings, I have reproduced the *SMw* version here, on the basis of its explicit claim to literalness and its standing at only a single remove from the original, rather than two. Significant variants in Thayer-Deiters's version are indicated by the inclusion of both versions in square brackets, the *SMw* reading always preceding; variants affecting orthography or punctuation alone are not included.

vorläufigen Regeln des Contrapunktes unbekannt war, so gab ich ihm das [altbekannte] [allbekannte] Lehrbuch von Josef [Fuchs] [Fux], *Gradus ad Parnassum,* zur Übersicht der weiter folgenden Übungen. Josef Haydn, der gegen Ende des vorhergehenden Jahres [vom Lande] [von London] nach Wien zurückgekommen [war] [only in Thayer], war beflissen seine Musse [sic] auf neue Kompositionen grosser Meisterwerke zu verwenden. In diesem rühmlichen Bestreben ist zu erachten, dass sich Haydn mit der Lehre der Grammatik nicht so leicht befassen konnte. Nun war mir's ernstlich angelegen, dessen Wissbegierigen Mitgehülfe zu werden. Bevor ich aber meine Lehre angefangen, machte ich ihm bemerkbar, dass unser beiderseitiges Zusammenwirken stets geheim gehalten werden. In Beziehung dessen empfahl ich ihm, jeden Satz, den ich durch meine Hand verbessert, wieder abzuschreiben, damit bei jeder Vorzeigung Haydn keine fremde Hand gewahren könne. Nach einem Jahre kam Beethoven mit Gellinek in Unfrieden. . . . Zufolge ihrer Uneinigkeit war Gelinek erbosst und offenbarte mein [Geheimnis] [Geheimhalten]. Beethoven und seine Brüder machten selbst kein Geheimnis mehr daraus.

12a.4   1792, anfangs August, habe ich bei meinem guten Louis das ehrenvolle Lehramt angetreten, und bis zu Ende Mai 1793 ununterbrochen fortgesetzt, als er eben den doppelten Contrapunkt in Octav vollendet hatte und sich nach Eisenstadt begeben. Wenn S. K. Hoheit seinen Schützling gleich zu Albrechtsbergers Leitung hingegeben hätte, so wäre sein Studium nie unterbrochen und ganz vollendet worden.

12a.5   [The following paragraph was later stricken in the manuscript; Thayer quotes only its final half-sentence, from "vielmehr":] Vor etwelchen Jahren wollte ein Jemand mit feierlichen Beteuerungen glauben machen: Beethoven habe seine Lehre noch bey Albrechtsberger ganz vollendet. Für Beethoven wäre das wohl nützlich gewesen, wenn er das getan hätte. Jedoch diese Aussage nach so vielen verflossenen Jahren war die erste, die mir je zu Ohren kam. Wenn ich aber das für wert befunden habe [sic; sense calls for "hatte"?], so wäre Abbé Gellinek vor allen anderen gewiss der erste gewesen, mir davon Kunde zu geben. So auch Beethoven, der jederzeit so gut und aufrichtig gegen mich gestimmt war, hätte diese Lobens werte Veränderung mir nie verheimlicht, vielmehr gestand er mir, dass er sich zu Herrn Salieri k. k. Hofkapellmeister hingegeben, um in der Komposition im freyen Stil Unterricht zu nehmen.

12a.6   Ungefähr nach halbem Mai tat er mir zu wissen, dass er [sich mit Haydn] [mit Haydn sich] bald nach Eisenstadt begeben werde und daselbst bis anfangs Winter [da] [only in Thayer] verweilen werde. Den Tag der Abreise wisse er noch nicht. Anfangs Juni kam ich zur gewöhnlichen Stunde wieder—allein mein guter Louis war nicht mehr zu sehen. [Thayer's quotation from Jahn breaks off here.] Er hinterliess mir folgendes Billetchen, welches ich Wort für Wort niederschreibe:

12a.7   Lieber Schenk!
Ich wünschte nicht, dass ich schon heute fort würde reisen nach Eisenstadt. Gerne hätte ich noch mit Ihnen gesprochen. Unterdessen rechnen sie auf meine Dankbarkeit für die mir erzeigten Gefälligkeiten. Ich werde mich bestreben, Ihnen alles nach meinen Kräften gut zu machen. Ich hoffe Sie bald wieder zu sehen und das Vergnügen Ihres Umganges geniessen zu können. Leben Sie wohl und vergessen Sie nicht ganz Ihren
                                    Beethoven.

12a.8   Es war meine Absicht mein Verhältnis zu Beethoven nur sehr kurz zu berühren; allein die obwaltenden Umstände, auf welche Art und Weise ich dazu gekommen, sein Wegführer in der musikalischen Composition zu werden, geboten mir, mich etwas ausführlicher zu erklären.

12a.9   Für mein Bemühen (wenn doch das Bemühen heissen sollte) erwarb ich mir von meinem guten Louis ein köstliches Geschenk, nämlich: das feste Band der Freundschaft, das bis an seinen Tod noch unverwelkt geblieben. [Translation of (12a.1-9): Thayer-Forbes, pp. 140–42.]

12b.1   [Schenk? (Version of autobiography from *Der Freischütz*, 1837; quoted from Thayer I, Vol. 1, pp. 380 ff.)]: Im Jahre 1792 sendete der Churfürst von Cölln seinen Schützling, Ludwig van Beethoven, nach Wien, um bei Joseph Haydn die Composition zu lernen. Der Abbe Gelinek, mit welchem Schenk häufig zusammenkam, erzählte diesem, dass er einen jungen Menschen kenne, der eine Virtuosität auf dem Pianoforte bewahre, wie sie, ausser bei Mozart, niemals gehört worden. Ein anderes Mal erwähnte er, dass Beethoven bereits vor einem halben Jahre bei Haydn die Lehre des Contrapunktes angefangen, aber wenig Fortschritte mache. Er endete mit der Bitte, Schenk möchte den jungen Künstler in seinem Studium behülflich sein. Vor allem wurde ein Zusammenkunft in Gelinek's Wohnung beschlossen. . . .

12b.2   [Beethoven's improvisation is described.]

12b.3   Den Tag nach der ersten Zusammenkunft besuchte Schenk den jungen Künstler. . . . Auf dem Pult lagen einige contrapunktische Uebungssätze, in denen Schenk, nach flüchtigem Ueberblick, einige Fehler bemerkte. Beethoven schien in einem etwas gereizten Zustande. Voll Eifer und Wissbegierde war er nach Wien gekommen; . . . er war an einen grossen Mann gewiesen, und doch wollte es in der Haupsache [sic] nicht recht worwärts. Das war aber sehr begreiflich. Haydn war oft abwesend, überdies zu sehr mit seinen bedeutenden Werken beschäftigt, um sich genau mit der Lehre der musikalischen Grammatik zu befassen, oder sich überhaupt viel um den jungen Feuergeist zu bekümmern, den ihm ein grosser Herr aufgebürdet und der ihm im Grunde lästig war. Beethoven verhehlte seine missmuthige Stimmung gegen Schenk nicht und wiederholte endlich, mit aller Freimüthigkeit, Gelinek's Antrag, den jener mit Vergnügen annahm, da er sich dadurch geehrt fühlte. Der *Gradus ad Parnassum,* von Joseph Fux, wurde vorgenommen und rasch an das Werk geschritten. Nun entstand wirklich ein sonderbares Verhältniss, indem er, der neue Lehrer, die nahe Grösse seines Schülers voraussehend, den höchsten Respect gegen ihn empfand, und sich selbst nur als das Werkzeug betrachtete, um zur theoretischen Ausbildung des künftigen Meisters sein Scherflein beizutragen. Indessen durfte Haydn nicht gänzlich übergangen werden; Beethoven schrieb also die von Schenk corrigirten Sätze immer wieder ab, damit jener keine fremde Schrift gewahre. Natürlich drang Schenk auch bei diesem Verhältnis auf das tiefste Geheimhalten. Im nächsten Jahre entstanden Uneinigkeiten zwischen Beethoven und Gelinek, und der letztere plauderte das Geheimniss aus, worüber sich Schenk gar nicht zufrieden geben wollte. Der Unterricht hatte noch kein Jahr gedauert und war im besten Gange, als Beethoven plötzlich nach Eisenstadt berufen wurde, um dort mit Haydn längere Zeit zu verweilen. Er liess in seiner Wohnung folgenes Schreiben zurück:

12b.4   "Lieber Schenk! . . . " [Thayer now refers to p. 262, where he quotes the letter, ostensibly from Seyfried's version (15.2), but with the variant for the first three words, "Ich wusste nicht," that occurs in *Der Freischütz,* in place of "Ich wünschte nicht" as in Schenk (12a) and Seyfried (15).]

12b.5   Späterhin bildete sich, bei aller Verschiedenheit, noch ein inniges Verhältniss zwischen den beiden Männern bis zu Beethoven's Tod.

13   Schenk [according to notes by F. Luib, reported by Jahn; quoted from Kerst, I, 29–30]: . . . dass Schenk . . . Beethoven bei Gelinek kennen lernte und phantasieren hörte, was ihn an Mozart erinnerte. Un-

mutig beklagte sich Beethoven oft, dass er in seinen kontrapunktlichen
Studien bei Haydn nicht vorwärts komme, da dieser [,] vielfach beschäftigt, seine Ausarbeitungen nicht gehörig nachsehe. Schenk erbot sich . . .
Beethoven Anweisung zu geben. . . .Anfang August 1792 begann
dieser Unterricht und dauerte bis Ende Mai 1793. Jede verbesserte Aufgabe musste Beethoven abschreiben und so Haydn vorlegen. Als Schenk
Anfang Juni 1793 zu Beethoven kam, fand er ihn verreist zum Besuch
beim Fürsten Esterhazy und ein Abschiedsbillet an ihn. Als Haydn
Beethoven an Albrechtsberger übergab, musste der geheime Unterricht
aufhören.

14a.1   Schindler [(1840), p. 31 f.]: . . . dass Beethoven bei seiner
Ankunft in Wien nichts vom Contrapuncte und wenig von der Harmo-
nielehre wusste. Seine Phantasie bereits mächtig rege, das Ohr scharf,
und Pegasus stets willig, schrieb er darauf los, ohne nach den unent-
behrlichen Schulregeln weiter zu fragen. So begann der Unterricht bei
Haydn, und Vater Haydn soll mit seinem neuen Schüler immer zufrieden gewesen seyn, weil er ihn thun liess, was dieser wollte; bis sich
das Blatt wendete, und der Schüler mit dem Lehrer unzufrieden wurde,
welches so kam:

14a.2   Unter den von Beethoven gekannten und geachteten
Künstlern war auch Herr Schenk, . . . ein sanfter, liebenswürdiger
Charakter und gründlicher Kenner der musikalischen Wissenschaften.
Herr Schenk begegnete eines Tages Beethoven, als er eben mit seinem
Hefte unter'm Arm von Haydn kam. Schenk warf einen Blick in das-
selbe, und sah da und dort manches Unrichtige. Beethoven darauf aufmerksam gemacht, versicherte, dass Haydn dieses Elaborat so eben cor-
rigirt habe. Schenk blätterte zurück, und fand in den früheren Elaboraten
die gröbsten Fehler nicht verbessert. Beethoven schöpfte nun Verdacht
auf Haydn und wollte den Unterricht bei ihm nicht weiter fortsetzen,
von welchem Entschlusse er sich aber abbringen liess, bis Haydn's
zweite Reise nach England schickliche Gelegenheit dazu gab. Seit jenem
Augenblicke schien keine freundliche Sonne mehr zwischen Haydn und
Beethoven. . . . Herr Schenk blieb seitdem der vertraute Verbesserer
der Elaborate Beethoven's, selbst dann noch, als Albrechtsberger seinen
Unterricht im Contrapuncte übernommen. . . . [Translation of (14a.1–
2): . . . that on his arrival in Vienna Beethoven knew no counterpoint
and only a little harmony. His fantasy already powerfully active, his ear
sharp, Pegasus always willing, he dashed off his thoughts without wor-
rying about the indispensable technical rules. Thus the studies with
Haydn began, and Papa Haydn was apparently always satisfied with his
new pupil, because he let him write whatever he liked;—until one day

the tables were turned, and the pupil became dissatisfied with the teacher, which came about thus:

Among the artists whom Beethoven knew and respected was a certain Herr Schenk, . . . a gentle, kind fellow and a thorough master of musical science. One day Schenk encountered Beethoven just as he was returning from Haydn, his notebook under his arm. Schenk took a look at it, and saw many errors in various places. When this was pointed out to him, Beethoven assured Schenk that Haydn had just corrected this particular exercise. Schenk flipped back through the pages, and discovered that in earlier exercises even the most egregious errors had not been corrected. Beethoven now became suspicious of Haydn and wanted to break off his studies with him, but he allowed himself to be persuaded to put off this decision until Haydn's second journey to England gave an appropriate pretext. From that moment on the relations between Haydn and Beethoven stood under a cloud. Afterwards Schenk remained the trusted corrector of Beethoven's exercises, even after Albrechtsberger had taken over his instruction in counterpoint.]

14b   [p. 32 f.]: Bei dem unstäten Leben Beethoven's geschah es nur zu oft, dass er selbst von recht guten Freunden und Bekannten jahrelang nichts wusste, . . . und . . . waren sie für ihn so gut wie gestorben. So traf es sich, dass . . . Anfang des Frühlings 1824 . . . uns der alte Herr Schenk begegnete, damals schon ein hoher Sechziger. Beethoven[,] ausser sich vor Freude, diesen alten Freund noch unter den Lebenden zu sehen, . . . fing nun an, alle Falten seines Herzens seinem verehrten Corrector aufzudecken. Redselig wie selten, tauchten eine Menge Geschichten und Anekdoten aus jener längst vergangenen Zeit in seiner Erinnerung auf, so auch jene Vorfälle mit Haydn, und der nun auch zur Majestät im Reiche der Tonkunst emporgestiegene Beethoven überhäufte den bescheidenen, in Dürftigkeit lebenden Componisten des "Dorfbarbiers" mit dem innigsten Danke für seine ihm damals bewiesene Freundschaft. [Owing to Beethoven's unsettled way of life, it happened all too often that for years on end he lost track even of very good friends and acquaintances, and for all he knew they were as good as dead. So it happened that in early spring 1824 we encountered old Schenk, by then already in his late sixties. Beside himself with joy at seeing this old friend still among the living, Beethoven began to reveal the innermost secrets of his heart to his admired corrector. Talkative as I had rarely seen him, [Beethoven] recalled story after story and anecdote upon anecdote from those far-off days, including those incidents with Haydn. And Beethoven, who in the meantime had ascended to majesty in the kingdom of music, overwhelmed the modest composer of *Der*

Dorfbarbier, living in straitened circumstances, with the most sincere thanks for the friendship granted him many years before.]

15.1   Seyfried [quoted from Schilling, 2nd ed. (1840), VI, 189 f.]: 1792 kam Beethoven nach Wien, und S[chenk] hörte ihn zum ersten Male in Abbe Gelinek's Wohnung fantasiren: ein Hochgenuss, der lebhaft Mozart's Andenken zurückrief. Unmuthig beklagte sich der lernbegierige Beethoven oftmals gegen Gelinek, wie er in seinen contrapunktischen Studien bei Haydn nicht vorwärts kommen könne, da dieser Meister, allzu vielseitig beschäftigt, den ihm vorgelegten Elaborationen die gewünschte Aufmerksamkeit zu schenken gar nicht im Stande sey. Jener sprach darüber mit S. und befragte ihn, ob er nicht geneigt sey, mit B. die Compositionslehre durchzumachen. Dieser erklärte sich höchst willfährig dazu, jedoch nur unter der Doppel-Bedingung, ohne irgend eine Vergütung und unter dem Siegel unverbrüchlicher Verschwiegenheit. . . . Anfangs August 1792 begann der theoretische Unterricht und währte bis Ende Mai des nächsten Jahrs ununterbrochen fort; jede verbesserte Aufgabe musste Beethoven, um auch den Schein fremden Einflusses zu vermeiden, vorerst eigenhändig abschreiben, und dann erst Haydn zum Gutachten vorlegen. Dieses wenig bekannt gewordene Verhältniss wird durch folgende Tatsache documentirt. Als nämlich S. in den ersten Junitagen zur gewohnten Stunde sich einstellte, fand er das Vögelein ausgeflogen nach Ungarn, auf Besuch zum Fürsten Esterhazy, dafür aber ein hinterlassenes Briefchen, welches, diplomatisch genau vidimirt, also lautete:

15.2   Lieber Schenk! Ich wünschete nicht, dass ich schon heute fort würde reisen, nach Eisenstadt. Gerne hätte ich noch mit Ihnen gesprochen. Unterdessen rechnen Sie auf meine Dankbarkeit für die mir erzeigten Gefälligkeiten. Ich werde mich bestreben, Ihnen Alles nach meinen Kräften gutzumachen. Ich hoffe, Sie bald wieder zu sehen u. das Vergnügen Ihres Umgangs geniessen zu können. Leben Sie wohl und vergessen Sie nicht ganz Ihren Beethoven. [Translation of (15.1-2): Schindler-MacArdle, 53–54 (Schindler quotes these paragraphs in his third edition).]

15.3   Da Haydn beim Antritt der zweiten Londoner Reise seinen Pflegbefohlenen Albrechtsberger'n übergab, unter dessen Aegide Beethoven das gesammte Harmonie-System recapitulirte und beendigte, im freien Style aber Salieri's erfahrungsreicher Leitung sich anvertraute, so konnte das frühere geheime Zusammenwirken nicht ferner

fortbestehen; reichliche Entschädigung fand jedoch S. in jenem Freund-
schaftsband[,] das unverwelkt auch noch fortblühte, als die von ihm so
sorglich gehegte Pflanze zum angestaunten Riesenbaume emporge-
wachsen war. . . . [Since Haydn, upon departing on his second journey
to London, gave his charge over to Albrechtsberger, under whose aegis
Beethoven recapitulated and concluded the entire system of harmony
(entrusting himself, however, to Salieri's experienced guidance in free
composition), the secret collaboration [with Schenk] could no longer be
maintained. But Schenk was richly rewarded by his bond of friendship
[with Beethoven], which bloomed without fading even after the sapling
he had so carefully tended had grown into an astonishingly mighty tree.]

16   Seyfried [*Beethoven's Studien*, Anhang, p. 23 f.]: Als Joseph
Haydns Kränklichkeit zunahm, besuchte ihn Beethoven immer seltener;
hauptsächlich aus einer Art von Scheu, weil er bereits einen Weg einge-
schlagen hatte, den jener nicht ganz, eigener Überzeugung zufolge, bil-
ligte. Dennoch erkundigte sich der liebenswürdige Greis häufig nach
seinem Telemach, und fragte oftmahls: "Was treibt denn unser Gross-
mogul?" [As Joseph Haydn's ill-health worsened, Beethoven visited him
less and less often, owing primarily to a kind of sensitivity, because he
had already struck out in a direction of which Haydn, according to his
own convictions, did not entirely approve. Nevertheless the kindly old
man often inquired about his "Telemachus," and often asked, "What is
our Grand Mogul up to?"]

17.1   [F. Lorenz; quoted from original]: . . . nur war mir gleich Anfangs die sehr ungleiche Werthschätzung aufgefallen, die [Schenk] ein-
zelnen musikalischen Autoren und ihren Werken angedeihen liess. Im
Ganzen gemässigt und gerecht über Italiener wie Deutsche urtheilend,
namentlich Mozart's und Beethoven's Namen nie ohne Verehrung aus-
sprechend, verfinsterte sich die Miene des sonst heiteren und
liebenswürdigen Greises doch allsogleich, sobald das Gespräch auf
Haydn kam; er hatte fort und fort nicht blos an dessen Werken, auch an
dessen Charakter zu mäkeln. "Mozart war ein seelenguter Kerl, aber
Haydn grundfalsch," sagte er mir eines Tages. . . .

17.2   Dennoch war ich Thor genug, . . . mich in den glühendsten
Lobpreisungen [der "Schöpfung"] . . . zu ergehen. Als er aber auch so-
gar für dieses widerwillig nur kühles Lob und verschiedene abträgliche
Bemerkungen in Bereitschaft hatte, platzte ich . . . mit den unhöflichen
Worten heraus: "Sie haben halt gegen meinen armen Haydn so einen
dummen Hass." "Und Sie sind ein ———," rief der alte Herr, das derbe
Kompliment noch derber erwiedernd. . . .

17.3   Ich halte . . . die Thatsache, dass Schenk tiefen Groll gegen Haydn hegte, . . . der Veröffentlichung werth, weil durch sie ein aufhellendes Streiflicht auf die bekannte Episode in Beethoven's Leben fällt. . . .

17.4   Der Grund dieser Abneigung ist nicht bekannt geworden. . . . [Man] weiss, aus welch' kleinen, ja kleinlichen Motiven zuweilen bei Künstlern und Schriftstellern zweiten und dritten Ranges ein blinder Hass gegen die Koryphäen entsteht, und mit welch' äusserster Vorsicht daher abträgliche Urtheile und Anekdoten aufgenommen werden müssen, wenn sie von jener Seite ausgehen. . . . [Translation of (17.1–4): But I at once noticed how variable were the opinions [Schenk] harbored towards individual composers and their works. Although by and large he judged both German and Italian [composers] fairly, and in particular never mentioned Mozart's or Beethoven's name with anything other than admiration, and was usually of cheerful and kind disposition, his face darkened at once whenever the conversation turned to Haydn. He constantly criticized not only his works, but also his character. "Mozart was a good soul," he once said to me, "but Haydn was false through and through. . . ."

Despite all this I was foolish enough to lose myself in glowing hymns of praise [of *The Creation*]. But he would praise even this masterwork in lukewarm terms at best, against his will, and with various negative qualifications; and once I sputtered at him impolitely, "But you bear such a grudge against my poor Haydn!" "And you are a ———!" cried the old man, repaying my rude compliment with interest.

I believe that it is worthwhile to publish the fact that Schenk bore a deep grudge against Haydn, because it throws an illuminating perspective on the familiar episode in Beethoven's life.

The basis for this aversion never came out. [One] knows all too well that inconsequential, even petty motives can engender blind hatred of the great, especially perhaps among second- and third-rate artists and writers; and that one must therefore regard negative judgments and anecdotes with the utmost caution when they emanate from such sources. . . .]

A Veiled Judgment of Beethoven by Albrechtsberger?

Martin Staehelin

The services that Elliot Forbes has performed for Alexander Wheelock Thayer's "classical" Beethoven research are so well known to musicology, especially in America, that they need not be elaborated here.[1] If I am not mistaken, however, this is not the only area in which Forbes feels united with Thayer. In addition to the labor of both scholars on Beethoven's biography, there is their common academic tie with Harvard University.[2] Both Thayer and Forbes have served this worthy institution, and the firmness of this connection in each case can be properly measured only by one who has extensive familiarity with the local relationships[3] and the special spirit at Harvard University from a personal viewpoint. I cannot claim that for myself, and so, as a "distant" European, I choose my theme for the following essay from that other realm where Forbes and Thayer come together—Beethoven's biography. Here I, too, with many another Beethoven-colleague, owe a debt of gratitude to Forbes and Thayer.

*　　*　　*　　*　　*

The relationship between Beethoven and his sometime teacher of composition, Johann Georg Albrechtsberger, has never been clarified to the extent that musicology would wish. To be sure, we know the basic

[1]Citations are from the third paperback printing of Thayer-Forbes, 1973.

[2]See Thayer's autobiographical sketches: Bonn, Beethoven Archives, SBH 230 (Ad 5 Thayer). Printed in Thayer-Forbes, pp. vii-viii.

[3]I was especially impressed to see, on my latest visit to Harvard University, that a building in Harvard Yard bears the name "Thayer Hall." After finishing the text, I was kindly informed by Phyllis Benjamin of Harvard University that this hall was built in 1870 by the Boston merchant Nathaniel Thayer in honor of his father, Reverend Nathaniel Thayer. Although the two families were apparently not related by blood, Alexander Wheelock Thayer's maternal grandfather, William Biglow, studied theology with Reverend Thayer during the 1790s.

facts and also much of the content of the instruction that Albrechtsberger gave to the young Beethoven from around the beginning of 1794 through the first half of 1795.[4] At the same time, the factors outside the bare biography of this relationship, as well as the reciprocal artistic and personal judgments of these two men, have been documented poorly, and sometimes even in a contradictory way. Thus, according to Ries, Beethoven acted willfully at his lessons and was not particularly receptive.[5] For that reason Albrechtsberger, according to Doležalek, was said to have declared that Beethoven had never learned anything in the proper way.[6] The veracity of both these reports may be strongly questioned in light of Beethoven's assiduous exercises, still preserved, that Beethoven prepared for Albrechtsberger. Further, three little-known letters of 1796–97 from Albrechtsberger to Beethoven[7] display, from the teacher's side, quite a friendly tone, and even a passing word of artistic recognition;[8] while on the side of the pupil, details in the reports of Potter and Hirsch show Beethoven's rather reverent approbation of Albrechtsberger.[9]

The little surviving evidence thus leaves us in the dark, not only on the question of this mutual relationship but already on questions of the value of the individual sources and the weight or the circumstantial nature of their comments. In such a situation, a letter from Albrechtsberger to the publisher Breitkopf in Leipzig may shed a welcome new light, and may even tell us something about Albrechtsberger's artistic judgment of Beethoven. Unpublished until now, it is presented here in its entirety,[10] without any further prefatory remarks:

[4]See especially Gustav Nottebohm, *Beethovens Unterricht bei J. Haydn, Albrechtsberger und Salieri*, Vol. I of *Beethovens Studien* (Leipzig and Winterthur: Rieter-Biedermann, 1873), especially pp. 45-203. For a chronology, see Douglas P. Johnson, *Beethoven's Early Sketches in the 'Fischhof Miscellany,'* Diss. Princeton Univ. 1973 (Ann Arbor: University Microfilms International, 1980), I, 447-54.

[5]See Wegeler-Ries, p. 86.

[6]See Friedrich Kerst, ed., *Die Erinnerungen an Beethoven* (Stuttgart: Hoffmann, 1913), II, 191.

[7]See Andreas Weissenbäck, "Drei noch unveröffentlichte Briefe Albrechtsbergers an Beethoven," *Musica Divina*, IX (1921), 10-11.

[8]For example, Albrechtsberger writes to Beethoven on June 8, 1797: "My dear Beethoven! I have just received your letter and am astonished that you have withdrawn your trio, when it was going so well for you. . . ." ["Mein lieber Beethoven! Ich erhalte soeben Ihren Brief und bin erstaunt, daß Sie das Trio zurückziehen, wo es Ihnen doch so gut gelungen ist. . . ."]

[9]Kerst, *op. cit.*, I, 225 f. and 230 f.

[10]SPK, Musikabteilung, Mus. Slg. Härtel 5. At this point, let me express my deep thanks to Dr. Rudolf Elvers for his kind permission to publish this letter. On the history of the Härtel collection, see Rudolf Elvers, "Breitkopf & Härtels Verlagsarchiv," *Fontes Artis Musicae*, XVII (1970), 24-28, especially p. 27 f.

Wien, den 17.ten
Augusti 798.

Wohl Edler Herr
von Breitkopf!

Dero Zeilen vom 3.ten August habe ich vorige Wochen rechtens erhalten. Jch danke Jhnen, und der ganzen wohlmeinenden Gesellschaft des neuen Jnstitutes, die einen der musickalischen Welt nüzlichen Plan zu machen Willens ist, vom Grunde meines biedermännischen Herzens, daß Sie auch mich dazu so sehnlich eingeladen haben. Dieser Ehre kan mein hohes Alter (wenn ich es doch kurz und aufrichtig sagen darf) nicht mehr theilhaftig werden; meine Geistes-Kräften nehmen von Tag zu Tag ab; und ein Mann nahe dem 63.ten Jahr, folglich auch dem Tode, denkt schon mehr auf die zeitliche und ewige Ruhe, als auf die Ehre: ein Lehrer oder *Criticus* zu seyn. Meine geringe Kenntnissen würden auch wenig beytragen den jeztigen Bittergeschmack in der Musick zu verbessern. Und der Heyland selbst hat uns schon längst vorgesagt: *Semper pauperes habebitis vobiscum:* ihr werdet mehr Schmierer, als reine Sätzer bei euch herum haben: derowegen gehe ich auch sehr selten zu häußlichen Akademien, weil sich fast jede mit einem faden Gassenliedel, oder gar teutschem Tanze endiget. Vor 32. Jahren, da ich nach Wien kamm, sprachen die Damen das Lob den Komponisten; jezt aber gar die Schusters Weiber und junge Windpursche aus. O Zeiten! O Sitten!

Welch alter Mann soll sich also einlassen, da alles kindisch und üppig in der Sätzkunst ist, seine Meinung laut zu sagen, oder gar schriftlich darwieder zu klagen? ich danke dem Himmel, wenn er mir noch so viele Kräften schenkt, daß ich meine große Familie und meine Kirchen Musick ehrlich und wohl besorgen könne: übrigens tröstet mich noch ein bisgen, daß es beyläufig noch ein Viertelhundert Männer in Wien giebt, die das künstliche, und erhabene der Musick zu schätzen wissen; bin auch überzeugt, daß es in Londen, Leipzig, und Berlin noch weit mehrere giebt, als in Wien. Wer kan für verdorbenen und faden Geschmack? ich, Sie, und viele andere unseres Gleichen gewiß nicht. Mir scheint die vielen Schaubühne sind es; oder wie Herr Hasse zu Wien vor einigen Jahren sagte: die *Opera buffa* ist der Sturz der künstlich—vernünftig— und gründlichen Musick.

Wegen der Schöpfung des Herrn Joseph Haydn und des 2.ten Theiles der Zauberflötte, oder Labyrinth, muß ich Sie berichten: daß das erstere sehr schön warr, das zweyte aber nicht aller Kenner Beyfall hatte. Wenn ich Jhnen mit neuen 4. 5. oder 6. stimmigen Geigenfugen, oder mit *Gradualen, Offertorien* oder andern Kirchen Stücken mit, oder ohne Orgel dienen kan, so stehe ich Jhnen um einen billigen Preis zu Diensten. Um die *Gallanteri*—oder Theater-Stücke habe ich mich in meinem

Leben wenig besorgt. Und jetzt desto weniger, da mein schwacher Kopf schon mehrere Ruhe verlangt. Nehmen Sie, ich bitte, meine aufrichtige Zeilen in voriger Wohlgewogenheit an! ich ersterbe sodann desto leichter Jhr aufrichtiger Freund und Diener *Georgius Albrechtsberger.*

[1]   Vienna, the 17th
                                                       of August, 1798

Most Noble Herr
von Breitkopf!

[5] I received in good order your lines of the 3rd of August last week. From the bottom of my Biedermann[11] heart, I thank you and all the members of the new institute for so warmly inviting me to join in a project so full of good intentions and so useful to the musical world. My advanced age (if I may put it briefly and directly) prevents me from
[10] sharing in this honor. The powers of my spirit diminish daily; and a man near his 63rd year, that is, near also to death, thinks more about temporal and eternal rest than about the honor of being a teacher or *criticus.* Besides, my meager knowledge would do little to improve the current sour taste in music. And our Savior Himself said to us long ago:
[15] *Semper pauperes habebitis vobiscum:* You will have more scribblers than pure composers around you. For that reason also I seldom attend domestic concerts, since nearly every one of them ends with an insipid street-song, or even a German dance. Thirty-two years ago, when I came to Vienna, ladies spoke the praise of composers; now shoemak-
[20] ers' wives and young windbags do so. O Tempora! O Mores!
      Since everything in the art of composition [nowadays] is childish and arrogant, what old man should allow himself to express his opinion out loud, much less to put his complaints in writing? I thank Heaven if I can just have strength enough to see to my large family and
[25] my church music honorably and properly. More than this, I comfort myself a little that there still exist a few dozen men in Vienna who know how to value the artistic and sublime in music; and I am convinced as well that there are many more such men in London, Leipzig, and Berlin than in Vienna. Who is responsible for this depraved and vacuous
[30] taste? Certainly not I, you, or many others of our type. It seems to me that the many theatres are to blame; or as Herr Hasse of Vienna said a few years ago: *opera buffa* is the ruin of artistic, rational, and fundamental music.
      Concerning Herr Joseph Haydn's Creation and the 2nd Part of The

---

[11]A "Biedermann" is a "man of honor and integrity." It is not to be confused with "Biedermeier," particularly not with the pejorative connotations of philistinism associated with that term.

[35] Magic Flute, or The Labyrinth, I can report to you that the former was very lovely, but the latter did not win the applause of all connoisseurs. If I can serve you with new 4-, 5-, or 6-voice fugues for strings, or with *Graduals, Offertories,* or other church pieces—with or without organ— then I am at your service for a cheap price. Throughout my life I have
[40] bothered little about *galanteries* or theatre pieces. And now I care even less, as my weak head demands more rest. Accept, I pray, my sincere lines in the spirit of my customary affection! Thus would I expire the easier, your honest friend and servant, *Georgius Albrechtsberger.*

This letter from Vienna must have been written in response to Breitkopf's letter of August 3, 1798, inviting Albrechtsberger to participate in the publisher's new undertaking, in the course of which he, as "teacher or *criticus*" (line 12 f.) would be asked to express his opinion, whether in writing or otherwise. It is not difficult to guess that Breitkopf had thought of having Albrechtsberger join the planned *Allgemeine Musikalische Zeitung.* In fact, the first number of this series appeared two months after this invitation, on October 3, 1798.

Aside from this insight into the motives of the correspondents, and perhaps aside from Albrechtsberger's brief references to Hasse's dictum on *opera buffa* (line 31 ff.) and the premieres of Haydn's *Creation* and Peter von Winter's continuation of *The Magic Flute* (line 34 ff.), this text offers no particulars. It is, however, marked throughout by the most gloomy pessimism in its judgment of the newer music composed or played in Vienna. Ostensibly due to its mixture of musical styles and genres, this music displays "depraved and vacuous taste" (line 29 f.),[12] and it lacks "the artistic and sublime" (line 27). Albrechtsberger obviously recognizes no individual among all the younger composers who brings the

---

[12]It is instructive to note that Albrechtsberger's conviction that the mixture of musical styles was an unhappy one grew stronger in the course of time. His view is emphatically and broadly discussed in Johann Georg Albrechtsberger, *Sämmtliche Schriften über Generalbass, Harmonie-Lehre, und Tonsetzkunst, zum Selbstunterrichte,* ed. Ignaz Ritter von Seyfried, 2nd ed. (Vienna: Haslinger, 1837), III, 136, in the chapter "Von dem Kirchen-, Kammer- und Theater-Style." However, first mentioned and only briefly regretted is this mixture of styles in a similarly titled chapter (which served as the basis for the later revision) in Johann Georg Albrechtsberger, *Gründliche Anweisung zur Composition . . .* (Leipzig: Breitkopf, 1790), p. 377. Incidentally, contemporary literary criticism also noticed the growing mixture of genres within its realm. Thus Goethe writes to Schiller on December 23, 1797: "It has . . . truly struck me, how we moderns are so inclined to mix genres, in fact, that we are never once in a position to distinguish them one from another." ["Es ist mir . . . recht aufgefallen, wie es kommt, das wir Modernen die Genres so sehr zu vermischen geneigt sind, ja daß wir gar nicht einmal imstande sind, sie voneinander zu unterscheiden."]

slightest hope, the tenderest gleam of light into the future. His sole consolation is that there remain a few connoisseurs and aficionados of true music in Vienna and a few other cities (line 25 ff.).

In light of Beethoven's former study with Albrechtsberger, the complete suppression of his name in this context is most striking. One gets the impression that while writing the letter, Albrechtsberger did not even think of Beethoven for a moment. It is inconceivable that he would not have recognized the gifts of the young man from Bonn; moreover, his above-mentioned letters to Beethoven hardly permit such a conclusion. Obviously, Albrechtsberger's main interest as a composer lay in church music; this comes out clearly in his letter to Breitkopf. But the works Beethoven composed and published between 1795 and the date of this letter were exclusively secular.[13] Albrechtsberger may well have sensed that despite Beethoven's diligent efforts in his lessons, his inclination did not lie with *stile antico*, counterpoint, and strict composition,[14] as Albrechtsberger would probably have liked. This may explain at least in part why Beethoven is not named in the letter to Breitkopf: Because of the opposing directions of their musical interests, Albrechtsberger simply did not think of the young composer from Bonn at that moment. On the other hand, there remains the question whether the absence of Beethoven's name here does not force the conclusion that Albrechtsberger would rather have repudiated his former pupil altogether as a composer. There is more evidence for such a conclusion when we consider the above-mentioned testimony, given by Doležalek, of how Albrechtsberger once set aside with disgust a proffered composition by Beethoven. He is reported to have said, "Ach, take that away; he has learned nothing and will never write anything substantial."[15]

To be sure, Albrechtsberger's letter neither specifies nor intimates an artistic valuation of his former student Beethoven. But perhaps the combination of the already known testimony and the evidence presented by our letter here, together with Doležalek's report, provides a stronger reason to suppose that while Albrechtsberger may have liked his pupil Beethoven well enough as a person, he seems to have thought little of the prospects for his further development as an artist. For his part, Beethoven may certainly have found Albrechtsberger's instruction nec-

[13]See the convenient overview in Thayer-Forbes, pp. 178–79, 201–2, and 217–18.

[14]See Nottebohm, *Beethovens Unterricht*, especially p. 196. Beethoven may be remembering his instruction with Albrechtsberger when, in his letter of January 22, 1825 to Schott, he mentions the "art of creating musical skeletons" [die "Kunst musikalische Gerippe zu schaffen"]. Albrechtsberger is called by name earlier in this letter.

[15]See Kerst, II, 191 ["Ach, gehen Sie mir dem, der hat nichts gelernt und wird nie etwas Ordentliches machen"].

essary. But he must have also sensed that his future in composition lay in a decidedly different direction. Perhaps the future will shed more light on this teacher-pupil relationship; but in any event, the letter presented here provides a welcome illumination of the musical situation of the time, as judged by Albrechtsberger.

—Translated from the German by David L. Schwarzkopf and Lewis Lockwood

A Beethoven Price List of 1822

Alan Tyson

In an appendix to the third volume of his biography of Beethoven, A. W. Thayer cites a price list that Beethoven had drawn up for a number of his unpublished (and in a couple of cases still unwritten) works.[1] Thayer appears to have known it only from a transcript made by Otto Jahn, and his printed text contains some errors. Fortunately it is possible to correct them, for the list is today in the Deutsche Staatsbibliothek, Berlin, catalogued as "Mus. ms. autogr. Beethoven 35, 80"; it came to the Berlin library in 1880 as part of Anton Schindler's *Nachlass*.

The list carries no date—not surprisingly, since as a document it was probably intended for Beethoven's eyes alone. It consists of a large sheet (45 by 51 centimeters) of coarse paper, folded vertically in the middle to make four sides, all of which have been used. Apart from three lines on page 4 and a few of the prices, which are in ink, the entries are entirely in pencil.

Thayer printed the list along with Beethoven's correspondence with Steiner and Haslinger from the years 1815–17, and added a somewhat enigmatic footnote to say that, according to indications in "the Steiner and the Streicher correspondence," the document belonged to the end of 1816. Thayer's dating was not challenged by Nottebohm.[2] Today, however, it is plain that the list must be placed over five years later.[3] The clearest evidence for a later date is contained in a letter that Beethoven wrote to the Leipzig publisher Carl Friedrich Peters on June 5, 1822 (Anderson number 1079). The letter has come down in two forms, both of which are now in the Beethovenhaus, Bonn: a draft wholly in Beethoven's hand

---

[1]Thayer III, pp. 487–88; reprinted unchanged in Thayer-Deiters-Riemann III, pp. 619–20.

[2]N II, p. 478, footnote.

[3]In its final form, as will become clear, it dates from around the middle of 1822. But Beethoven may have started to compile it a little earlier, adding unpublished works from time to time as they came to mind.

(except for one word), and the fair copy that was dispatched to Peters, in a different hand but signed by Beethoven.[4]

Beethoven's letter, which was in reply to an inquiry that Peters had made on May 18, 1822 about the possibility of entering into business relations with the composer and publishing some of his music, began by declaring that "the *greatest* work that I have composed to date is a grand mass with choruses, four obbligato voices, and a large orchestra." But after stating his price for the *Missa solemnis*, Beethoven went on to describe a large number of compositions that were for sale, along with their prices; the works, and in most cases the prices for them, correspond closely with the contents of the list. (In some cases the extra information provided by the list or by the letter enables more precise identifications to be made.)

There follows a transcription of the price list. The various items have been numbered on the right from [1] to [20], for the purpose of the succeeding commentary.

[Page 1]

Gesänge 1 für jeden fürs Klawier allein 12#	Von Hast du[nicht] liebe zu[–] gemeßen u darauf wüßt ich *c moll, dur*	[1]
2 "	Ich wiege dich in meinem Arm	[2]
3 "	meine lebenszeit verstreicht *in g moll*	[3]
4 "	*E dur* Ich der mit flatterndem Sinn bisher	[4]
mit *accomp* von 4 Stimen 5 "	*italienische No, non torbati o Nice*	[5]

[4]Beethovenhaus, Sammlung H.C. Bodmer, BBr 73 (= SBH 309) for the draft, BBr 35 (= SBH 308) for the final text. A description of the former may be found in Georg Kinsky, *Manuskripte—Briefe—Dokumente von Scarlatti bis Stravinsky; Katalog der Musikautographen-Sammlung Louis Koch* (Stuttgart, 1953), pp. 112–14. The best text of the latter is in Thayer-Deiters-Riemann IV, pp. 249–52, which also cites the variants in the draft.

[Page 2]

	"	*duetto* *ne' giorni* *tuoi felici* *in E dur* mit ganzem *orchester*	[6]
	"	*Elegie* zu 4 Singstim̄en	[7]
	"	*germania*	[8]
	"	Prüfung des Küssens 16# [in ink]	[9]

	"	Mit mädeln
		  ~~herumgeschlagen~~
		sich vertragen
		  16# [in ink]
			[10]

[Page 3]

	"	Marsch tarpeja für ganz großes	[11]
12# [in ink]		*orchester*	
		Romanze für *Violin solo* 15# [in ink]	[12]
	"	chor der	[13]
noch nicht		Derwische	
das Honorar		aus der	
bestim̄t		ruinen	
		von *athen*	
	"	*Regiments*märsche	[14]

[Page 4]

	"	*terzetto* für 2 *oboen*	[15]
30#		Englischhorn	
	"	*Bagatellen*	[16]

für die neuen *Variationen*
  30#

für ein neue *solo sonate*
  40#
——————————s *quartett* 50#
für die 2 im 20 guldenFuß

"bej chloen war ich ganz
allein " von gleim——

[all in ink] ⎱ [17] [18] [19]

[20]

In the following commentary, the price list is cited as "the List"; and where appropriate, the descriptions of the same works in Beethoven's letter to Peters of June 5, 1822 (cited as "the Letter") have been added.

The first page of the List already contains surprises: for it begins with four "Gesänge" for voice and piano, with German words, at a price of 12 ducats each—and two of the songs seem to be unknown.[5] The Letter speaks of several extended or "worked-out" songs ("ausgeführte Gesänge"), one of which contains a recitative, at 12 ducats each, but does not identify them further; a "Lied" (strophic song?) could be obtained for 8 ducats.

[1] = WoO 118. "Hast du nicht Liebe zugemessen" and "Wüsst ich" are the opening words of two poems, "Seufzer eines Ungeliebten" and "Gegenliebe" by G. A. Herder, which Beethoven combined into a single setting in 1794–95.[6] The song begins with a recitative (as referred to in the Letter); the principal theme of "Wüsst ich" was later used by Beethoven in 1808 for the Choral Fantasia, Op. 80. Published by Diabelli in 1837.

---

[5]Another early song by Beethoven that has not survived, though it was evidently completed, is "An die Freude"—no doubt a setting of part of Schiller's *Ode*. It is listed, in a letter written on September 15, 1803 by Ferdinand Ries in Vienna to Nikolaus Simrock in Bonn, as one of eight songs composed four years earlier and now ready for sale (the others are Op. 52, nos. 2-4 and 6-8, and WoO 117). See Cecil Hill, ed., *Ferdinand Ries: Briefe und Dokumente* (Bonn, 1982), p. 60. The first leaf of an *Abschrift* of these eight songs, consisting of the title page ("Verschiedene Lieder Vür das Clavier") and the first 5½ measures of the first song ("Feuerfarb'," Op. 52, no. 2), was auctioned by J. A. Stargardt of Marburg on March 23, 1983 (Katalog 628, no. 769), and is now in the Beethovenhaus, Bonn. The title page also carries an inscription by Beethoven, dated October 7, 1803, assigning the ownership of the eight songs (and also of the F minor prelude WoO 55) to his brother Johann.

[6]Douglas Johnson, *Beethoven's Early Sketches in the 'Fischhof Miscellany,'* (Ann Arbor, 1980), I, 440.

[2] "Ich wiege dich in meinem Arm." No Beethoven song with these words is known. It must be assumed that this was a song which was once completed, but which has not survived. The author of the words has not so far been identified.

[3] "Meine Lebenszeit verstreicht," in G minor. These are the opening words of C. F. Gellert's "Vom Tode." A setting of this poem in F♯ minor was completed by 1802 and published by Artaria in August, 1803 as No. 3 of the six Gellert songs known today as Beethoven's Op. 48. But no setting by Beethoven in G minor appears to have survived.

There is, however, a draft of a complete setting of the same text, in D minor, on folio 13^r and 13^v of Grasnick 1 (late 1798), and there are also a few sketches for another version in E minor on folio 58^v of Landsberg 6 (late 1803). It is not impossible that one of these versions eventually became a setting in G minor.

[4] = WoO 114. "Ich der mit flatterndem Sinn" is the first line of J. W. L. Gleim's poem "Selbstgespräch." Beethoven sketched this song in Bonn, perhaps in 1792, and completed an autograph score in the early Vienna years (1793?).[7] The song remained unpublished until the appearance of the Supplementband to the Gesamtausgabe in 1888.

[5] = WoO 92a, "No, non turbarti, o Nice." This scena and aria to words from Metastasio's *La tempesta*, with an accompaniment of four strings, was set by Beethoven in 1801–02, but remained unpublished until Willy Hess brought out his edition of it in 1949.

The Letter mentions "a little Italian cantata with recitative" on offer at 12 ducats—the same price as in the List.

[6] = WoO 93. The duet for soprano and tenor "Ne' giorni tuoi felici," to a text from Metastasio's *Olimpiade*, was composed at the end of 1802 (and perhaps not completed before the beginning of 1803). The work remained unpublished until Willy Hess's edition appeared in 1939. It is not mentioned in the Letter.

The ditto marks at the beginning of this entry and the following ones appear to indicate that the price of the items on this page was originally intended to be the same as that of the page 1 items—i.e., 12 ducats.

[7] = Opus 118, the *Elegischer Gesang* for four voices and string quartet that Beethoven wrote in July, 1814 for the third anniversary of the death of

---

[7]*Ibid.*, pp. 251 and 91.

Eleonore von Pasqualati, wife of his friend Johann Baptist Freiherr von Pasqualati. Published by Haslinger in July, 1826. In the Letter, Beethoven asks a sum of 24 ducats for the work.

[8] = WoO 94. "Germania" is the concluding number, for bass soloist and chorus, of a *Singspiel* by G. F. Treitschke, *Die gute Nachricht*, first performed in April, 1814. A vocal score was issued in June, 1814, but the full score did not appear until the Gesamtausgabe in 1864. Not mentioned in the Letter.

[9] = WoO 89, the aria for bass and orchestra "Prüfung des Küssens." This was written in Bonn c. 1790–92,[8] but not published before the Supplementband to the Gesamtausgabe in 1888. The price of 16 ducats added to the List in ink corresponds to the price in the Letter, where the aria, though not named, is mentioned as one similar to WoO 90 (see next item).

[10] = WoO 90, the aria for bass and orchestra "Mit Mädeln sich vertragen" (words by Goethe), also written in Bonn c. 1790–92,[9] and also unpublished until the 1888 Supplementband to the Gesamtausgabe. The price of 16 ducats added in ink corresponds to that in the Letter. The deleted word "herumgeschlagen" arose through a lapse of memory on Beethoven's part; it comes from the second line of the poem ("Mit Männern 'rumgeschlagen").

[11] = WoO 2a. This march, written in March, 1813 for Christoph Kuffner's tragedy *Tarpeja*, was published in parts by Haslinger in 1840. The price of 12 ducats added in ink corresponds to that given in the Letter (where a piano arrangement is included in the offer).

[12] The "Romanze für Violin Solo," with the price of 15 ducats added in ink, is a puzzle. It must be the same work as the "Violin-Romanze (Solo mit ganzem Orchester)" offered at the same price in the Letter. Two works answering to such a description are Beethoven's Op. 40 and Op. 50; but they had been published in December, 1803 and May, 1805, respectively. The only known composition for violin and orchestra unpublished at this time was the Violin Concerto WoO 5, written in Bonn c. 1790–92. All that has survived of it is a fragment of the first movement, though since the score breaks off at the end of a gathering, it is likely that there was once more of it. Perhaps its slow movement was

[8]*Ibid.*, p. 264.
[9]*Ibid.*, pp. 275 and 284.

still in existence when the List was compiled, and was the "Romanze" referred to here.

[13] = Op. 113, no. 3. The "chorus of Dervishes" is among the music for Kotzebue's *Die Ruinen von Athen* that Beethoven wrote in August and the first half of September, 1811; it did not appear until 1846, when Artaria published a full score. In the List the fee for the chorus is "not yet fixed," but in the Letter it is given as 20 ducats.

[14] The "Regimentsmärsche" are described in the Letter as "4 militärische Märsche mit türkischer Musik"; the fee is not stated but "could be quoted if desired." Although Beethoven introduced some degree of mystification into his subsequent correspondence with Peters, declaring on February 15, 1823 (Anderson number 1137) that instead of four marches he was sending three tattoos ("Zapfenstreiche") and one march, it is not clear whether he ever had any other "marches" than the ones he sent. These were doubtless the March WoO 24 that he wrote for the Viennese Artillery Corps in May–June, 1816 (published in piano reductions by Cappi & Czerny in April, 1827, but in full score not until the Gesamtausgabe, 1864), and the three Zapfenstreiche WoO 18, WoO 19, and WoO 20.

WoO 18 and WoO 19 were written in 1809 and 1810 respectively; they are described both as "Marsch" and as "Zapfenstreich" on different autographs. The date of WoO 20 is uncertain, though it may have been written at the same time as the others. All three were published in the 1888 Supplementband to the Gesamtausgabe.[10] A score of WoO 18 had appeared from Schlesinger in Berlin around 1818–19 as No. 37 in a series of marches; it is possible, however, that that edition was not authorized by Beethoven.

[15] = WoO 28. Neither in the List nor in the Letter (where the same price of 30 ducats is asked) is it stated that the terzetto consists of variations on "La ci darem la mano" from *Don Giovanni;* but this is mentioned in a later letter to Peters of December 20, 1822 (Anderson number 1111). The variations were probably composed in 1795,[11] but found no taker in Beethoven's lifetime. They even escaped the Gesamtausgabe, and were finally published by Breitkopf & Härtel in 1914.

[16] The "Bagatelles," which appear in the Letter as "Bagatelles oder

[10]Trios to WoO 19, probably written in 1823, were not published until 1961 (Supplemente zur Gesamtausgabe, IV).

[11]Johnson, 'Fischhof,' p. 411.

Kleinigkeiten für Clavier allein," were a portfolio of separate piano pieces, some dating back as far as the 1790s. Beethoven had hopes of getting at least some of them into print; but when Peters expressed an interest in buying two or three of them, he could not decide which ones to send. By the end of July Beethoven had undertaken to send four; but four months later he was hoping that Peters would take more, and on December 20, 1822 (Anderson number 1111) he wrote: "As to the bagatelles, there are now exactly six of them, and you only want four. I am reluctant to make this division, for indeed I have treated them as belonging together. But if you insist on taking only the four, well then I must make a different arrangement." The six that he selected from the much larger number available to him, it is clear, are the ones now known as Op. 119, nos. 1–6; he worked them into a set at this time, the autograph being dated "1822 Novemb." They were sent to Peters on February 8, 1823, but Peters expressed no interest in them and returned them.

Beethoven also sent them in February to Ferdinand Ries in London, together with five other bagatelles (Op. 119, nos. 7–11) which had already been published in Vienna in the spring of 1821 as a contribution to Friedrich Starke's *Wiener Piano-Forte-Schule,* Part 3. Ries passed both sets to the firm of Clementi & Co., which published them in June, 1823 as "Trifles for the Piano Forte, Consisting of Eleven pleasing Pieces, Composed in Various Styles."[12]

[17] The "new variations" are the "Diabelli" Variations, Op. 120, published by Cappi & Diabelli in June, 1823. In the Letter, where the same fee of 30 ducats is asked, the work is described as "Variationen über einen Walzer für Clavier allein." There were said in the Letter to be many variations, but at this time the work was not yet completed, so their exact number could not be stated.

[18] The "new solo sonata" (for piano), which the Letter also prices at 40 ducats and promises that Peters could have very soon, was in fact never written.

[19] The "new quartet," for which the Letter also asks 50 ducats, is also promised to Peters very soon; but in a letter to Peters written a month later on July 6, 1822 (Anderson number 1085), Beethoven describes it as "not yet quite finished, because something else intervened." The ultimate stimulus to return to string quartet writing came from the letter of

[12]See Alan Tyson, "The First Edition of Beethoven's Op. 119 Bagatelles," *The Musical Quarterly,* XLIX (1963), 331–38.

November 9, 1822 from Prince Nikolai Galitzin in St. Petersburg, inviting Beethoven to compose one, two, or three quartets for a fee to be determined. It seems most unlikely that Beethoven was working on any quartet in the spring or summer of 1822; even Galitzin had to wait until 1825 to receive his first quartet, Op. 127.

[20] = Op. 128, a setting of C. F. Weisse's "Der Kuss," the first line of which is "Ich war bei Chloen ganz allein." Sketches for the song, dating from the end of 1798, are to be found on folio 6ʳ of Grasnick 1. Beethoven revised the work at the end of 1822; the autograph of the final version is dated "1822 in decemb." [13]

The song is not mentioned in the Letter, and may have been added to the List at the time that the work was revised. Beethoven sent it on approval to Peters on February 15, 1823 (Anderson number 1137); but Peters did not want it, and it was published by Schott early in 1825.

The mention of Gleim rather than Weisse in the List as the author of the words seems to be merely a slip on Beethoven's part.

[13]London, Heirs of Stefan Zweig; on deposit at the British Library.

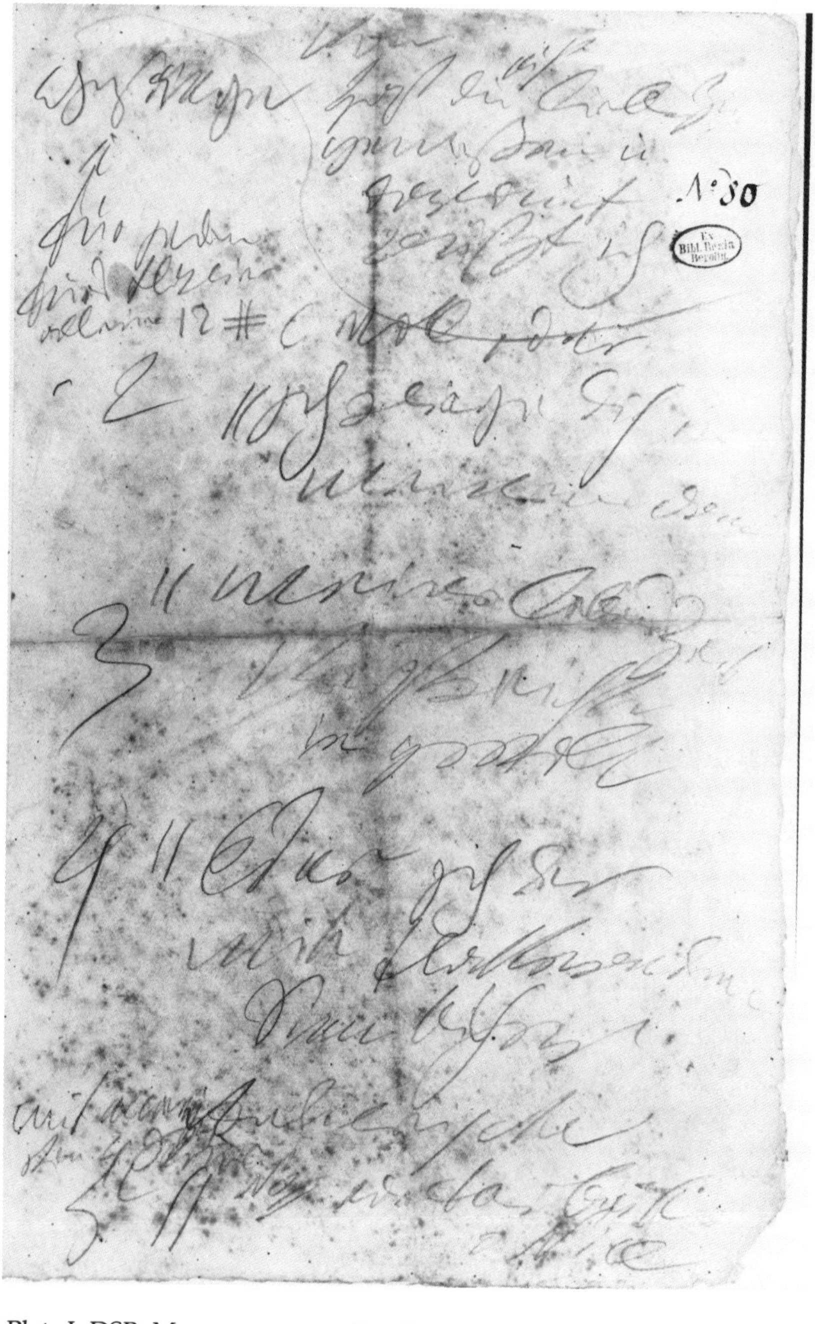

Plate I. DSB, Mus. ms. autogr. Beethoven 35, 80, page 1

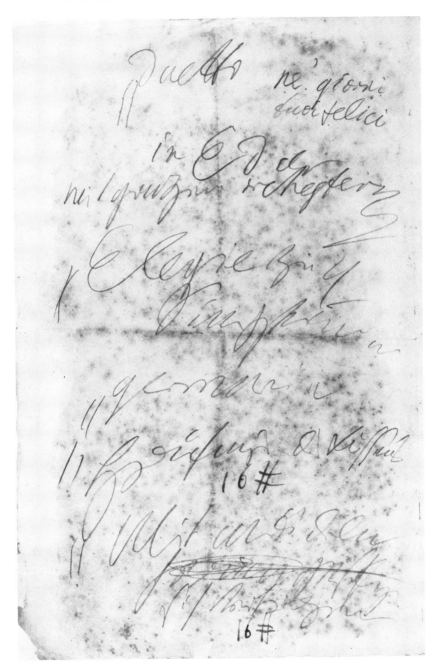

Plate II. DSB, Mus. ms. autogr. Beethoven 35, 80, page 2

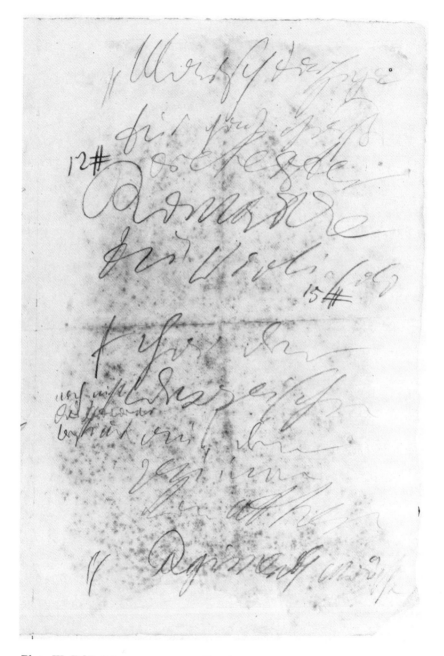

Plate III. DSB, Mus. ms. autogr. Beethoven, 35, 80, page 3

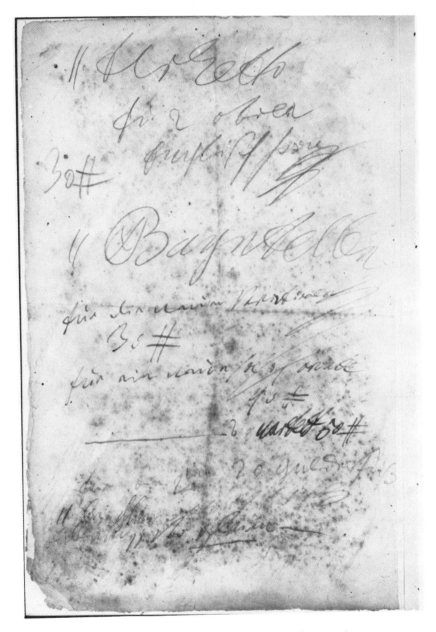

Plate IV. DSB, Mus. ms. autogr. Beethoven, 35, 80, page 4

Sonneck and Krehbiel: A Beethoven Correspondence

Maynard Solomon

The publication history of Alexander Wheelock Thayer's biography of Beethoven carries a rather Darwinian lesson—one not inappropriate either to its time or to its author's outlook. For *Beethovens Leben* managed to surmount obstacles to its survival that would have proven fatal to a project of less vigorous genetic stock. Foremost among these was its author's insistence on extending his investigations beyond any reasonable time necessary for their completion. Next was his inability—really, his inhibition—actually to compose the latter portions of the work during the decades after his research had been concluded in all essential respects. Despite the public's inexhaustible interest in Beethoven's life, few publishers could have been expected to share Thayer's long view: indeed, Schneider, who inaugurated the project in 1866, wearied after one volume, and Weber, who published Volumes II and III in 1872 and 1879, respectively, and the revision of Volume I in 1901, was unable to stay the full course, finally relinquishing the torch to a third publisher of proven longevity.

With Thayer's death in 1897, the opportunity finally arose to carry his project to completion. His erstwhile associate and translator, Hermann Deiters, took up the task with missionary zeal and within a relatively few years had revised Volume I and drafted the concluding volumes, which, after Deiters's death in 1907, were edited by Hugo Riemann. The now-familiar five-volume set appeared by 1911, published by Breitkopf & Härtel, who had purchased the rights from Weber.

In the more than forty years that elapsed between the publication of Volume I and Volume V, an English edition could be contemplated only with difficulty, although there was a very ready market in both England and the United States for multivolume biographies of great men; among composers, Jahn's *Mozart*, Kreissle's *Schubert*, Niecks's *Chopin*, Spitta's *Bach*, and May's *Brahms* had quickly found their way into print. Indeed, publishers, eager to satisfy the subscription libraries, often preferred multiple-volume formats, issuing in two volumes such relatively short works as Kreissle's *Schubert* and Charlotte Moscheles's *Life of Moscheles.* Clearly, however, few would be eager to undertake an incomplete biography, especially one that had unpredictable prospects for conclusion. Nevertheless, several publishers did express interest—only to be rebuffed by Thayer himself, for he did not seriously pursue publication of the book in English. Consistently self-defeating, he rejected an offer from Novello, Ewer & Co. to provide him with a literary secretary to aid his work; and though Sir George Grove had interested a publisher in issuing the already-published volumes, Thayer demurred, complaining that the work of preparing the edition was too great for him to undertake.

At bottom, Thayer did not want to complete his life's work, perhaps because in some obscure way he had come to identify its completion with his own mortality. Fortunately, the man who did render Thayer's *Beethoven* in its native tongue did not share its originator's inhibitions; rather, he tenaciously pursued his goal, hoping to see it in print before his own death, and secure in the knowledge that it was to be the most important work of a long and productive career.

Henry Edward Krehbiel[1] was born on March 10, 1854, in Ann Arbor, Michigan. Largely self-educated, he briefly studied law, but turned to a journalistic career in 1874 as a reporter and music critic on the *Cincinnati Gazette.* In 1880 he came to New York as music critic of the *New York Tribune,* an influential post which he held continuously until his death in 1923. For twenty years he was also program annotator for the New York Philharmonic Society. Krehbiel's many books include *Studies in Wagnerian Drama* (1891), *The Pianoforte and its Music* (1911), and *Afro-American Folk-Songs* (1914); he also wrote several books on opera and prepared English versions of librettos to operas by Mozart, Wagner, and others. Most of his work, though perceptive and intelligent, has long been superseded or forgotten—the common fate of the journalist music critic. But several works survive, for Krehbiel also had a scholar's instincts. His *Music & Manners in the Classical Period* (1898) long served as the only source in English for Haydn's "London Notebooks"; it still contains precious and unique extracts from Thayer's notebooks, the originals of which have long since vanished.

Thayer, too, had once worked on the *New York Tribune,* as a member of Horace Greeley's editorial staff in 1852–54, and he remained a faithful reader thereafter. Thayer opened a correspondence with Krehbiel during the later 1880s: "Ever and anon after that until shortly before his death," wrote Krehbiel, Thayer "gave evidence that he was following the

---

[1]For Krehbiel's biography, see *Dictionary of American Biography,* X (New York, 1933), 504–5; H. T. Finck, Obituary of Krehbiel, *New York Evening Post,* March 21, 1923.

current of musical affairs in America by reading *The Tribune*'s columns."[2]
In his proud—but, as we shall see, premature—announcement of his
edition of Thayer's *Beethoven* to his readers in 1914, Krehbiel judged it
highly appropriate that "what a writer for *The Tribune* began a writer for
The Tribune has brought to completion."[3]

It was only natural that Thayer's niece and heir, Mrs. Jabez Fox, turn
to the influential Krehbiel for assistance in sifting Thayer's voluminous
materials on Beethoven, which came to her upon her uncle's death, "in
order that all that was needful for the work of revision and completion"
of the German edition might be "placed in the hands of Dr. Deiters."[4]
Krehbiel had long been concerned about Thayer's failure to finish the biography; indeed, it was he who had persuaded the publisher Novello to
offer to provide Thayer with a literary secretary. Not surprisingly, therefore, he eagerly accepted Mrs. Fox's proposal of a contract for the preparation of an English edition of Thayer's *Life of Beethoven*.

Krehbiel's task occupied him for ten summers; but, as he wrote, he did
not "go systematically to work until publication of the German edition
had been completed."[5] His manuscript was delivered to the publisher
Charles Scribner's Sons in July, 1914, with the understanding that manufacture would begin at once. But it was an unfortunate moment to publish a monumental appreciation of a German composer, for its delivery
coincided with the outbreak of World War I, with its attendant arousal of
anti-German sentiment in the United States and England. In August,
Scribner's advised Krehbiel that it seemed inadvisable to print just then
because of the war and the fact that an English sale could no longer be
counted upon.[6] "For three years," lamented Krehbiel in 1917, "the manuscript . . . has been locked up in the vaults of a publishing house wait-
ing for a time more propitious than the present for its publication." He
continued, with a slightly excessive appeal to national pride: "When
American readers shall be privileged to peruse in their own tongue the
history which has brought them so much honour and put to shame the
Beethoven biographers of Europe can not be predicted."[7] Perhaps, he
suggested, only " 'When the hurlyburly's done,/When the battle's lost
and won.' " Even before the war's end, Krehbiel obtained what he believed was a publication commitment from the American branch of

---

[2]Krehbiel, Introduction to "The Last Days of Beethoven: Chapters from a Great Biography," *New York Tribune*, June 28, 1914, sec. III, p. 6.

[3]*New York Tribune*, loc. cit.

[4]*New York Tribune*, loc. cit., slightly revised in Thayer-Krehbiel, pp. xiv–xv.

[5]*New York Tribune*, loc. cit.; Thayer-Krehbiel, p. xv.

[6]Letter from Krehbiel to Harold Bauer of December 26, 1919.

[7]Krehbiel, "Alexander Thayer and His Life of Beethoven," *The Musical Quarterly*, III
(1917), 629.

Breitkopf & Härtel, but that firm canceled its agreement by March, 1918. We learn of this from a letter of March 12, 1918, by Krehbiel at the start of a lengthy and very interesting correspondence with the outstanding American musicologist and editor, Oscar G. Sonneck. This correspondence survives in the files of the Beethoven Association of New York, an organization of musicians and music-lovers founded by the pianist Harold Bauer in 1918.[8] Through the forty-five letters from Sonneck to Krehbiel, forty-eight letters from Krehbiel to Sonneck, and numerous collateral letters and documents, we can trace the process that eventuated in the publication by the Beethoven Association in 1921 of the three-volume set we now know as "Thayer-Krehbiel"—a set which was in turn revised and updated by Elliot Forbes.

O. G. Sonneck was born in New Jersey on October 6, 1873, but moved to Germany at an early age and received his musical education there.[9] Returning to the United States, he was appointed head of the music division of the Library of Congress in 1902 and, within a space of fifteen years, raised its archives and collections to world rank. During those same years he energetically applied the critical disciplines of European musicology to music of the United States, publishing numerous bibliographies, including *Bibliography of Early Secular American Music* (1905), and writing standard works on early American concert life (1907), on Francis Hopkinson and James Lyon (1905), and on "The Star-Spangled Banner" (1909, rev. 1914), as well as an influential scheme of music classification (1904, 1917). In 1915, under the auspices of G. Schirmer, Inc., he founded *The Musical Quarterly* and became its first editor. In 1917, "embittered by the neglect of his American studies and harassed by the government (because of his German education and anti-war sentiments)"[10] he resigned

[8]The Beethoven Association maintained clubrooms in New York City for its membership, which, during the 1920s, averaged 125 active and 120 associate members. Although the Association was actually founded in late 1918, its first series of concerts commenced on November 4, 1919. Through its concerts and dues, the Association raised and distributed more than $150,000 in gifts to needy musicians and various musical institutions. As its librarian, Sonneck accumulated a superb library of books pertaining to Beethoven, which was complete save for a few rare works. The Association ceased activities in 1938 and was formally dissolved in 1940; its collections of books, artworks, and instruments were donated to the New York Public Library, along with the copyright to the English edition of Thayer-Krehbiel. See Harold Bauer, *His Book* (New York, 1948), pp. 239–40; *New York Public Library Bulletin*, XLV (1941), 90–91, 176, and 208–9. The correspondence is quoted by permission of the New York Public Library, Astor, Lenox & Tilden Foundations, and with special thanks to Susan T. Sommer and Frank C. Campbell.

[9]For Sonneck's biography, see *Dictionary of American Biography*, XVII (New York, 1935), 395–96; Carl Engel, "A Postscript," *The Musical Quarterly*, XV (1929), 149–51; idem., "Oscar G. Sonneck," *The Musical Quarterly*, XXV (1939), 2–5.

[10]Jon Newsom, "Sonneck," *New Grove*, XVII, 525.

from the Library of Congress to become director of the publications department of G. Schirmer, Inc., where he remained as vice-president until his death.

In the fall of 1919, as secretary and librarian of the Beethoven Association, Sonneck suggested to Bauer that the Association's surplus funds be utilized to subsidize the publication of Thayer's biography of Beethoven. Bauer expressed interest and in December exchanged letters with Krehbiel about the project, but as yet without making any definite offer. On March 11, 1920, Sonneck asked Scribner's if it would publish Krehbiel's edition of Thayer, provided the manufacturing costs were underwritten. Scribner's declined to do so, but in a letter of March 15 offered to "transfer our rights in the book to any other publisher or organization disposed to undertake its manufacture and publication." Confident that another publisher could readily be found, Sonneck wrote to Krehbiel on April 1:

> The fate of Thayer's Beethoven worried me for years and so it occurred to me that the Beethoven Association could not possibly do a worthier thing with its funds than to make the publication at last possible. Mr. Bauer took to that idea quickly and he told me today that the project looks bright, so far as the votes of the members look at present.
>
> In the meantime I sounded Scribner's twice asking them on what terms they would go ahead with your edition of Thayer. . . . Their attitude was wholly negative, except to state that they would assign the rights to whatever organization might wish to assume the burden. . . .
>
> That is the status of the affair. The annual meeting of the Beethoven Association takes place on April 15 and unless I or Mr. Bauer have something concrete to propose to the members, there is a danger of my losing out.

He asked Krehbiel to inform him about the length of the text and to state the financial terms which would be agreeable to him and to Mrs. Fox. "As soon as I have these data, I shall approach such publishers as Holt, Putnam, MacMillan with the same questions as I did Scribner's."

Within a few days, Krehbiel had obtained the information from Scribner's (526,000 words) and, in letters of April 7 and 11, 1920, he stated Mrs. Fox's royalty requirements ("7% on the list price after the first 500 copies"). He added: "There would be no trouble in satisfying me—so eager am I to see the Beethoven in print." For him, the proposal was too good to be true: "I anticipate objections to the scheme [from the Association's membership] on personal grounds—especially from Stokowski. . . ." Sonneck immediately opened negotiations with the Macmillan Company and on April 12 received from that publisher a proposal of its conditions for the subsidized edition. On April 15 he gave a lengthy address to the Beethoven Association at its annual meeting.

Mindful that he was addressing a group of performing artists, some of whom may have been stung by the *Tribune's* reviews, he diplomatically noted: "Needless to say, I very often disagree with Mr. Krehbiel's critical estimates." And he couched his appeal in terms sure to strike a responsive chord in his audience:

> The world looks to you, the artists, as the true and inspired interpreters of Beethoven's genius, to you as the guides to Beethoven's temple of beauty. But if the world desires a scholarly and truthful picture of Beethoven, the man, then Alexander Thayer remains to this day the main fountain of our knowledge. . . .

After some fulsome praise of Harold Bauer and of his "wonderful success in getting all of you and us together, just for the unselfish, idealistic, artistic fun of it, under the banner of Beethoven," Sonneck turned to the practical side of the undertaking, carefully describing his negotiations with publishers and setting out the projected costs and returns. In light of what he described as "the constellation of circumstances"—the greatest biography of Beethoven, the 150th anniversary of the composer's birth, and a Beethoven Association made up of altruistic musicians—he confessed that "it seems almost impossible to me that our association will not grasp this wonderful opportunity."

Of course the Association could not resist Sonneck's appeal, which already had Bauer's full support. On April 17 Krehbiel wrote to Judge Jabez Fox, the husband of Thayer's niece, telling him of the good news:

> Quite unexpectedly to me, but to my great happiness despite the fact that it will burden me with a great load of unremunerative labor, . . . the Beethoven Association, a body of professional musicians headed by Harold Bauer, at a meeting night before last resolved to assume the cost of bringing out my version of Thayer's 'Life of Beethoven.'. . .

He asked Judge Fox to arrange the formal transfer of rights to the Beethoven Association: "Please, my dear Judge Fox," he wrote, "do this and let us see the light shine at last." It was a busy day for Krehbiel: he signed a memorandum of agreement assigning to the Beethoven Association all of his "right, title and interest" in the manuscript, and he wrote to Scribner's requesting return of the manuscript and proudly announcing the new publication plans. Not without a tinge of reproof, he expressed his

> sincere regret that you did not deem it advisable to undertake the publication yourselves. The musicians who have embarked upon the enterprise without suggestion from me or help, are obviously prompted by artistic motives alone, since their only reward can be the satisfaction

which they will derive from giving to English readers a standard and monumental work, the result of more than fifty years of enthusiastic and unrecompensed labor.

The next weeks were spent in concluding formal arrangements for the transfer of Scribner's rights and in negotiation of the terms of a contract with Macmillan. The drafting of an agreement acceptable to both the new publisher and the Beethoven Association took some time and required several drafts; it was not until July 19 that copies were forwarded to Krehbiel and Mrs. Fox. Meanwhile, Krehbiel had arranged to spend the summer at Blue Hill, Maine, hoping to revise the manuscript there. On May 30 he wrote to Sonneck:

> Tell me—would you in my case—since this is to be my last publication if it is to be published at all—make use of some of the titles which might either ornament or disfigure the title-page, such as M.A. Yale (Hon. Causa) Member of the Beethovenhaus Verein, Bonn, Chevalier of the Legion of Honor, Musical Editor of The N.Y. Tribune for nearly forty years, author of etc etc? Modesty says "No"; but I have been modest to my detriment all my life and this is the one work of which I hope to be proud.

Sonneck replied with his customary bluntness:

> My candid opinion is that a Henry E. Krehbiel need not make use of his titular attributes on the title-page. It is not, in my eyes, a question of modesty but of good taste. Don't, don't! Leave that sort of thing to the small potatoes and prize cows. (Letter of June 1, 1920)

But Sonneck himself was not altogether immune to such vanities: when Krehbiel submitted copy for a dedication page with Harold Bauer's name placed before Sonneck's, he objected, prompting Krehbiel to explain:

> I set them down as I did because I fancied that the President of the Association might think that he ought to be mentioned first because of his official dignity, not that I thought your deserts less than his. (Letter of July 3, 1920)[11]

However, problems more serious than these were soon to endanger the entire project. First came several minor technical and contractual delays, leading Krehbiel to complain: "Hope deferred maketh the heart sick; and when the body is as sick as mine is the combination becomes almost intolerable. I am beginning to regret that the plan to publish the

---

[11]Neither name appears on the dedication page; instead, Krehbiel expressed his "grateful appreciation to The Beethoven Association. . . ."

'Beethoven' ever was conceived" (letter of June 19, 1920). Then, Mrs. Fox, wary of potential legal entanglements, refused to take full responsibility for guaranteeing that Krehbiel's edition did not "infringe any copyright nor violate any property rights, nor contain any scandalous or libellous matter," as stated in the proposed agreement. Evidently she and Judge Fox were particularly worried that the edition might infringe upon the rights of Breitkopf & Härtel, inasmuch as large sections of the work were translated from the later volumes of the German edition. Climaxing these difficulties, Macmillan, which found that it had underestimated the typesetting costs, used Mrs. Fox's hesitancy to sign the warranty as a pretext for canceling the agreement. Thus, on October 5, 1920, Krehbiel wrote to Sonneck:

> I enclose a letter from Mrs. Fox just received. It was the first information received that my project was dead. I have not the heart to write. If there was some way to get a guarantee, or quit-claim, or assignment, or something of the kind from B&H I suppose matters might yet be arranged. I do not know. I suffer too much pain and exhaustion to run around much.

Characteristically, Sonneck was undaunted. "If you think that such a little thing like Macmillan's desertion leaves me panicky you do not know me," he replied on October 6. This was not mere bravado, for Sonneck had already prevailed upon his employer, G. Schirmer, Inc., to print the book on behalf of and at the expense of the Beethoven Association. As for Mrs. Fox's caveat, he suggested that a formal cession of her rights to Krehbiel be arranged so that the latter might himself provide the necessary warranties. And he advised Krehbiel not to worry about a potential claim of infringement by Breitkopf & Härtel: "We had better not arouse the sleeping dogs."

On November 3, Bauer wrote to Gustave Schirmer:

> Mr. Sonneck has informed me that G. Schirmer, Inc. are willing to set, print and bind for the Beethoven Association Thayer's "Life of Beethoven" in three volumes under certain conditions. In behalf of the Beethoven Association I accept these conditions and authorize you to proceed with the work at your earliest convenience.

He enclosed a check for five thousand dollars as an advance payment on a cost "not to exceed eight thousand dollars," the balance payable upon "completion of the job."[12] Within a week, Krehbiel received a formal assignment of all rights in Thayer's biography from Mrs. Fox (letter from

---

[12]Macmillan had been guaranteed only $5400. To meet the additional cost, Bauer raised funds from sources outside the Beethoven Association.

Krehbiel to Sonneck of November 10, 1920). On November 16, Sonneck wrote to Krehbiel: "Well, at last we can go ahead."

Sonneck served as editor and production coordinator of the project, setting out the procedure for copy-editing; arranging for Dr. Theodore Baker of Schirmer's to assist Krehbiel and his friend, the critic Richard Aldrich, with the proofreading; selecting the Beethoven portraits to illustrate each volume; and negotiating terms of a British agency with Novello. As such he had to deal with an ailing author, one who was impatient with the pace of production and disgruntled about the typographical design. In particular Krehbiel objected to use of *The Musical Quarterly*'s page layout for his book:

> It still seems to me that a book page like that of the Quarterly will be homely and the volume unwieldy; but I have not the spirit left to object to anything, or urge anything. I am in too much misery of body and mind. So go ahead as you think fit. (Letter of November 21, 1920)

Sonneck responded with some asperity:

> As to the homeliness of the page, that is, of course, a matter of taste. The page was adopted at the time by Mr. Edward Edwards, who as an art-designer and a designer of books for bibliophiles ranks, as you know, very high in his profession. (Letter of November 22, 1920)

Krehbiel yielded without much grace: "I shall have to shut my eyes when I read the Beethoven. . . . I am . . . too much chagrined to care to know about the paper—Trimmed margins, I suppose!" (letter of November 23, 1920). Sonneck did not reply. Half apologetically, Krehbiel wrote a few weeks later: "I feel that I am breaking down; the pains affect my nerves to such an extent that I fear they may give way unless I take a complete rest for a space" (letter of December 10, 1920). On his return from a vacation in Bermuda, he was not yet reconciled to the layout but had partially recovered his sense of humor: " 'Bruckner trousers' is . . . what I fear our pages are going to look like" (letter of January 29, 1921). (The reference was not as obscure to Sonneck as it may be to us, for it was a matter of amusement between them that when young Sonneck first visited Krehbiel, at the turn of the century, he was wearing a pair of shapeless knickerbockers reminiscent of those habitually worn by Anton Bruckner.)

Mainly technical details occupy the numerous letters of 1921. Krehbiel and Baker attended to stylistic issues: "I have written a note to Dr. Baker concerning capitalization," wrote Krehbiel on January 24:

> Thayer's indiscriminate use of 'Clement' and 'Clemens' (which escaped me in editing his pages) is annoying; so is his careless punctuation—too many commas and frequent dashes where commas

or semi colons would have been the right thing. (Letter of January 24, 1921)

The typesetting, proofreading, and preparation of the page proofs were virtually completed by the last week of August, and Krehbiel mailed the final copy for the indexes on September 18, calling forth a "Te Deum! sapienti sat!" from Sonneck (letter of September 21, 1921). But Krehbiel was somehow discouraged by the completion of his task:

> I have scarcely energy enough for this letter. And I haven't had time to think what I shall do. . . . There is much virtue in peace of mind. But may I have it? I don't know.

Again he expressed his dissatisfaction with the design:

> The vol. looks precisely as I told you I thought it would—not like a literary work but like a Pub. Doc. The shorter line which I wanted would have produced an entirely different effect. However, I am not worrying over the thing for I am too glad that the ghost that has haunted me for 17 years is about to be laid at last.

In his response of September 21, Sonneck wrote:

> It is a terrible disappointment to me that you are so disappointed in the looks of the book. Indeed, it was a most unpleasant shock, for the reason that all of us here feel entirely different in the matter. . . . How you can feel that the book does not look like a literary work, but like a public document is apparently beyond me. Every one to whom I have shown the work here was impressed with its good looks and congratulated me on the appearance of it. . . . I make so bold as to believe that your disappointment finally will wear off. . . .

On November 19, Sonneck sent Krehbiel a bound set of the work, advising that formal publication would take place on December 5 "for legal reasons connected with the British copyright regulations." The publication was a financial as well as a critical success. The first edition, consisting of 1037 copies, was exhausted by mid-1922, and a slightly corrected second edition of 565 copies appeared before the end of the year. Novello's allotment added 750 copies to the total. By March 31, 1923, the Beethoven Association had recovered over eighty percent of its investment, and ultimately, it had a net gain on its publication of a book that permanently altered the perception of Beethoven's life and character among English-speaking peoples.

Of course, Krehbiel understood well that it had been Oscar Sonneck's determination and foresight that had carried the day. However, it was not in his nature to express his gratitude in an effusive way. On learning that Schirmer would undertake the edition following Macmillan's defection, he had written: "I thank you for your letter and marvel at your persistence. . . . I wish I could see some reward coming to you" (letter of October 13, 1920). Shortly thereafter he succeeded in thanking Sonneck in a fashion more certain to be appreciated: "I had occasion yesterday. . . to read your essay [on Italian music] in 'Suum cuique,' " he wrote, "and found it full of information. I have quoted it with ample credit to you. I wish you were doing work on your old lines but I fancy you are glad that the need of that is over" (letter of October 29, 1920).[13] Sonneck was delighted, naturally, and responded with a revealing letter:

> My stock joke is: the O.G. Sonneck you knew died in August 1917. He is not to be confused with the gentleman of the same name whom you are addressing.
>
> The late O.G.S. cannot even get a second volume of essays, more historical than the first, printed. . . . The present O.G.S. sometimes feels the itch to walk in the foot-steps of his 'Namensvetter', but he fears that the stuff is not in him, even if he had time. (Letter of October 30, 1920)

Sonneck, sometimes called Oscar "Gloom" Sonneck by his friends,[14] was here being overly pessimistic, for his *Miscellaneous Studies in the History of Music* was indeed published, in 1921.

Unfortunately, the later stages of the relationship between these men were marred by Krehbiel's dissatisfaction with the book's design and his unreasonable complaints about production delays. Of course, Sonneck's righteous and commanding manner was difficult to take. "Occasionally," wrote Carl Engel of him, "he appeared irritable and could irritate."[15] And so there is no plain letter of thanks to Sonneck following publication of Thayer's *Life of Beethoven*. It was a year later that Krehbiel brought himself to express his feelings: not knowing that Sonneck had been ill, he looked for him in vain at musical events: "I suppose you're so busy that you never go to concerts," he wrote. "I miss you behind me at the Beethoven Association affairs" (letter of [November 21] 1922).

Krehbiel's final letter to Sonneck, written on February 23, 1923, again shows him reaching out to his erstwhile collaborator for sympathy and renewed contact. He tells of an "impertinent individual" who had com-

---

[13]Sonneck, "Signs of a New Uplift in Italy's Musical Life," in: *Suum cuique: Essays in Music* (New York, 1916), pp. 215–71; Krehbiel, "Reflections Concerning the Development of Italian Music," *New York Tribune*, October 31, 1920, sec. III, p. 6.

[14]*The Musical Quarterly*, XXV (1939), 4.

[15]*The Musical Quarterly*, XV (1929), 150.

plained to the editor of the *Tribune* about Krehbiel's penchant for remarks on such unmusical subjects as German war reparations. Krehbiel grumbled: "He had no more business trying to tell the Tribune editors and writers what to do than I have to tell G. Schirmer how to run its business." The busy Sonneck responded the very next day, but only with a short note signed "In haste." Thus ended the correspondence, for Krehbiel died on March 21, 1923.

Prior to his own death on October 30, 1928, Sonneck completed three books on Beethoven, which have become permanent contributions to the Beethoven literature: *Beethoven: Impressions of Contemporaries* (New York, 1926); *Beethoven Letters in America* (New York, 1927); and *The Riddle of the Immortal Beloved* (New York, 1927). In the last of these, Sonneck linked himself to Thayer and Krehbiel as their posthumous collaborator and continuator, for the work, set in the familiar *Musical Quarterly* page design, is subtitled: *A Supplement to Thayer's 'Life of Beethoven.'*

A. W. Thayer, the Diarist, and the Late Mr. Brown: A Bibliography of Writings in *Dwight's Journal of Music*

Michael Ochs

In a letter to his translator dated August 1, 1878, Alexander W. Thayer listed his published books to date: "A volume (small one) of musical novelettes in English, my *Chron[ologisches] Verzeichniss* of Beethoven's works, and the two volumes of his biography."[1] Volume 3 of the biography, moreover, was just five months away from publication. It may seem curious then to find, two sentences earlier in the same document, the statement: "My writings have been almost exclusively for periodicals and most of all, newspapers; especially for Dwight's Journal of Music and the New York Tribune."[2] But Thayer's contributions to these and to other periodicals, including the *New-York Musical Review and Gazette*, the *London Musical World*, and the Boston *Courier* and *Transcript*, number well into the hundreds. This extensive body of writings has remained relatively unnoticed in later research into the period.[3]

The aim of this bibliography is to draw attention to a large portion of these writings—those appearing in *Dwight's Journal of Music*. Thayer's contributions span the entire twenty-nine-year run of *Dwight's*, which was published weekly at Boston for eleven years beginning in April, 1852, then fortnightly until its demise in September, 1881. Its founder and sole editor, John Sullivan Dwight, printed an article by Thayer on the "Eroica" Symphony in the fledgling journal's second issue.[4] The next few months brought a characteristic diversity of writings by Thayer: a sketch of composer Antonio Salieri; a description of a "pilgrimage" to

---

[1] Letter to Hermann Deiters, quoted in Thayer-Forbes, p. viii.

[2] *Ibid.*

[3] An important exception is Christopher Hatch, "The Education of A. W. Thayer," *The Musical Quarterly*, XLII (1956), 355–65. See also Marcia Wilson Lebow, "A Systematic Examination of the *Journal of Music and Art* Edited by John Sullivan Dwight: 1852–1881, Boston, Massachusetts" (Diss. Univ. of California, Los Angeles, 1969), pp. 107–16.

[4] "Beethoven and his Third Symphony," *Dwight's*, I (1852), 9–10.

Beethoven's tomb; biographical sketches of four contemporary *prime donne;* a letter on various subjects, including oratorio practice and American voices; observations on the state of classical music in Rochester, Buffalo, Detroit, and towns in between; a translation from the diary of composer Johanna Kinkel; and Thayer's first publication in the guise of the "Diarist." Over half of all Thayer's contributions to *Dwight's* were to appear under the Diarist pseudonym, even though the author's identity had been hinted at and then revealed early on by the editor.[5] Thayer's use of another pseudonym, "the late Mr. Brown," for a group of fictional musical sketches can be regarded as an amusing affectation that was not meant to disguise their authorship.

Perusal of the bibliography quickly reveals not only Thayer's wide-ranging interest in musical subjects, but also his readiness to address any issue, great or small. His writing, especially when he comments on current musical events and ideas, may be humorous, reflective, or argumentative, but it is always informed and never dull. It often betrays the author's special pleasure, mingled with righteous indignation, in rooting out and denouncing the "humbug" wherever he finds it. But he also praises eloquently those works, performances, and practices that he admires. He does not shun controversy; indeed, some of his consciously opinionated derogations of Italian opera generated heated responses from dissenting readers—much to the editor's delight.

Through 1861, Thayer produced more column-inches in the pages of *Dwight's* than anyone save the prolific Dwight himself. After that, the number of his contributions dwindled sharply. An extensive study of Salieri appeared during 1864 as Part 2 of a projected six-part series on Beethoven's contemporaries that was not, in fact, carried further. The following January saw Thayer installed as United States Consul in Trieste. The appointment, however welcome, was to make considerable demands upon his time and energy, and the issues of *Dwight's* from then on carry only an occasional article or letter of his. Dwight eventually took to printing excerpts from the Beethoven biography, which had been published in German and had to be translated back into English—though not without noting the absurdity of the effort. Thayer's final article in *Dwight's*, a reprint from the *London Musical World*, dealt like the first with a Beethoven subject; it appeared in the journal's sixth to last issue.[6]

Many of the titles in *Dwight's* convey little to describe the content of the articles they head (e.g., "From my Diary, no. 15"). Happily, the index pages often compensate for this lack by providing brief phrases that can

---

[5] In *Dwight's*, III (1853), 31, and V (1854), 111, respectively.
[6] "The Archduke Rudolf," *Dwight's*, XLI (1881), 73–74.

serve as explanatory subtitles. Titles in this bibliography have been liber-
ally augmented by such phrases (which accounts for the seeming lack of
consistency in capitalization). When even the indices fail us, suitable
phrases have been supplied in square brackets. "See also" references
provide the necessary links to other items in *Dwight's* that are specifically
referred to by Thayer in a given item.

I. "Diarist" Writings

Writings, most of which purport to be diary entries; unsigned, except as
noted. Most fall within one of several series, which are listed chronologically. The remaining items are listed alphabetically.

A. Writings in Series

From my Diary [ser. 1, published Sep., 1852–July, 1854]

[No. 1:] Funeral marches; Notices of Beethoven more sentimental
than true; Woodbury's *Absalom.* 1 (1852): 188–89.

No. 2: Concerts at Newport; Trashy programmes; Gungl's abuse of
us; Singing hymns "in the *German* manner"; Indian music; A new
psalm-book. 1 (1852): 196.

No. 3: About "everybody learning to read music in Germany";
Czerny's anecdotes of Beethoven; A "sacred concert" programme!
1 (1852): 204–5.

No. 4: Little Urso; Sontag; Overture to "Martha"; Schubert's *"only"*
symphony; A singer's harvest. 2 (1852–53): 13.

No. 5: Mr. Wyzaker at Sontag's concert; "Old and new," a few dates. 2
(1852–53): 20–21. [Part 1 reprinted: *Signor Masoni and Other Papers of
the Late I. Brown,* ed. Alexander W. Thayer (Berlin: F. Schneider;
Boston: A. Williams, 1862), pp. 231–35.]

No. 6: The "gloomy" Beethoven; "Fidelio." 2 (1852–53): 28–29.

No. 7: How should orchestras and choruses be arranged on the stage?
2 (1852–53): 35.

No. 8: Dr. Franklin and the harmonica; Cecilia Davies. 2 (1852–53): 44–
45.

No. 9: Drumming in New York streets; Notices of Balfe; How Weber
wrote for the voice; Ludwig Fischer. 2 (1852–53): 53.

No. 10: Rode; Haydn's remains; Music at Webster funeral procession;
Dialogue about two music journals. 2 (1852–53): 60–61.

No. 11: Sontag's dress rehearsal; Philharmonic rehearsal; Gade; Mendelssohn cut into psalm-tunes; the Misses Tourny. 2 (1852–53): 69.

No. 12: Paul Jullien and young Mozart; Quicksteps at funerals; Anecdote of Sontag. 2 (1852–53): 75.

No. 13: Macfarren's notice of Beethoven's "Ruins of Athens." 2 (1852–53): 93–94.

No. 14: Alfred Jaell; "Positive, comparative, superlative"; Alboni's "sacred" concert. 2 (1852–53): 124.

No. 15: Zeuner's psalmody; Boston Music Hall; *Choral Symphony;* American vocal schools. 2 (1852–53): 140–41.

No. 16: "Engedi" [English setting of Beethoven's *Mount of Olives*]; "Choral Symphony," &c. 2 (1852–53): 149.

No. 17: Rhythm for psalmody; Sontag and the clergy. 2 (1852–53): 156.

No. 18: Onslow; Salomon. 2 (1852–53): 164–65.

No. 19: Beethoven's 7th Symphony; Yankee Doodle be-devilled. 2 (1852–53): 173.

No. 20: The sisters Milanollo. 2 (1852–53): 180.

No. 20 [*bis*]: [Names of Zeuner's psalm-tunes; *Mount of Olives* choruses translated; "Provincial" Boston and "progressive" New York.] 2 (1852–53): 188–89.

No. 21: "Arrangements" from Beethoven. 2 (1852–53): 196–97.

No. 22: Lack of oratorios in New York. 3 (1853): 4–5.

No. 23: Joseph Vernet and Pergolese. 3 (1853): 12.

No. 24: Lindpaintner; Prussian decree about music directors; the Germanians at Washington. 3 (1853): 28–29.

No. 25: Schumann's music. 3 (1853): 36.

No. 26: "Midsummer Night's Dream" with Mendelssohn's music; Classical concerts in Boston. 3 (1853): 53.

No. 27: Music in the West; Beethoven's *Studien;* Jullien's Beethoven night. 4 (1853–54): 5.

No. 28: A story; Rub-a-dub!; Mendelssohn night at Jullien's. 4 (1853–54): 20–21.

No. 29: Mendelssohn's melodies; *Tannhäuser.* 4 (1853–54): 37.

No. 30: Jullien, Rossini, Berlioz, &c.; Beethoven musical relics. 4 (1853–54): 45.

No. 31: Gongs. 4 (1853–54): 60.

No. 32: Original edition of the "Messiah." 4 (1853–54): 69.

No. 33: "Samson." 4 (1853–54): 77.

No. 34: American voices. 4 (1853–54): 83–84.

No. 35: Jullien's concerts; Fry's symphonies. 4 (1853–54): 91.

No. 36: Philharmonic rehearsals; Jullien. 4 (1853–54): 100.

No. 37: Mason's letters; "Charles Auchester." 4 (1853–54): 125.

No. 38: A Philharmonic concert; Bryan Gallery. 4 (1853–54): 131–32.

No. 39: American voices and psalmody. 4 (1853–54): 156–57.

No. 40: The Fry-Willis controversy. 4 (1853–54): 165. [*See also:* Letter from the Diarist in answer to Mr. Fry (Section I.B).]

No. 41: Beethoven's waltzes. 4 (1853–54): 180–81.

No. 42: Eisfeld's soirées. 4 (1853–54): 187–88.

No. 43: New York criticism, &c. 4 (1853–54): 197.

No. 44: Attacks on N.Y. Philharmonic; Metropolitan Hall to be rebuilt; the *Lon[don] Mus[ical] World's* life of Mendelssohn. 5 (1854): 4.

No. 45: Mendelssohn's name. 5 (1854): 21.

No. 46: Errors in Fétis' sketch of Beethoven. 5 (1854): 28.

No. 47: "Old Hundredth." 5 (1854): 44–45. [*See also:* Old Hundred, and Mr. Havergal's Letter (Section I.B).]

No. 48: "Pennyroyal tunes"; Jullien's "Prima Donna" in church; Amateur orchestras. 5 (1854): 68–69.

No. 49: Music at the N.Y. Institution for the Blind. 5 (1854): 100.

No. 50: Dr. Tyng's church; Anna Stone; Beethoven's last hours. 5 (1854): 108–9.

Diary Abroad [ser. 1, published Oct., 1854–Jan., 1856]

No. 1: Music in Berlin; Liebig's Sinfonie concerts; Quartet party; Inundation in Silesia and music in the Thiergarten. 6 (1854–55): 11–12.

No. 2: Hanover; The *Prophète.* 6 (1854–55): 51–52. [*See also:* No. 9.]

No. 3: Cassel; *Der Unbekannte,* opera by J. J. Bott. 6 (1854–55): 59.

No. 4: *Fidelio* and Johanna Wagner. 6 (1854–55): 67–68.

No. 5: Beethoven and Bellini. 6 (1854–55): 90.

No. 6: Poverty of music in Paris; One month's music in Berlin. 6 (1854–55): 100–101.

No. 7: Making psalm-tunes from Beethoven, &c. 6 (1854–55): 115–16.

No. 8: The "Choral Symphony" at Berlin. 6 (1854–55): 123–24.

No. 9: Reply to "A Subscriber" about the *Prophète.* 6 (1854–55): 131–32. [*See also:* No. 2; "A Subscriber's" letter, 6 (1854–55): 58–59.]

No. 10: Allegri's *Miserere.* 6 (1854–55): 164–65.

No. 11: Reminiscences; Old musical journals; "Wonder-children"; Joachim. 6 (1854–55): 189.

No. 12: Joachim. 6 (1854–55): 196–97.

No. 13: Rubinstein. 6 (1854–55): 204–5.

No. 14: Rubinstein's Symphony. 7 (1855): 2.

No. 15: *Don Juan;* Music in Paris. 7 (1855): 10–11.

No. 16: Graun's *Tod Jesu;* Breslau; Amateur club; The mass. 7 (1855): 60.

No. 17: Opera in Berlin; Gluck, Meyerbeer, Mozart, Beethoven, Wagner; Schneider's *Last Judgment.* 7 (1855): 116–17.

No. 18: Reminiscences; Young Meyerbeer. 7 (1855): 150–51.

No. 19: Liebig's concerts, &c. 7 (1855): 159.

No. 20: Prof. Dehn; Rossini; His respect for Germans, &c. 7 (1855): 4.

No. 21: Berlin, the Dom Choir; Mozart's sacred music. 8 (1855–56): 13.

No. 22: Notes on *Don Juan*; Rossini's *Tancredi*. 8 (1855–56): 20–21.

No. 23: *Des Adler's Horst;* The *Messiah*. 8 (1855–56): 35–36.

No. 24: Mendelssohn as a creative genius. 8 (1855–56): 44–45.

No. 25: Alleged discoveries of works by Weber and Handel. 8 (1855–56): 51–52.

No. 26: Italian opera; Strictures on the *Tribune*. 8 (1855–56): 59–60.

[No. 27: *See:* How shall the Orchestra or Choir be Placed? (Section IV.B).]

[No. 28: *See:* Musical Correspondence. Berlin, 1855: Oct. 30 (Section III).]

No. 29: Lenz on Beethoven; The spider story. 8 (1855–56): 83.

No. 30: Lenz's book on Beethoven again. 8 (1855–56): 91–92.

No. 31: Chorley's "Music in Germany"; Haydn's "Farewell Symphony"; Mozart's father. 8 (1855–56): 132–33.

From my Diary [ser. 2, published May, 1857–Mar., 1858]

[No. 1:] Handel; Concert at Cambridgeport; Luther. 11 (1857): 43–44.

No. 2: The Handel and Haydn festival. 11 (1857): 53.

No. 3: Union among artists. 11 (1857): 69–70.

No. 4: First oratorio in Boston. 11 (1857): 76.

No. 5: A scheme for orchestral concerts. 11 (1857): 84–85.

No. 6: Bells; Rellstab, the critic; Mozart's *Ave Verum Corpus*. 11 (1857): 100–101.

No. 7: Rellstab on Mozart; "Old Hundred." 11 (1857): 116–17.

No. 8: The steam "calliope." 11 (1857): 126.

No. 9: Recitative and spoken dialogue in opera. 11 (1857): 132–33.

No. 10: Corey's Hill. 11 (1857): 140–41. [Reprinted as: A Park for Boston: Corey's Hill, 35 (1875–76): 39.]

No. 11: Trip to Montreal, Lake Champlain, &c. 11 (1857): 180–81.

No. 12: Considerations for singers. 11 (1857): 199.

No. 13: Schoelcher's life of Handel. 12 (1857–58): 237.

No. 14: Concerts and operas in New York; Congregational singing. 12 (1857–58): 283–84.

No. 15: Puffs of young artists. 12 (1857–58): 291.

No. 16: Stradella's works. 12 (1857–58): 298.

No. 17: [A conversation.] 12 (1857–58): 318.

No. 18: Lilla Linden's "Linden Harp"; Satter's concert in Cambridge; Carl Formes. 12 (1857–58): 322–23.

No. 19: Lilla Linden again; L. H. Southard and his "Omano." 12 (1857–58): 333–34.

No. 20: [Concert at Chickering's Rooms; View of Harvard.] 12 (1857–58): 340.

No. 21: The "pupil nuisance." 12 (1857–58): 347.

No. 22: German Trio concert; Rubinstein. 12 (1857–58): 356.

No. 23: A Beethoven concert for a musical library. 12 (1857–58): 362–63.

No. 24: Duty of singing teachers, &c. to musical journals. 12 (1857–58): 379–80.

No. 25: Verdi's popularity. 12 (1857–58): 391.

No. 26: Cost of the *Huguenots*. 12 (1857–58): 395.

No. 27: Voices; Where to learn to sing. 12 (1857–58): 405–6. [*See also:* American Voices (Section I.B).]

From my Diary [ser. 3, published Apr.–July, 1858]

No. 1: [Church music.] 13 (1858): 5–6.

No. 2: [A fancy sketch for the Handel & Haydn Society.] 13 (1858): 15.

No. 3: [An annual series of orchestral and vocal concerts; Haydn's "Creation" in Holliston.] 13 (1858): 27–28.

No. 4: [August Fries leaves the Boston Quintet Club.] 13 (1858): 38.

No. 5: [Poor choral singing; Teaching music in common schools;] Old Hundred; Miss E. W. Bruce. 13 (1858): 44.

[No. 6: Omitted in numbering.]

No. 7: S. W. Dehn. 13 (1858): 61–62.

No. 8: [A Clara Schumann anecdote.] 13 (1858): 68.

No. 9: [Musical instruction in schools; Songs by Miss Bruce's sister.] 13 (1858): 99–100.

No. 10: [The musical service in Christ Church, Oxford.] 13 (1858): 124.

The Diarist Abroad [ser. 2, published Oct., 1858–Mar., 1859]

[No. 1:] The voyage. 14 (1858–59): 209–10. [Signed: A. W. T.]

No. 2: A fortnight in London. 14 (1858–59): 217–19.

[No. 3:] At sea. 14 (1858–59): 238–39.

No. 4: Wolfenbüttel. 14 (1858–59): 242–43.

No. 5: Berlin. 14 (1858–59): 252–54.

[Nos. 6–10: Omitted in numbering.]

No. 11: Notes and a query. 14 (1858–59): 281–82.

No. 12: Notes. 14 (1858–59): 321–22.

No. 13: A Monument to Weber; Zelter. 14 (1858–59): 337–38. [Signed: A. W. T.]

No. 14: What do we mean by "Classic"? 14 (1858–59): 354. [Signed: A. W. T.]

No. 15: An Imaginary Conversation with "John." 14 (1858–59): 361.

No. 16: Notes. 14 (1858–59): 377–78.

No. 17: Notes. 14 (1858–59): 385. [Part 3, Johann Wenzel Tomaschek, reprinted 28 (1868–69): 412, signed: A. W. T.]

No. 18: Berlin. 14 (1858–59): 401–2.

The Diarist Abroad [ser. 3, published Apr., 1859–Dec., 1860]

Feb. 21, 1859, Berlin: [History of the Royal Opera House and the Theatre in Berlin.] 15 (1859): 9–10.

March 28, 1859, Berlin: [Hamburg; Memory of East Cambridge bridge.] 15 (1859): 33–34.

April 9, 1859, Berlin: [The Symphony; Is ignorance bliss?; Americans in Berlin.] 15 (1859): 41–42.

[Mid-Apr. (?), 1859, Berlin:] Notes [Macfarren's sketch of Beethoven; Ludwig Erk.] 15 (1859): 57–58. [Signed: A. W. T. *See also:* Macfarren's sketch, 14 (1858–59): 395–96, 402–3, 412–13; 15 (1859): 3, 11–12, 18–19.]

April 20, 1859, Berlin: [Beethoven's Mass in D.] 15 (1859): 110–11. [Signed: A. W. T.]

April 17–May 18, 1859, Berlin: Notes [Bach's "St. Matthew Passion"; American tourists.] 15 (1859): 116.

May 11, 1859, Berlin: Trip to Breslau. 15 (1859): 146–48, 153–54. [Signed: A. W. T.]

[June, 1859,] In Prague: Dr. Edmund Schebeck; Dr. August Wilhelm Ambros; Johann Friedrich Kittl. 16 (1859–60): 321–22.

July 14–Oct. 19, 1859, Vienna: ["Private music" parties; Evening at Herr Halm's; &c.] 16 (1859–60): 362. [Signed: A. W. T.]

Oct. 23–Dec. 16, 1859, Vienna: ["Euterpe" concert; Beethoven's Ninth Symphony in the Redouten Saal; Rosa Suck's concert; &c.] 16 (1859–60): 372. [Signed: A. W. T.]

Dec. 1859–Jan. 12, 1860, Vienna: [Alfred Jaell; Helmesberger's Quartet concert; Vieuxtemps' Quartet concert; &c.] 16 (1859–60): 380–81. [Signed: A. W. T.]

Feb., 1860, Berlin: Notes [Haydn's "Farewell Symphony"; Madame Zimmermann.] 16 (1859–60): 406–7. [Signed: A. W. T.]

Feb., 1860, Berlin: Notes [Oubilicheff upon Mozart's *Zauberflöte.*] 16 (1859–60): 410–11. [Signed: A. W. T.]

Feb., 1860, Berlin: Notes [Concert at the King of Prussia's.] 17 (1860): 4. [Signed: A. W. T.]

Feb. 17–Mar. 4, 1860, Berlin: [Laub's concert; The Leipzig Conservatorium; American students in Berlin.] 17 (1860): 23. [Signed: A. W. T. *See also:* Musical Correspondence, Vienna, June 16, 1860 (Section III).]

Mar. 22, 1860, Vienna: [Schubert's Quintet, op. 114; Handel's "Israel in Egypt"; Julia Swoboda; Michael Glinka.] 17 (1860): 27–28. [Signed: A. W. T.]

May 12, 1860, Vienna: Notes [Elise Polko's Leonora sketch, &c.] 17 (1860): 99–100. [Signed: A. W. T. *See also:* Polko's sketch, 17 (1860):

33–34; Editor's comment, 17 (1860): 38; and Polko's letter to the Diarist, 17 (1860): 145–46.]

[May or June, 1860:] Beethoven and Paer. 17 (1860): 119. [Signed: A. W. T.]

[June–Sep., 1860:] Utile et Dulce. 17 (1860): 153–54, 163–65, 169–71; 18 (1860–61): 225–27. [Signed: A. W. T.]

Sept. 9, 1860, Bonn: [Beethoven stories.] 18 (1860–61): 234–35. [Signed: A. W. T.]

Sept. 1860, Bonn: [A music festival at Brühl;] A Great Man. 18 (1860–61): 241–43. [Signed: A. W. T.]

[Mid-Nov., 1860, Paris:] Neither Utile nor Dulce. 18 (1860–61): 297–99. [Signed: A. W. T.]

Nov. 26, 1860, Paris: [American painters in Paris.] 18 (1860–61); 306–7. [Signed: A. W. T.]

Nov. 27, 1860, Paris: [Offenbach's "Orphée aux Enfers"; Gluck's "Orpheus"; Halevy's "Vale of Andorra"; "The Hen that Laid the Golden Eggs"; "The Prophet."] 18 (1860–61): 313–14. [Signed: A. W. T.]

The Diarist in Paris [published Jan.–Feb., 1861]

Dec. 26, 1860: [Alexis Azevedo on M'lle Sax, Ronconi, Mario, Mad. Viardot; Dufresne's l'Hotel da la Poste.] 18 (1860–61): 346–47.

Dec. 28, 1860: [*Trovatore* at the Italian Opera; Paladilhe; Wekerlin's *Les Poemes de la Mer;* Joseph Wieniawski's concert at the Salle Pleyel.] 18 (1860–61): 354–56.

Jan. 4, 1861: [Theatre-going in Paris: Boulanger's l'Eventail.] 18 (1860–61): 363–64.

Jan. 4 [*i.e.* 9], 1861. Maillart's *Les Pecheurs de Catane;* Offenbach's *le Roi Barkouf.*] (1860–61): 370–71.

The Diarist in London [published July–Aug., 1861]

Jan. 31–Feb. 14, 1861: Light Reading for Hot Weather. 19 (1861): 130–32.

Feb. 26, 1861: Le Domino Noir—Light Reading for Hot Weather. 19 (1861): 137–39.

Feb. 27–Mar. 8, 1861: Concert of the Musical Society of London; On the Great Increase of Musical Societies, &c. in London; Kemp's "Old Folk's" [sic] in London; Wallace's Amber Witch; Elijah. 19 (1861): 145–47.

Mar. 9–Apr. 10, 1861: [A Beethoven concert in Sydenham; New Philharmonic concert; The "Vocal Association"; Beethoven night; "Exeter Hall National Choral Society"; Mendelssohn's "First Walpurgis Night."] 19 (1861): 153–55.

Apr. 12–May 10, 1861: [The Sacred Harmonic Society: New Philharmonic; Mr. Walter Macfarren's concert; Haydn's "Creation" at the Crystal Palace; Concert of the Musical Society; Rossini's "Tell"; Handel's "Israel in Egypt" by the London Sacred Harmonic Society.] 19 (1861): 161–62.

[May or June (?), 1861:] Music in England; Arabella Goddard, Sims Reeves, and Other Singers; Cathedral Choirs. 19 (1861): 169–71. [Signed: A. W. T.]

B. Miscellaneous Writings

American Voices; Musical Conventions. 13 (1858): 13. [A lengthy question from "Phi." with a brief answer signed Diarist. *See also:* From my Diary, ser. 2, no. 27.]

Beethoven's "Egmont" Music. ("From my Diary.") 9 (1856): 61–62.

The Diarist in Vienna. 17 (1860): 49–50. [Signed: A. W. T.]

Diary at Home: Singers with Italianized names. 11 (1857): 20.

Emma of Nevada. 40 (1880): 198–99. [Signed: A. W. T.]

From the Diarist: Notes on Gluck. 23 (1863–64): 132. [Signed: A. W. T.]

How the D[iarist] Went Pleasuring. 15 (1859): 161–63; 16 (1859–60): 289, 305–7, 313–15. [Signed: A. W. T.]

The humble apology and plea for mercy of the "Diarist," in a note to his honored Mentor, "C." of the Boston *Atlas*. [Part 2 of : A Complaint and an Apology.] 2 [1852–53]: 10–11. [*See also:* Dwight's comment, 2 (1852–53): 15; A word from "C." of the *Atlas*, 2 (1852–53): 18–19.]

Letter from the Diarist: Dr. Chrysander's labors on Bach and Handel. 10 (1856–57): 37–38. [Signed: A. W. T.]

Letter from the Diarist [in answer to Mr. Fry]. 4 (1853–54): 196–97, 203–5; 5 (1854): 4–5, 18–20. [*See also* the following earlier items, all in vol. 4 (1853–54): Fry letter to Willis, 138–40; Dwight editorial, 140–42; Willis reply to Fry, 146–47; Fry rejoinder to Willis, 163–64; "Diarist" comment on Fry rejoinder (From my Diary, ser. 1, no. 40), 165; Dwight comment on Fry rejoinder, 166–67; Willis reply to Fry, 171–73; Dwight comment on Willis reply, 173–74; and Fry letter to Dwight answering "Diarist's" and Dwight's comments, 186–87.]

The Normal Music School at North Reading. 11 (1857): 133–34. [Signed: A. W. T.]

Old Hundred, and Mr. Havergal's Letter. 5 (1854): 99–100. [Signed: Alexander W. Thayer. *See also:* From my Diary, ser, 1, no. 47; Havergal's letter, 5 (1854): 90–91.]

A Private Letter of the D[iarist]. 15 (1859): 195–96.

II. "BROWN" PAPERS

Fictional sketches, unsigned; most subsequently collected and reprinted in: *Signor Masoni and Other Papers of the Late I. Brown,* ed. Alexander W. Thayer (Berlin: F. Schneider; Boston: A. Williams, 1862) [hereafter *Brown*].

From the Private Papers of the late Mr. Brown [title varies: From the Brown Papers; etc.]

An Evening in the Hartz. 8 (1855–56): 2–4, 10–12. [Reprinted: *Brown,* pp. 48–72.]

The Magic Flute. 14 (1858–59): 265–67, 273–75.

Monsieur Paul. 15 (1859): 196–98, 201–3; 16 (1859–60): 209–11. [Reprinted: *Brown,* pp. 236–71.]

Mrs. Smith and Elizabeth. 13 (1858): 113–15. [Reprinted: *Brown,* pp. 194–206.]

A New Acquaintance. 13 (1858): 185–87. [Reprinted: *Brown,* pp. 207–21.)

On the Structure of Italian Opera. (From "Brown's Letters Upon the Poetry and Music of the Italian Opera." 8 (1855–56): 162–63.

Our Music-teacher. 12 (1857–58): 353–54, 361–62, 369–70. [Reprinted: *Brown,* pp. 83–103.]

The Philister's Reminiscence. 13 (1858): 1–2, 9–10. [Reprinted: 21 (1862): 172–73; *Brown,* pp. 272–82.]

A Prima Donna's Triumph in "Fidelio." 11 (1857): 1–2.

Somewhat from the Private Papers of Mister Brown: [Wyzaker.] 7 (1855): 179–81. [Reprinted: *Brown,* pp. 222–31. *See also:* From my Diary, ser. 1, no. 5.]

Signor Masoni. 8 (1855–56): 98–100, 106–8, 114–16, 121–22, 129–31. [Reprinted: *Brown,* pp. 1–47.]

The Story of Don Juan. 14 (1858–59): 297–99, 305–6.

Susan Bedloe. 10 (1856–57): 185–86. [Reprinted: *Brown,* pp. 73–82.]

Wyzaker. *See:* Somewhat from the Private Papers of Mister Brown; From my Diary, ser. 1, no. 5.

III. MUSICAL CORRESPONDENCE

Writings appearing in the columns headed "Musical Correspondence" (or occasionally, "Correspondence" or "Foreign Correspondence"). Signed A. W. T., except as noted. Other contributions in letter form are included in other sections of this bibliography.

Berlin, 1854

Nov. 4: Music and Missions; Great Collections in the Royal Library; Importance of Musical Libraries. 6 (1854–55): 66–67.

Nov. 12: [Heinrich Dorn; Wilhelm Taubert.] 6 (1854–55): 99–100.

Nov. 18: Weber's "Euryanthe"; Gluck's "Orfeo." 6 (1854–55): 91–93. [Unsigned. By Thayer?]

Nov. 22: The Sing-Akademie; Mendelssohn's Lauda Sion; Cherubini's Requiem; Compared with Mozart's. 6 (1854–55): 108–9.

Berlin, 1855

Jan. 9: [Handel's "Samson" at the Sing-Akademie.] 6 (1854–55): 148.

Jan. 19: [Zimmer's thoughts on the Bach Society's edition of Bach's works.] 6 (1854–55): 171–72, 179–80.

Mar. 9: Beethoven's Choral Fantasia and Mass in D. 7 (1855): 12.

Oct. 30: [Alfred Jaell's concert.] 8 (1855–56): 77. [Probably intended by Thayer to serve as Diary Abroad, ser. 1, no. 28.]

Nov. 10–12: Clara Schumann's concerts with Joachim. 8 (1855–56): 77–78, 85.

Nov. 12–Dec. 1: [Concert by Clara Schumann and Joachim; Rellstab; Mozart's grave.] 8 (1855–56): 93.

Berlin, 1856

Mar. 16–17: [A Fortnight in Dresden and Leipzig: Meyerbeer's "North Star"; Visits with Moscheles and C. F. Becker; A Gewandhaus concert.] 9 (1856): 13–14, 20–21.

Berlin, 1858

Sep. 17 ["Everybody away"; The study of music in Germany.] 14 (1858–59): 244–46.

Sep. 26: Sketch of Prof. Dehn. 14 (1858–59): 256, 259–61, 268–69.

Nov. 8: [Opera and oratorio in Berlin; Robert Radecke's concerts.] 14 (1858–59): 285–86.

Nov. 10: [The Royal Orchestra concert, &c.] 14 (1858–59): 293.

Nov. 15: [The Laub-Radecke Quartet.] 14 (1858–59): 293–94.

Nov. 22: [Gluck's "Orpheus and Eurydice"; The Laub-Radecke Quartet; Liebig's concert.] 14 (1858–59): 304.

Nov. 22: [Cherubini's *Requiem*; Hermann Zopf; Death of Mrs. Kinkel; Carl Holz; An anecdote.] 14 (1858–59): 309.

Dec. 13: [Laub's concert, &c.] 14 (1858–59): 324–25.

Nov. [*i.e.* Dec.] 23: [A Latin and Spanish Bible of 1574.] 14 (1858–59): 325.

Berlin, 1859

Jan. 5: [The "Association of Berlin-Artists" exhibition; The "Gesellschaft der Musikfreunde" in Vienna.] 14 (1858–59): 360.

Jan. 9: [Trautwein Book and Music Store; Radecke's concert; Answers to Mr. Blank.] 14 (1858–59): 367–68.

Jan. 16: [Howard Vaughan; How to improve singing in our country.] 14 (1858–59): 371–72.

Jan. 20: ["Chaos" at the Sing-Akademie; Hans von Buelow's concert.] 14 (1858–59): 380–81.

Jan. 26: [Hans von Buelow, &c.] 14 (1858–59): 388.

Feb. 4: [A Dom-chor concert; Festival Overture by Hugo Ulrich; Radecke's concert.] 14 (1858–59): 388–89.

Feb. 9: [Madame Zimmermann's musical evening; Instruction in singing.] 14 (1858–59); 397–98.

Feb. 10: [An English school of singing.] 14 (1858–59): 405.

Feb. 26–Mar. 1: [Dreams during the Dom-chor concert; The Mass in B minor at the Sing-Akademie; The Stern Society's "Creation"; Woldemar Bargiel.] 15 (1859): 8.

Mar. 8: [Schumann's *Faust* music; Robert Radecke; Theodore Kullak; Haupt.] 15 (1859): 12–13.

Apr. 1: [Halle.] 15 (1859): 36–37.

Apr. 2. [Leipzig; Chrysander.] 15 (1859): 45.

May 2: [Prof. Fischoff's collection; A Homer library.] 15 (1859): 64.

Berlin, 1860

Feb. 5: The New Edition of Handel's works. 16 (1859–60): 413.

Frankfort on the Main, 1854

Oct. 20: Beethoven's Biographer; Oratorio for Boston; Weigl's "Swiss Family." 6 (1854–55): 60.

Leipzig, 1855

June 21: [August Gockel; *Ave Maria* by Liszt; Beethoven's *Sonata Appassionata.*] 7 (1855): 127.

New York, 1852

Nov. 15: First concert of the Philharmonic Society—Beethoven's Eighth Symphony, Gade's Overture, &c. 2 (1852–53): 51–52.

Paris, 1860

Nov. 10: [Opera in Paris.] 18 (1860–61): 292.

Vienna, 1860

June 16: [Response to Dwight's comment on the Leipzig Conservatorium.] 17 (1860): 160. [*See also:* The Diarist Abroad, ser. 3, Feb. 17–Mar. 4, 1860; Dwight's comment and O. W.'s letter, 17 (1860): 79; and a letter to Thayer, 17 (1860): 160.]

July 6: [Music at Darmstadt; Joseph Dessaur's "Domingo"; Leopold von Meyer; Gustav Pressel's "The Night of St. John"; &c.] 17 (1860): 159–60.

Vienna, 1861

Aug. 18: [In the old room again.] 19 (1861): 190.

[Western New York, &c.,] 1852

June 10: Notes of a Short Tour Westward. 1 (1852):84.

IV. Miscellaneous Writings

Writings not included above. Signed with Thayer's initials or name, except as noted.

A. Writings About Beethoven

The Archduke Rudolph. 41 (1881): 73–74. [Reprinted from the *London Musical World*.]

Beethoven and his Third Symphony. (Extract from an unpublished work.) 1 (1852): 9–10.

Beethoven and the Height of his Productivity (1807–9). (Translations from Thayer's Third Volume.) 39 (1879): 75–76, 90–91.

Beethoven Literature. 9 (1856): 149–50, 158–59.

A Beethoven Matter [his Schottische Lieder]: Notes upon a Preface. 20 (1861–62): 274–75.

Beethoven's Early Sonatas. 10 (1856–57): 119. [*See also:* Beethoven's "First Work"; Letter from F. W. M., 10 (1856–57): 155–56.]

Beethoven's Famous Love-Letter. 37 (1877–78): 153–55. [Translated from Thayer's *Beethoven*, vol. 3.]

Beethoven's "First Work." 10 (1856–57): 102–3. [*See also:* Beethoven's Early Sonatas.]

Beethoven's Letters. 26 (1866–67): 296.

Beethoven's Music for the Opening of the National Theatre in Pesth. 17 (1860): 41–42.

Beethoven's Schottische Lieder. *See:* A Beethoven Matter.

Beethoven's Sonatas: A card. 9 (1856): 135, reprinted 143.

Beethoven's Violin. 40 (1880): 166.

A Critical Contribution to Beethoven Literature. (Read before the Schiller-Union in Trieste.) 37 (1877–78): 121–23, 129–31, 137–39, 145–46, 151. [Translation of: *Ein kritischer Beitrag zur Beethoven-Literatur; vorgelesen im "Schillerverein" zu Triest* (Berlin: W. Weber, 1877).]

[Letter on his Life of Beethoven.] 16 (1859–60): 400.

[Letter on his Life of Beethoven.] 26 [1866–67]: 288.

[Letter on his Life of Beethoven.] 26 (1866–67): 312.

The Life of Beethoven. 9 (1856): 167.

Music in Vienna in the Year 1793. (Translated from Thayer's Life of Beethoven.) 27 (1867–68): 33–34, 41–42, 49–50.

A Pilgrimage to Vienna and the Tomb of Beethoven. 1 (1852): 89–90.

Portrait of Beethoven by Kriehuber. 26 (1866–67): 279–80.

The Schindler-Beethoven Papers. 40 (1880): 166–67.

Some Notes from A. W. Thayer: [Beethoven; "Gott erhalte unsern Kaiser."] 35 (1875–76): 95–96.

To Piano-Forte Players. 9 (1856): 168, reprinted 176, 184, 192, 200, 208; 10 (1856–57): 8, 16, 24, 31. [Advertisement.]

B. Other Writings

About Old Books. 14 (1858–59): 335–36.

Antonio Salieri. 1 (1852): 190.

Canova's Violin. 33 (1873–74): 87.

Chaucer's Verse. 38 (1878): 265. [*See also:* article and comment by George T. Bulling, 38 (1878): 233–34, 279.]

Chimes. *See:* From a Lecture on Bells.

A Christening of Bells, at Bonn on the Rhine. 12 (1857–58): 218–19.

The Cologne Cathedral. 6 (1854–55): 37–38, 41–42.

Composers of "Stabat Mater." 21 (1862): 21.

Dehn's Counterpoint. 16 (1859–60): 374, 380–81.

Dussik, Dussek, Duschek. 20 (1861–62): 211–12, 218–19, 225–27, 233–34, 241–42.

English Cathedral Music. (From the Remarks read by A. W. Thayer at the Concert of the Boston Choristers' School, April 15 [1857].) 11 (1857): 27–28, 34–35.

From a Lecture on "Bells." 10 (1856–57): 148–49; 12 (1857–58): 225–26, 233–34. [Part 3 entitled: Chimes.]

From the Country: Letters from Natick. 9 (1856): 94–95; 10 (1856–57): 20–21, 59–60, 78–79.

A Genealogical Disquisition (Which Leaves Everything at Loose Ends): The Basilli family and Adelina Patti. 21 (1862): 19–20.

"God Save the King." 37 (1877–78): 53. [*See also:* Two or Three Notes and Queries.]

A Good Suggestion: Corey's Hill. 10 (1856–57): 150. [*See also:* A Letter from an Old Contributor.]

The Greek Writers on Music. 34 (1874–75): 233–34.

Half a Dozen of Beethoven's Contemporaries

    1. Adalbert Gyrowetz. 23 (1863–64): 73–76, 81–82, 89–92, 97–99, 105–7, 113–14, 121–22.

    2 (preliminary). Opera in the Family Hapsburg. 23 (1863–64): 153–54, 161–62, 169–70, 177–78.

    2. Antonio Salieri. 23 (1863–64): 185–87, 193–95, 201–2; 24 (1864–65): 209–10, 217–18, 225–26, 233–34, 241–42, 249–50, 257–58, 265–67, 273–75, 289–90, 297–98, 321–22, 330–31, 337–38, 345–47.

No more published.

Haydn and Boccherini. 36 (1876–77): 400.

Haydn's Diaries in England. 22 (1862–63): 281–83, 289–91, 307–8, 315–16, 322–24.

A Hint to Choirs. 10 (1856–57): 174–75. [Signed: A Lover of Psalmody.]

Hints for Choirs. 9 (1856): 159. [Signed: *.]

"Home, Sweet Home." 11 (1857): 3.

How it [Wagner's "Walküre"] Struck A. W. T. 38 (1878): 260–61.

How shall the Orchestra or Choir be Placed? 8 (1855–56): 67–68. [Signed: A. W. T. Probably intended by Thayer to serve as Diary Abroad, ser. 1, no. 27.]

How the Books were Secured. 14 (1858–59): 357. [Signed: A. Reprinted from the (Boston) *Transcript*.]

The Hungarian Orchestra. 1 (1852): 19.

Johann Wenzel Tomaschek. *See:* The Diarist Abroad, ser. 2, no. 17.

A Letter about some of the Prime Donne: [Jette Trefftz, Cornelia von Holossy, Elena Angri, Claudia Fiorentini]. 1 (1852): 193–94.

A Letter from A. W. T. on Oratorio Practice, American Voices, &c. 1 (1852): 170.

A Letter from an Old Contributor: [Corey's Hill.] 10 (1856–57): 193–94. [*See also:* A Good Suggestion.]

Letter from Leipzig. 7 (1855): 118–19.

Lowell Mason. 39 (1879): 186–87, 195–96. [Reprinted in Theodore F. Seward, *Lowell Mason, Doc. Mus.* (n.p.: n.p., 1885?), pp. 24–32.]

Madame Johanna Kinkel. 13 (1858): 69.

More about Musical Libraries. 6 (1854–55): 156–57.

Mozart and "The Messiah." 30 (1870–71): 424.

Mozart's "Magic Flute." 14 (1858–59): 257–58.

Mozart's Son. 12 (1857–58): 339.

Mozart's "Twelfth Mass." 10 (1856–57): 73.

Musical Libraries. 14 (1858–59): 287.

Musical Tales and Romances. 9 (1856): 102–3.

New Works on Music: Letter from A. W. Thayer. 27 (1867–68): 31.

Note on Weber's Euryanthe. 16 (1859–60): 213.

Notes on a Passage in Hawkin's [sic] History of Music. 12 (1857–58): 260–61, 267.

Old Hundred. 9 (1856): 190–91; 10 (1856–57): 131. [*See also:* Comment, 10 (1856–57): 175.]

The "Origin of English Opera." 39 (1879): 186.

Original MSS. of Great Composers. 21 (1862): 43.

Paragraphs from Vienna. 23 (1863–64): 55, 59–60.

A Park for Boston: Corey's Hill. *See:* From my Diary, ser. 2, no. 10.

Pierre Rodé [sic]. 2 (1852–53): 73–74.

The Salzburg "Kapelle." 10 (1856–57): 103, 106–8.

Schubert's Musical Remains. 20 (1861–62): 279. [*See also:* Schubert's Manuscripts (Section V.A).]

A Sketch from the Diary of a Composer, By Madame [Johanna] Kinkel, of Bonn on the Rhine. 1 (1852): 26–28. [Translated by Thayer.]

Some Notes from A. W. Thayer. *See* Section IV.A.

The Stage of the Music Hall. 10 (1856–57): 180–81.

Sussmayr and Mozart's Requiem. 17 (1860): 2–3, 10.

A Title Page. 31 (1871–72): 95.

Two or Three Notes and Queries: ["God Save the King"; "Gott erhalte unsern Kaiser"; Wagner, &c.] 37 (1877–78): 103, 110. [*See also:* "God Save the King"; John W. Morre's "God Save the King," 37 (1877–78): 71.]

Weber's "Last Waltz" Again. 30 (1870–71): 219–20. [*See also:* "Weber's Last Waltz," 29 (1869–70): 178.]

V. THAYERIANA

Editorial and other writings dealing with Thayer and his publications; arranged chronologically.

A. Writings About Thayer

[An American named "Taylor."] 3 (1853): 31.

Welcome Back! 4 (1853–54): 6.

For Europe! 5 (1854): 111.

Friends and Music in Berlin. 10 (1856–57): 91. [Letter from "W—x." Reprinted from the St. Louis *Intelligencer.*]

Musical Chit-Chat: [Thayer sails for Europe.] 13 (1858): 118.

[Compliments to Thayer.] 13 (1858): 134.

"Mr. Brown's" Den. 14 (1858–59): 415–16. [Letter from "Bostonian."]

The Diarist in England. 18 (1860–61): 383. [Reprinted from the *Athenaeum.*]

Schubert's Manuscripts. 20 (1861–62): 295. [*See also:* Schubert's Musical Remains (Section IV.B).]

"Our Diarist" (A W T). 24 (1864–65): 351.

A. W. Thayer. 27 (1867–68): 207. [Letter from the Rev. Dr. H. W. Bellows. Reprinted from the *Christian Enquirer.*]

Jottings: [Thayer on leave in Boston.] 31 (1871–72): 79.

A False Report. 33 (1873–74): 88. [Reprinted from the *London Musical World.*]

Music Abroad: Vienna. [Date of Beethoven's birth.] 35 (1875–76): 189.

B. Writings About Thayer's Publications

The Brown Papers. 20 (1861–62): 252.

["The Brown Papers."] 20 (1861–62): 295.

"The Brown Papers." 21 (1862): 159.

["The Brown Papers."] 21 (1862): 176. [Reprinted from the Worcester *Palladium.]*

Thayer's New Beethoven Catalogue. 25 (1865–66); 49–50. [Review by Dr. Laurencin.]

[Thayer's Life of Beethoven, vol. 1.] 26 (1866–67): 359.

Thayer's Life of Beethoven [vol. 1]. 26 (1866–67): 393–94, 409–10; 27 (1867–68): 1–2, 9. [Chiefly an abstract of the book. Translated from the Leipzig *Allgemeine Musikalische Zeitung.*]

Of Thayer's "Beethoven" [vol. 1]. 26 (1866–67): 407–8. [Reprinted from the *Athenaeum.*]

Beethoven [Thayer's *Chronologisches Verzeichniss* and *Leben,* vol. 1]. 27 (1867–68): 120. [Reprinted from the *Church Choirmaster and Organist,* London.]

A. W. Thayer's Life of Beethoven [vol. 2]. 31 (1871–72): 140–41. [Review by Dr. Eduard Hanslick. Translated from the *Neue Freie Presse,* Vienna.]

A. W. Thayer's Life of Beethoven: German Criticisms [of vol. 2]. 37 (1877–78): 42–43, 49. [Translated from the *Allgemeine Zeitung,* the *Neue Berliner Musik Zeitung,* and the *National Zeitung.*]

[Thayer's Life of Beethoven, vol. 3.] 39 (1879): 24. [Review by George Grove (?). Reprinted from the *Crystal Palace Programme,* London.]

Toujours Perdrix [on Nohl's criticisms of Thayer's *Beethoven,* vol. 3]. 39 (1879): 114–15. [Article by Prof. Franz Gehring. Translated from the *Deutsche Zeitung,* Vienna.]

Thayer's "Beethoven" [vol. 1 (!)]. 40 (1880): 29–30. [Editorial comment on London *Times* review.]

Beethoven:

Studies of Works

A Cadenza for Op. 15

Edward T. Cone

Beethoven completed two cadenzas for the opening Allegro of his so-called "First" Piano Concerto, Op. 15. Since the longer of the two is widely admired and played (Tovey considered it a masterpiece among Beethoven's cadenzas),[1] and since the shorter is available to those who prefer a less elaborate interpolation, why should anyone try to compose yet another?

One obvious reason, of course, would be the desire of a pianist to exploit certain elements of his own technique. A composer, on the other hand, might enjoy manipulating Beethoven's materials in a new way. In attempting a new cadenza I acknowledge both of those aims for myself, but my approach has also been that of the analyst. In fact, my chief motivation has been to make the cadenza clarify an important but somewhat obscure formal relationship that might otherwise go unnoticed, at least during an actual performance.

Beethoven's cadenza for the first movement of his Third Piano Concerto may be cited as an authority for this strategy. After an opening flourish it embarks (measure 3) on an imitative development of the principal motive of the first theme. A comparison of this passage in the cadenza (example 1a) with the one starting in measure 9 of the movement proper (example 1b) reveals the origin of that apparently contrasting counterstatement—a derivation that might otherwise have escaped the listener's attention.

In the First Concerto the relationship I have in mind is less obvious, more complex, and possibly more problematic. Yet I am convinced that the connection is real, and moreover that it involves a formal parallelism that Beethoven, according to the evidence of the other concertos, was careful to articulate. With the apparent exception of the First Piano Con-

---

[1] "[It] is one of the most splendid successes in recording the style of an extemporization." Donald Francis Tovey, *Concertos,* Vol. III of *Essays in Musical Analysis* (London, 1936), p. 65.

Example 1

certo, all of Beethoven's mature compositions in that genre (i.e. those with opus numbers) share a common feature in the construction of their opening movements. In each, two crucial entrances of the solo instrument—those that initiate the exposition (after the ritornello) and the development—present similar material, similarly treated. Most frequently this entrance is simultaneously a bridge and an introduction, somewhat like an improvisatory *Eingang*: the upward scales of the Third Concerto, the tritone elaboration of the opening motif in the Fourth, the rising chromatics of the Fifth. In the Violin Concerto, this transition is expanded into a substantial cadenza. All these are duly repeated (in a new key, of course) when the solo inaugurates the development. In contrast, the opening piano solo of the Second Concerto is devoted to a new theme rather than transitional material; yet it too recurs at the beginning of the development, as happens in Concertos Three, Four, and Five. Finally, the same principle is maintained in the Triple Concerto, the only one that allows its soloists to plunge without mediation into the opening theme after the ritornello: Each takes it in turn, forming a quasi-fugato, in both exposition and development (although the cello is allowed an introductory phrase in the latter).

What, then, of the First Concerto? Is it a lone exception, as one is led to believe by the contrast between the four-square solo theme of the exposition (measures 106–18) and the rhapsodic arpeggiations that inaugurate the development (measures 266–80)? Was the composer perhaps reverting here to the model he had used for his juvenile effort, the Piano Concerto in E♭ (WoO 4), in which the soloist injects a new episode at this same point? On the contrary; closer attention to the melodic flowerings of the First Concerto's arpeggiations will discover there a variation of the theme of the exposition (see example 2a–b). If this interpretation is valid, then the exception is only an apparent one that does indeed confirm the rule. Such a conclusion is supported by another reference to the same theme during the development: The staccato triplets that enter in measure 293 suggest both a further variation and a quasi-diminution (example 2c).

It seemed worthwhile to bring all these identifications into the open, not just as an act of analysis, but also as a musical demonstration. The revelation of relationships between these passages might well constitute the climax of a cadenza. I was encouraged to write one by the fact that Beethoven himself had already done half the work for me in a third cadenza, which he left unfinished; it breaks off after sixty measures, during a passage of increasing excitement that might well have led to its climax. So I began where Beethoven left off and very soon (measure 74) found an opportunity of introducing the crucial material. In addition to the resem-

Example 2

blances outlined above, I suggested two more: the obvious kinship between the solo theme and the second theme of the exposition (example
2d), and the amusing echo—probably coincidental—of another familiar
C major concerto in Beethoven's closing theme (measures 87–90).

Because of the wide keyboard range (F′ to c′′′′) used by Beethoven in
his three cadenzas, it is generally agreed that they were written long after
the concerto itself.[2] In my continuation I have taken advantage of this
range, but I have not exceeded it. I have added a few dynamic markings
and articulations (in square brackets) to Beethoven's sparse ones. Otherwise the first sixty measures are as he left them, with the exception of my
octave transposition of the last three notes in the left hand at measure 60.

Tovey issued a challenge, as it were, when he wrote: "I cannot help
wondering whether Beethoven could not have made something almost
as great [as the long cadenza] out of his first cadenza, which he left unfinished just after it had developed on lines calculated to bring certain
discursive passages of the tutti into closer organic connexion with the
whole."[3] I am not sure just what Tovey had in mind, but in a sense I have
picked up his gauntlet by trying to demonstrate an organic relationship
between two apparently disparate sections of the movement.

[2]Kinsky-Halm (p. 36) suggests 1809 as a probable date.
[3]Tovey, *op. cit.*, p. 65.

Cadenza

Presto

Some Gray Areas in the Evolution of Beethoven's Piano Concerto in B♭ Major, Op. 19

Geoffrey Block

The arduous odyssey of Beethoven's B♭ major concerto began at least eleven years before its composer, who held the finished work in great disdain, reluctantly and apologetically offered it at half price to Hoffmeister for publication as Op. 19 in 1801.[1] Nevertheless, despite Beethoven's considerable labor over its five distinct compositional stages (1790, 1793, 1794–95, 1798, and 1801), the surviving sources (outlined in the table below) present inconclusive testimony as to how most of the concerto actually sounded before 1798.[2] Extant autograph sources from the period that preceded Beethoven's arrival in Vienna late in 1792 are confined to one page of an autograph score, Bibliothèque Nationale Ms. 61 (Paris 61), containing twelve measures of the first movement (Allegro con brio). Early Viennese autograph sources, including those from 1795, are also disappointing. For the Allegro con brio there exists a combined record of only twenty-five measures in the two autograph sources: British Museum Add. 29801 (Kafka), folio 89ʳ; and SBH 609. Allegro sketches from before 1798, on the other hand, appear on a number of pages; but they are limited to passages either labeled "cadenza" by Beethoven or suggesting cadenza material, and to a few fragments on diverse sheets con-

---

[1]Beethoven offered his septet in E♭ major (Op. 20), the symphony in C major (Op. 21), and the piano sonata in B♭ major (Op. 22) to Hoffmeister for twenty ducats each, the B♭ major concerto (Op. 19) for only ten. See Anderson no. 44.

[2]The most thorough discussions, with transcriptions, of the various stages of Op. 19 are contained in Geoffrey Holden Block, "The Genesis of Beethoven's Piano Concertos in C Major (Op. 15) and B-flat Major (Op. 19): Chronology and Compositional Process," 2 vols., Diss. Harvard 1979; Douglas P. Johnson, Beethoven's *Early Sketches in the 'Fischhof Miscellany,' Berlin Autograph 28*, 2 vols., Studies in Musicology, No. 22 (Ann Arbor: UMI Press, 1980); and Hans-Werner Küthen, "Probleme der Chronologie in den Skizzen und Autographen zu Beethovens Klavierkonzert Op. 19," *Beethoven-Jahrbuch 1973/77*, IX (1977), 263–92. The dates used in the Table of Sketch and Autograph Manuscripts are based on the sources cited above.

taining various themes.[3] Sketches for both the Adagio and Rondo movements in 1795 include rough continuity drafts in two contiguous and complementary sources, but there are no extant autographs for these movements prior to Autograph 13 in 1798.[4]

In contrast to the fragmentary record for the concerto in the sketches and autograph scores from the Bonn and early Vienna years, abundant compositional work from 1798 is found in the sketches of Grasnick 1, folios 19–21; Kafka, folios 64–65; and Autograph 13, the first autograph score that is nearly complete.[5] Because they can be placed in relationship to Beethoven's previous work in 1795, an examination of these 1798 sketches will be of some help in reconstructing the B♭ concerto of 1795, at least the Allegro and Rondo. A study of the 1798 sketches will also clarify many of the first-movement corrections and revisions that appear in Autograph 13 and throughout SBH 524, an 1801 source.[6] The Grasnick 1 sketches are particularly important for the Allegro because the earlier sources are so fragmentary. In fact, the Grasnick 1 sketches show such a substantial reworking of this movement that, were it not for the sketches and autograph fragments, Paris 61, Kafka folio 89[r], SBH 609, and Bibliothèque Nationale Ms. 70, the pages in Grasnick 1 could be interpreted as sketches for a completely new work rather than a revision. The Grasnick

---

[3]For transcriptions and critical commentary on Kafka 29801, see Joseph Kerman, ed., *Ludwig van Beethoven. Autograph Miscellany from circa 1786–1799. British Museum Additional Manuscript 29801, ff. 39–162 (the "Kafka Sketchbook")*, 2 vols. (London: British Museum, 1970); see especially folios 40[r], 45[r], 46–47, 55[v], 89, 97, 127, 134, 139[v], 147–48, and 154. For a description of SBH 609 see SBH.

Since half of the measures in SBH 609 present the same material, bars 248–60, as the Bonn autograph, Paris 61, it is possible to trace a small portion of the Allegro con brio over a five-year period, 1790–95. There are no sketches from the Bonn or early Vienna years for the Allegro that are continuous for more than a few measures.

[4]The Adagio continuity drafts are found in Kafka, folios 134 and 148[v]; Rondo continuity drafts are found in Kafka, folios 97[r], 147[v], and 148[r]. Autograph 13 in the Staatsbibliothek Preussischer Kulturbesitz, Berlin, is the only extant full orchestral score autograph for Op. 19; it also contains a partial piano part in two distinct ink hues: reddish-brown and gray. See Hans-Günter Klein, *Ludwig van Beethoven—Autographe und Abschriften Katalog* (Berlin: Merseburger, 1975), pp. 60–61; also the Block, Johnson, and Küthen works cited in note 2.

[5]For descriptions and discussions of Grasnick 1, DSB, see Eveline Bartlitz, *Die Beethoven-Sammlung in der Musikabteilung der Deutschen Staatsbibliothek* (Berlin: Deutsche Staatsbibliothek, 1970); Block, *op cit.*; Douglas P. Johnson and Alan Tyson, "Reconstructing Beethoven's Sketchbooks," *Journal of the American Musicological Society*, XXV (1972), 137–57; N II, pp. 476–81; and Erna Szabo, "Ein Skizzenbuch Beethoven aus den Jahren 1798–99," Diss. Bonn Universität 1951.

[6]SBH 524, Beethovenhaus, Bonn, contains a complete piano part with orchestral reduction for Op. 19; see SBH.

1 sketches contain the full range of compositional activity found normally in a new movement: tentative fragments and short continuous sketches, followed by a thorough continuity draft of most of the exposition and development.

For the Allegro con brio it is not possible to compare the 1798 sketches with the 1795 version except in a few measures of the development; but it can be shown, nevertheless, that the extensive continuity draft in Grasnick 1 most probably contains major ideas that were unformed before 1798. At the very least, Beethoven made several significant alterations in the key structure in 1798, and he juxtaposed his principal themes in the ritornello differently from the way he had in 1795. One infers from the Grasnick 1 sketches that the largest compositional development occurred *within* 1798 between Grasnick 1 and Autograph 13, although most of this process cannot be observed directly in either manuscript. The roots, however, of several discrepancies between Grasnick 1 and Autograph 13 can be traced to 1795 material. It is also reasonably certain from the sketches following the continuity draft in Grasnick 1 that Beethoven had not yet made several major decisions concerning harmony, thematic shapes, and the ordering of material by the time he had completed his final thoughts in Grasnick 1.

The pivotal importance of the 1798 sketches and Autograph 13 is thus unquestionable. Although the Adagio remained substantially unchanged after 1795, the B♭ major concerto as we know it today is for the most part a product of 1798 rather than 1795.[7] This is true even for the piano part, which Beethoven refined considerably only in 1801, when he first wrote it out in completed form in SBH 524. This source contradicts neither the structure nor the substance of the piano part Beethoven had worked out in the Grasnick 1 and Kafka sketches and in Autograph 13. Furthermore, revisions in SBH 524 that cannot be traced back to Autograph 13 can in most cases be linked to ideas that Beethoven had sketched in 1798.

Changes in SBH 524 usually result from a synthesis of ideas that Beethoven had worked out previously in the 1798 sketches or in Autograph 13, rather than from a new idea. In fact, the development of Op. 19 from 1798 to 1801 demonstrates repeatedly one of the most crucial as-

---

[7]The only Adagio passages that Beethoven had not substantially worked out in 1795 were bars 9–11 (sketched in Grasnick 1) and bars 61–69. Beethoven had planned a quasi-improvisatory passage for bars 61–69 in 1795 (Kafka, folios 134 and 148ᵛ), but the main compositional activity for this complex chromatic passage took place in 1798 in Grasnick 1, folios 20ᵛ–21ʳ, and Kafka, folio 64ᵛ. The relative neatness of the piano part in bars 61–69 of Autograph 13 reflects this earlier labor. Nevertheless, Beethoven did not settle every detail of the passage until 1801, in SBH 524.

pects of Beethoven's compositional process, at least for the 1790s and the first years of the nineteenth century: Beethoven's persistent reluctance to discard his early thoughts, despite valiant attempts at creating new ideas.

In the case of Op. 19, nowhere is this unwillingness more clearly revealed than in the autograph score, Autograph 13, which Beethoven composed in at least three discrete compositional phases over the period between 1798 and 1801. The evidence for such a separation is provided by three ink hues and textures: reddish-brown, gray, and thick brown-black. The reddish-brown hue, the main ink used throughout the autograph, can be dated 1798. Both the gray and the brown-black inks, which can be shown by the spacing to have been added after the reddish-brown, are used in a limited way for marking details, almost exclusively in the Allegro. The exact date cannot be determined for the gray ink additions, but the brown-black ink can be placed in 1801, *after* Beethoven had copied all but a small portion of SBH 524—three years later than the reddish-brown ink of Autograph 13.[8]

Despite its infrequent usage, Beethoven's third ink, the thick brown-black hue, is indispensable to an understanding of the evolution of the orchestral score between 1798 and 1801. Beethoven's orchestral revisions in Autograph 13 usually pertain to details in the inner voices; these parts are omitted in the tutti sections of SBH 524, where Beethoven writes out only the outer voices. Since the solo sections in SBH 524 rarely show any orchestral material at all, the brown-black hue provides a major clue to one of the central questions posed by the incomplete autograph SBH 524: To what extent was the orchestra part revised after 1798?

The clue occurs in measure 30 of Autograph 13, in the form of a seemingly insignificant octave transfer from f to f' on the first beat in the cello part. In SBH 524 Beethoven duplicated this revision on the bass staff. Since a direct comparison between the orchestral parts of Autograph 13 and SBH 524 is not usually possible, any minor revision is theoretically important. On the surface, however, it shows only that Beethoven remained indecisive about a small detail for nearly three years.

But a closer examination reveals something unexpected. The deletion and addition in Autograph 13 are in different inks, whereas there is no distinction in ink between the original and revised versions in SBH 524. The appearance of this new ink, the thick brown-black one, suggests a

[8]The gray ink is clearly confined to the Allegro in Autograph 13, but it also appears in at least one other source: Kafka, folio 152 (Kerman's paper type 16t, Johnson's paper type III-I$_{16}$), which dates from 1799. The significance of the gray ink is discussed in Johnson, 'Fischhof,' pp. 374–75, and Küthen, *op. cit.*, pp. 286–92.

different chronology for the revisions in the measure: that Beethoven entered the revision in Autograph 13 *after* he had completed his revisions in SBH 524. Such a hypothesis cannot of course be advanced as fact, but it is supported by other appearances of the brown-black ink: tempo directions and some phrase markings for the Allegro and Adagio, and the title of the concerto—notations that Beethoven probably added only after the completion of SBH 524 in 1801.[9]

If Beethoven entered the thick brown-black additions in Autograph 13 after he had completed his revisions in SBH 524, then the orchestral revisions he made in Autograph 13 after SBH 524 were few and confined mainly to the Allegro. We can be sure in any case that Beethoven scarcely altered the orchestra part between the main layer of Autograph 13 and SBH 524, because several specific mistakes appear in the Hoffmeister orchestra parts due to a misreading of an ambiguous passage in Beethoven's hand in Autograph 13. Clearly Autograph 13 was a *Stichvorlage* for Hoffmeister's edition (1801) of the orchestra parts.

Beethoven's use of the gray ink in the Allegro con brio presents intriguing problems. Although the gray ink additions can be considered revisions—second thoughts added after the reddish-brown ink—Beethoven almost without exception discarded these changes before he began SBH 524. The gray ink additions thus comprise a unique body of revisions, a virtual dead end in the compositional process.

The gray ink notations fall into two compositional categories: deletions and alterations. In the first, Beethoven cross-hatched out a total of forty measures without indicating alternative readings. Only four of these measures, bars 381–84, contain a piano part in gray (see example 6). Some of these deletions also contain Beethoven's common direction *Vi-*, but only one is completed with the expected *-de*. Beethoven did not attempt to efface the deleted passages altogether. In contrast to his usual practice of eradicating a discarded measure with heavy scrawls,

---

[9]The other definite appearances of the thick brown-black ink are less conclusive, but they do not contradict the theory, inferred from bar 30, that Beethoven added this ink after he had completed SBH 524. They include, in the Allegro, the *"f:"* in bar 5; the alterations of the inner voices in bar 11; the flute and oboe additions in bars 45–50 (within a large section excised in gray); the rubric "fagotti col. basso" in bars 75–77 (also within an orchestral passage deleted in gray); and, finally, an addition in the second violin part in measure 85, which, like most gray excisions, will be restored in SBH 524 without a trace. More ambiguous late additions in the Allegro, possibly written in the thick brown-black ink, occur in the strings in bars 145–46, 155–56, and 337–40, and the cello alone in bar 175. Aside from the tempo indication and phrase marks, the only clearly discernible thick brown-black ink in the Adagio appears in the first four measures of the bassoon part. In the Rondo, Beethoven's use of the thick brown-black ink is still more conjectural; see bars 11, 14–16, and 19–20.

Beethoven deleted these forty measures with simple X's that extend to the four corners of the canceled measure or passage.[10]

It is not known whether Beethoven wrote out replacement versions of the canceled material; but the edited passages would make no musical sense without such alternatives. It is reasonable to hypothesize that he did compose substitutes for the forty measures deleted in gray, and then rejected the second thoughts in favor of the original ideas.[11] Unfortunately, only the piano revisions in bars 381–84 are extant in gray. What remains is the startling fact that the original versions in reddish-brown, underneath the gray deletions and *Vi-de* marks, were almost invariably the versions that Beethoven would retain in SBH 524.

Beethoven uses the gray ink for alterations in seventy measures altogether, twenty in the orchestra and fifty in the piano part. With one exception, the orchestral revisions in gray ink, nearly all of which are from the opening ritornello, will be dropped before the final version. The first appearance of gray ink, bar 19 of the cello part, typifies Beethoven's procedure (see example 1). The gray ink revision represents Beethoven's final version for the cello part in 1798, but he will use the original reddish-brown version in SBH 524 in 1801.[12] Unfortunately, there is no visual trace of the process by which Beethoven worked out this decision.

Example 1. Autograph 13, folio 2[r]
Unless otherwise noted, all examples are in reddish-brown ink, with gray ink revisions shown on small staffs. For all examples, x = deletion made with gray ink, o = deletion made with prevailing ink.

[10]The deletions made with gray ink are outlined below:

bar 63	A *Vi-* appears to the left of the first violin part, without a *-de*. No change or deletion is actually notated.
bars 81–84	*Vi-* and hatch marks. No *-de*.
bars 136–37	Several parallel vertical lines are drawn through the string parts.
bars 198–200	*Vi-* and *-de* above the first violin part in bar 198 and in the right-hand margin following bar 200, respectively.
bars 214–22	*Vi-* in bar 214, and diagonal hatch marks. No *-de*.
bars 230–32	*Vi-* and *-de* in bars 230–31, and hatch marks.
bars 378–83	Hatch marks in bars 378–80 and vertical lines in bars 381–83.

[11]Küthen (*op cit.*, p. 288) assumes that Beethoven sketched the passages deleted in gray on sheets that are no longer extant.

[12]The Hoffmeister edition follows SBH 524 here, i.e., the reddish-brown version, both in the piano reduction and in the cello and bass parts.

The second appearance of gray ink revisions in the orchestra, bars 41–48, constitutes a late stage in Beethoven's efforts to achieve a modulation from C major to E♭ major (see example 2). In Grasnick 1, folios 19ᵛ and 20ʳ, Beethoven experimented only with a modulation to an E♭ major statement of the theme that appears in the final version in D♭ major beginning at bar 43. There are no D♭ major sketches for this theme any place within Grasnick 1 or in any source before Autograph 13. Beethoven's final choice of the flat mediant rather than the subdominant for this theme in the opening ritornello was perhaps the major compositional decision of 1798 for the Allegro, yet no sources exist between Grasnick 1 and Autograph 13 to give us a glimpse of the process by which he arrived at this choice.[13] Nevertheless, Beethoven clearly achieved his final version of the modulation to D♭ major in bar 41 in the reddish-brown ink, that is, before he revised the passage in gray.

Example 2. Autograph 13, folios 3ᵛ-4ʳ

At the return of this theme in E♭ in the development, measures 230–36, Beethoven intended originally to state the present bar 232 before the present bars 230–31. He did this in the original reddish-brown ink, then canceled the measure with hatchmarks in gray and a definitive "aus." In the former passage (bars 41–47), Beethoven returned to the original reddish-brown version, with slight changes in viola figuration; in the parallel passage (bars 230–36) he wrote a "new" version, in reddish-brown, which also conformed closely to his original version. Thus the parallel passages were made to correspond after much intervening labor.

[13]See Block, *op cit.*, pp. 257–61, and Johnson, 'Fischhof,' p. 381.

After Autograph 13 Beethoven did not attempt to revise either passage. He retained the reddish-brown version in SBH 524 without a trace of the process by which he removed the gray ink revisions.

Beethoven did not relinquish his next gray ink revisions, bars 75–80 (the end of the opening ritornello) so readily (see example 3a). In fact, at bar 77 Beethoven would eventually keep the revised gray version in SBH 524; this is the only measure of an orchestral passage containing gray ink that he would retain. SBH 524 also contains visual signs of Beethoven's vacillations over the revisions. At bars 78–80 in SBH 524, Beethoven copied the gray version first before he discarded it and put his original version from Autograph 13 in its place. The other gray ink revision in Autograph 13 for these five measures—the removal of the cello syncopation in bars 75–76—Beethoven discarded in SBH 524 without notating it first. Here too the last corrections made in Autograph 13 were in gray, but Beethoven used his original reddish-brown ink version in SBH 524.[14]

Example 3(a). Autograph 13, folio 6ʳ (upper staff); SBH 524, p. 4 (lower staff)

Example 3(b). Autograph 13, folio 15ᵛ

The remaining orchestral measures with gray ink after the opening ritornello, bars 204–6 and bars 372–73, require only a brief note. The parallel bars 204–6 refer directly back to bars 75–76, and the gray in bar 206 serves to delete a second thought composed originally in the reddish-brown ink rather than to record a new idea (see example 3b).[15] Finally, Beethoven added bassoon parts in bar 372 and oboe parts in bar 373 (see example 4). In the former measure he intended to anticipate the piano

[14]When faced with such a discrepancy in an orchestral part, Hoffmeister always chose the version in SBH 524.

[15]Here too Hoffmeister followed the original reddish-brown sixteenth notes in his first violin part.

part of Autograph 13 (also in gray), two octaves lower and harmonized a third above (see example 6); the lower bassoon and oboe parts foreshadow the left hand, which does not appear until SBH 524. In keeping with his usual practice of abandoning ideas in gray, Beethoven eventually rejected the bassoon and the oboe parts in measures 372–73.

Example 4. Autograph 13, folio 29ʳ (see example 6 for piano part)

Although the first two movements as copied in Autograph 13 contain enormous gaps in the piano part, the extant portions in Autograph 13 nevertheless provide the major link in the evolution of the B♭ concerto between 1798 and 1801, the years of Beethoven's unavailing attempts to achieve a completed work that satisfied him. Without the gray ink notations in the piano part of the Allegro con brio, much of this compositional history would be lost. Not only does the piano part in this movement contain the highest proportion of gray ink revisions (fifty measures out of a total of seventy measures), but these fifty bars constitute all but five of the total number of measures of the Allegro in Autograph 13 that contain any piano part at all.[16]

The piano measures in gray form several units varying in length from four to fourteen measures. Significantly, all of these gray measures occur in parallel passages in the latter part of the exposition and recapitulation, and all but seven measures, bars 330–36, are duplicated in reddish-brown ink throughout most of both passages.

The first of these gray units, bars 167–73 (paralleled in bars 351–57), comprises seven measures of continuous gray matter, the first three of which, bars 167–69, also appear on staffs 10 and 11, where the piano part is usually sketched, in reddish-brown ink (see example 5a). At bar 167 the gray version occupies the twelfth staff, and the twelfth and thirteenth in measures 168–73. Wherever the reddish-brown and gray versions ap-

[16]With the exception of bars 381–84, the fifty measures with gray ink in the piano part do not overlap with the forty orchestral measures deleted in gray. Five measures (bars 359–63) are exclusively reddish-brown, and at least ten measures contain a piano part in both gray and reddish-brown (bars 167–69, 184–87, 351–52, and 358). The right hand in bars 353–55 is probably also in reddish-brown, above a left hand that is clearly in gray. Including the overlapping of reddish-brown and gray, there are at most seventeen reddish-brown measures in the piano part of the Autograph 13 Allegro, compared with fifty in gray.

pear in the same measure, Beethoven will eventually discard all of the gray revisions and reinstate all of the reddish-brown material.[17] Again the early version prevails.

Example 5(a). Autograph 13, folios 12^r-13^r

Example 5(b). Autograph 13, folio 28^r

In the parallel passage, bars 351–57, Beethoven repeats the procedure. The reddish-brown material in bars 351–52, also on staffs 10 and 11, is nearly identical to its parallel passage, bars 167–68.[18] Beethoven again crosses out the entire reddish-brown passage with gray hatch marks and adds the same alternative gray version, on line 12, that he had used in the exposition. For the next three measures, bars 353–55 (parallel to bars 169–71), Beethoven uses both inks, reddish-brown for the right hand (staff 10)

[17]There are, however, several measures that contain gray revisions *without* any reddish-brown. These revisions are all retained in some form: The piano melody in gray in bar 168 is given to the first violin and the flute in Autograph 13; the gray right-hand part in bars 169–72 will be duplicated in SBH 524; and the sixteenth notes in measures 172–73 anticipate the melodic shape of the right hand in SBH 524.

[18]The third measure in the recapitulation (bar 353) does not include the quarter note on the first beat from the parallel measure in the exposition (bar 169).

and gray for the left (staff 11); the final two measures, bars 356–57/172–73, appear in the right hand only, in gray. Besides omitting the left hand entirely from these two measures, Beethoven also alters the melody slightly in bar 357 from bar 173 (see example 5b).

The greatest difference between the exposition and recapitulation occurs after bar 173/375. Only in the recapitulation does Beethoven indicate the five measures that follow (plus one extra beat in the right hand in measure 363). Unlike bars 167–69/351–52, Beethoven did not delete in gray these additional measures of reddish-brown ink; by the time he reached the recapitulation he knew what he wanted.[19]

Bars 184–97 form the largest single continuous piano unit in Autograph 13.[20] (Its parallel passage, measures 368–84, is interrupted by one of the gray ink deletions in bars 378–80 [see example 6], where Beethoven does not indicate a piano part.) There are several other notable discrepancies between these "parallel" passages. Beethoven notates the recapitulation entirely in gray, but the exposition contains a touch of reddish-brown as well in bars 184–86, the only measures of the piano part where Beethoven would eventually discard his reddish-brown version and re-

Example 6. Autograph 13, folios 29ʳ–30ᵛ

---

[19]The only measure of Autograph 13 to show gray ink between bars 358 and 363 is measure 358 on folio 28ʳ, where Beethoven sketched a passage on staff 12 nearly identical to the reddish-brown version he would finally adopt:

[20]See Küthen, *op cit.*, pp. 289–92, for a transcription of bars 184–97 and a discussion of their antecedents in Grasnick 1.

tain the gray.[21] The exposition also contains an added measure, bar 187, which upsets the parallel alignment between exposition and recapitulation (bars 188–90 of Autograph 13 correspond to bars 187–89 of SBH 524 and the final version), although the net total of measures in each source remains equal. The alignment in the recapitulation of Autograph 13, however, corresponds exactly with SBH 524 in bars 368–73.

The discrepancies between Autograph 13 and SBH 524 within this passage are due more to the structural differences between the exposition and recapitulation than to the actual musical material found in Autograph 13. In the recapitulation, four measures of gradually descending triplets are followed by three measures of an ascending chromatic scale. The triplets correspond to bars 374–77, the scale to bars 381–84. The passage makes musical sense even without the three measures that Beethoven eventually inserted between the triplets and the scales. The absence of a *Vi-* here suggests that Beethoven's decision in this passage, after he had composed the orchestral parts to fill in bars 378–80 (the piano staffs being blank here), revolved around the possibility of removing these three inserted measures, rather than composing an entirely new version.[22]

Beethoven's piano part for this extended passage in Autograph 13 digresses somewhat from the compositional path outlined in Grasnick 1. Therefore in SBH 524 Beethoven would not so much create a new version as return to a version that predates Autograph 13 by a few months. Grasnick 1, folio 20ᵛ, staffs 9–11, presents the version which Beethoven will adopt in SBH 524 for bars 194–98, abandoning the gray version in Autograph 13.[23]

The last piano section in the Allegro, measures 330–36, sketched entirely in gray for right hand only, stands alone without a notated parallel statement (see example 7). Here too it can be observed that Beethoven had formed most of the details of this passage in Grasnick 1 (folio 20ʳ, staff 15), where he sketched the parallel passage, bars 146–52. For five measures this final piano section in Autograph 13 corresponds in almost every detail to the sketch (transposed, of course), as well as to SBH 524 and the version published by Hoffmeister. In the last two measures Beethoven attempted to depart from the sketch, and it was not until 1801

[21]Beethoven does also retain, however, the gray ink piano part from bars 188–90, 330–36, and 369–73, where no reddish-brown version exists.

[22]Beethoven also made some revisions within these measures. He deleted the cello part and altered the rhythm of the upper strings by inserting a tie between bars 379 and 380 that would eliminate the quarter rest on the first beat of bar 380. The material of the present measures 382–83 of Op. 19 may have been originally condensed into only one measure of Autograph 13.

[23]Grasnick 1 also corresponds perfectly to SBH 524 for bars 184–88.

that he resolved bar 335. These revisions mark a compositional change, not an oversight, and thus demonstrate as clearly as any measures in the B♭ major concerto the strong ties between Autograph 13 and SBH 524.

Example 7. Grasnick 1, folio 20ʳ (top line); Autograph 13, folio 25ᵛ (2nd line); SBH 524, p. 21 (bottom lines)

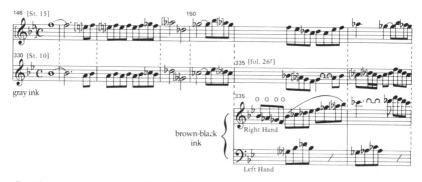

Beethoven began bar 335 in SBH 524 with the same descending scale he had used on the first two beats in the right hand of Autograph 13. The composer then decided to ascend one octave higher in measure 336 than he had in Autograph 13. He accomplished this by rising from the first B♭ in bar 335. Finally, Beethoven neatly aligned his left hand under the revised scale in bar 335 of SBH 524. This indicates that the revision decision occurred only after he had copied the descending beats in the right hand of SBH 524 in bar 335.[24] Aside from this revision, Beethoven maintained this gray ink passage of Autograph 13 intact in SBH 524.

Thus, despite his elaborate plans to revise the Allegro, shown by the deletions and additions in gray ink in Autograph 13, Beethoven ultimately altered the concerto in B♭ major only marginally after 1798 in SBH 524. Considering the obstacles that inhibit a systematic comparison between these two autographs, the observable interdependence between Autograph 13 and SBH 524 is extraordinary. Although SBH 524 presents the piano part complete to the last detail, it only contains a simple piano reduction for the orchestral parts, excluding inner voices and scoring indications other than "tutti" and "solo." In Autograph 13 Beethoven enters the piano part only sporadically in the first two movements. A thorough evolutionary study of either the piano or orchestra parts therefore seems impossible.

The difficulties in comparing Autograph 13 and SBH 524 can be par-

[24]In bar 336 of Autograph 13 Beethoven writes out the turn; in the same measure of SBH 524 he indicates the turn by a sign ∿, which presumably designates the same execution.

tially resolved by the thick brown-black ink markings of 1801, which indicate only negligible orchestral revisions. Surprisingly, the absence of full orchestra in SBH 524 does not severely handicap an attempt at understanding the orchestral revisions between 1798 and 1801, such as they were. Beethoven's piano reduction in SBH 524 of the orchestral parts of Autograph 13 appears almost revision-free; and if the amount of work shown in SBH 524 accurately reflects Beethoven's labor in reducing the orchestration of 1798 to a two-voice piano texture in 1801, the transcription was almost effortless.[25]

Difficulties do occur in trying to reconstruct the missing piano passages of Autograph 13. The extant piano parts and compositional processes in the sketches of 1798, Autograph 13, and SBH 524 suggest some solutions, although the element of improvisation in performance makes the pre-1801 versions more difficult to determine for the piano part. Nevertheless, an important clue is offered by two related phenomena: The piano passages revised within SBH 524 usually appeared earlier in Autograph 13; and the piano passages in SBH 524 for which Beethoven did *not* notate a piano part in Autograph 13 are generally little revised. These points bear out the general observation that areas most extensively sketched are also among the most heavily revised in Beethoven's early autographs. The sketch process rarely saved Beethoven time and labor; more often his sketches, among which the gray ink notations in Autograph 13 might well be included, generated further compositional activity or else reflected a prolonged indecisiveness.

One final feature in Beethoven's compositional process from Autograph 13 to SBH 524 should be mentioned: In those piano passages where antecedents exist in Autograph 13 but for which Beethoven composed a new version in SBH 524, the *process* of these revisions is indicated only rarely in 1801. Thus without Autograph 13, an early version for

---

[25]There are a few rough spots in the reduction. In measures 37–38 of the Allegro Beethoven decided not to incorporate the flute part with the first violin; he deleted the flute part from his reduction and substituted quarter-note rests. In bar 48 he decided to combine the first and second violins, as he had in bars 46–47 and would again in bars 49–50; the deletion of the rests from the second violin is shown in SBH 524. Beethoven also deleted the half-note rest in bars 127 and 179, but not at the parallel measures, bars 311 and 363–64, where he omitted the first violin part entirely from the piano reduction. Finally, in the Allegro, as an afterthought, Beethoven added the *d'* from the violin in bar 228 to replace a half-note rest.

The only change in the piano reduction of the Adagio occurs in measure 74, where it appears that Beethoven started to write a basso continuo and then changed his mind. Scoring alterations in the Rondo in SBH 524 are limited to Beethoven's removal of the second bassoon's dotted half note on *f* in bar 29 and the transposition of the violin part one octave lower for purposes of contrast in bar 241.

these passages might not even be suspected, and certainly not reconstructed.[26]

The importance of Autograph 13 for the understanding of Beethoven's revisions in SBH 524 is therefore undeniable. Since most of the major revisions in SBH 524, all of which are found in the piano part, can be compared directly with Autograph 13, the main outlines of Beethoven's compositional process for the piano part as well as for the orchestra can in fact be determined from the extant evidence.[27] This evidence reveals two significant features of Beethoven's compositional process: his frequent return to earlier ideas, and his use of earlier material (especially the sketches and Autograph 13 of 1798) as an impetus to create new ideas at the last compositional moment.[28]

Beethoven must have worried in 1801 that the B♭ major concerto was being revised too far away from his original conception. How better to preserve the character of this work than by synthesizing its compositional history? It is clear from his letters to his friends Amenda and Wegeler in 1801 that Beethoven himself considered the period from 1798 to 1801—the years also of the Op. 18 quartets and the First Symphony—a time of major compositional growth.[29] Thus when the composer described his B♭ major concerto to Hoffmeister as "ein Konzert fürs Klavier, welches ich zwar für keins von meinen besten ausgebe" ["a concerto for pianoforte, which, it is true, I do not make out to be one of my best"],[30] we have no reason to doubt his sincerity. In his letters to Hoffmeister, Beethoven claimed that he wanted to save his "better" piano concertos for his exclusive use on future concert tours. His increasing deafness, however, would inhibit both future journeys and the composition of these better concertos. Instead Beethoven decided in 1801 to publish the B♭ concerto in much the same form that Vienna had heard it in 1798, adding a modestly revised piano part and only a touch of gray.

---

[26]This phenomenon is best illustrated in the Rondo of Autograph 13; in SBH 524 Beethoven most often offers a different version without indicating the stages by which he arrived at the new reading.

[27]Beethoven's frequent return to earlier ideas and his use of earlier material as an impetus for new ideas at the last moment of composition are among the most significant features of his compositional process for the Second Concerto. While this discussion has centered on the Allegro, striking examples may also be found in the Rondo, especially at bars 82–95 and the parallel passage at measures 254–60.

[28]These features are most easily observable in the Rondo parallel passages, measures 82–95/254–60 (see Block, *op. cit.*, pp. 347–59.

[29]Anderson nos. 51–54.

[30]Anderson no. 41.

Chronological Table of Sketch and Autograph
Manuscripts for Op. 19 (1786–1809)

1786	*BM 29801 (Kafka), f. 75* British Library, London
	Rondo: sketches
	Rondo in B♭, WoO 6 (early finale to Op. 19?)
	mm. 138–50, 172–77 f. 75ᵛ/st. 12–15
1786–90	*Autograph 28 (Fischof), f. 15* SPK
	Allegro: cadenza sketches?
	rhythm of opening incipit f. 15ʳ/9–10, continued on
	f. 15ᵛ/9–10
1790	*Paris 61* Bibliothèque Nationale, Paris
	Allegro: full-score autograph fragment with piano part
	mm. 248–60 f.2ᵛ/1–12
1793	*Kafka, f. 40*
	Allegro: sketch fragments
	early version of mm. 136 ff. in B♭ minor f. 40ʳ/15–16
	Kafka, f. 46
	Allegro: sketch fragments
	cadenza? f. 46ʳ/1–2
	early version of mm. 136 ff. in B♭ f. 46ᵛ/9–10
	Kafka, f. 89
	Allegro: autograph and sketch fragments
	full-score autograph fragment with piano part,
	mm. 282–86 f. 89ʳ/1–13
	opening incipit and cadenza sketch fragments?
	f. 89ᵛ/1–8
	A3 GdM
	Rondo: full orchestral autograph score with piano part
	Rondo in B♭, WoO 6 (early finale to Opus 19?)
1794–95	*Paris 70* Bibliothèque Nationale, Paris
	Allegro: cadenza sketches
	"Cadenz Anfang" rubric appears on the recto between
	staffs 10 and 11
	rhythmic foreshadowing of mm. 90 ff. recto/3-4
	early version of mm. 136 ff. in D♭ recto/6–8
	mm. 85–87 recto/11–12

Kafka, f. 97
Rondo: sketches

mm. 1–8, 23–26	f. 97^r/1–2
mm. 44–46	f. 97^r/3
mm. 93–96	f. 97^r/3, 9
mm. 148–61	f. 97^r/4, 6–7
mm. 236–39	f. 97^r/8?
mm. 262–63	f. 97^r/8
mm. 268–70	f. 97^r/10

Kafka, f. 134
Adagio: sketches

mm. 18–26, 30	f. 134^r/8–9
mm. 51–60	f. 134^v/5–6
mm. 61–63	f. 134^r/11 "Cadenz"
mm. 83–84, 87–88	f. 134^r/7

Kafka, f. 147–48
Allegro, Adagio, Rondo: sketches
Allegro

mm. 259–68	f. 148^v/14–15

Adagio

mm. 18–26, 37–47, 51–53, 61, 68–69	f. 148^v/8–12

Rondo

mm. 23–27	f. 147^v/3
mm. 33–46	f. 147^v/3–5; f. 148^r/7–8, 12–13
mm. 49–56	f. 148^r/14
mm. 64–76	f. 148^v/10–11
mm. 65–67	f. 147^v/11
mm. 148–49	f. 147^v/10
mm. 237–40	f. 147^v/14
mm. 241–45	f. 148^r/14
mm. 268–70	f. 147^v/7
mm. 283–84	f. 148^r/12
mm. 298–305	f. 147^v/15–16

SBH 609   Beethovenhaus, Bonn
Allegro: full-score autograph fragment with piano part

mm. 248–55	recto/1–12
mm. 256–68	verso/1–12

1795   *Kafka, f. 45*
Allegro: sketch fragments

"Cadenza" sketches in B♭	f. 45^r/5–14
mm. 135–37 in G, marked "adagio"	f. 45^r/13

Kafka, f. 127
Adagio: projected version
    "Concerto in B dur adagio in D dur" on f. 127$^\mathrm{v}$ between
    staffs 5 and 6 (may link f. 127$^\mathrm{r}$/1–16 with a discarded adagio
    for Op. 19)

1796   *Fischof, f. 16*
Adagio: sketch fragments
    bassoon part only for mm. 88, 89?   f. 16$^\mathrm{v}$/2

1798   *Grasnick, 1 f. 19–21*   DSB
Allegro
    opening incipit and sketch fragments   f. 19$^\mathrm{r}$/6; f. 19$^\mathrm{v}$7,
    16; f. 20$^\mathrm{r}$/3–4, 9; f. 20$^\mathrm{v}$/4
    cadenza sketches?   mm. 136ff.   f. 21$^\mathrm{v}$/1–3
    continuity drafts and other sketches

mm. 1–67	f. 20$^\mathrm{r}$/3–9 and fragments on f. 19$^\mathrm{v}$/12–14
(mm. 23–25) and f. 19$^\mathrm{v}$/1–3 (mm. 35–62)	
mm. 81–89	f. 19$^\mathrm{v}$/6–7
mm. 81–86	f. 19$^\mathrm{v}$/16
mm. 81–85	f. 21$^\mathrm{r}$/2
mm. 90–99	f. 20$^\mathrm{r}$/10–11
mm. 90–95	f. 19$^\mathrm{v}$/9
mm. 90–94	f. 19$^\mathrm{r}$/9; f. 19$^\mathrm{v}$/4
mm. 90–99	f. 19$^\mathrm{r}$/5
mm. 106–28	f. 20$^\mathrm{r}$/10–11
mm. 143–73	f. 20$^\mathrm{r}$/15–16; f. 20$^\mathrm{v}$/1
mm. 143–44	f. 19$^\mathrm{r}$/11; f. 19$^\mathrm{v}$/14
mm. 161–73	f. 19$^\mathrm{v}$/11–12
mm. 168–73	f. 20$^\mathrm{v}$/12
mm. 179–98	
mm. 179–83	f. 19$^\mathrm{v}$/12
mm. 180–90	f. 20$^\mathrm{v}$/1–3
mm. 180-83	f. 20$^\mathrm{v}$/2
mm. 187–98	f. 20$^\mathrm{v}$/9–10
mm. 194–95	f. 20$^\mathrm{v}$/9–10
mm. 195–98	f. 20$^\mathrm{v}$/3
mm. 198–203	f. 20$^\mathrm{v}$/3–4
m. 198	f. 20$^\mathrm{v}$/11
mm. 198–203	f. 20$^\mathrm{r}$/2
mm. 207–38	f. 20$^\mathrm{v}$/4–7 (mm. 220–27 omitted)
mm. 312–16	f. 19$^\mathrm{v}$/3
m. 326	f. 19$^\mathrm{v}$/4
mm. 342–45	f. 19$^\mathrm{v}$/15–16
m. 384	f. 19$^\mathrm{r}$/6–7

Adagio: sketches

mm. 9–12	f. 21^r/4
mm. 10–11	f. 21^r/9
mm. 61–69	
mm. 61–68	f. 21^r/13–15; f. 21^r/6–7
mm. 63–68	f. 21^r/10–11
mm. 65–68	f. 20^v/12–14
mm. 65–67	f. 21^r/8, 16
mm. 66–68	f. 21^r/3

Rondo: sketches

mm. 207–13	f. 21^v/5–6

Kafka, f. 64–65

Adagio: sketch fragment

mm. 68–69	f. 64^v/1–2

Rondo: continuity drafts and sketches

mm. 1–48	f. 64^v/11–13
mm. 23–34	f. 64^v/4
mm. 41–48	f. 65^r/7
mm. 49–52	f. 64^v/4–5
mm. 57–64	f. 65^r/7
mm. 57–60	f. 65^r/15
mm. 64–76	f. 64^v/5
mm. 82–89	f. 64^v/5–6
mm. 90–95	f. 64^v/14
mm. 116–65	f. 65^r/9–14
mm. 125–29	f. 64^v/15
mm. 133–40	f. 64^v/15
mm. 144–65	f. 64^v/16–17
mm. 161–64	f. 65^v/2
mm. 195–204	f. 64^v/18
mm. 207–13	f. 65^v/4–5; f. 65^r/8
mm. 214–20	f. 65^r/17
mm. 261–70	f. 65^r/2
mm. 273–312	f. 65^r/2–6

Autograph 13   SPK

full orchestral score autograph with incomplete piano part

1801	*SBH 524*	Beethovenhaus, Bonn
	piano part and orchestral reduction	
1809	*SBH 525*	Beethovenhaus, Bonn
	Allegro: autograph score of the cadenza	

Ends and Means in the Second Finale to Beethoven's Op. 30, no. 1

Christopher Reynolds

Establishing a goal and charting a path to that goal are complementary facets of musical composition. A listener's sense of direction depends equally on a composer's capacity to envision musical goals and on his ability to work toward them. "Work" is here used in two senses: In the finished opus, the "working out" of a musical statement may be defined as the organization of ideas so as to clarify a sense of order in the presentation of those ideas; and in the evolving opus, "work" may be defined as the composer's progress toward that ordered presentation. Studies of the compositional process based on sketches begin with an investigation of work on the evolving opus, documenting early, middle, and late phases of the composer's progress. And if musical goals can be deduced from an analysis of the finished opus, so too can they be induced from the internal details of the work's evolution. It seems axiomatic for any creative endeavor that the more substantial the ultimate goal, the more susceptible it is to change, to unsuspected alterations and sidetracks as the work pursues paths unforeseen at the outset. The smaller, the more clearly defined the challenge, the lesser the likelihood of deviation from an initial conception.

In Beethoven's sketches for the second finale to his A major violin sonata, Opus 30, no. 1, I shall isolate two compositional goals. One is localized, limited to a single variation; the other is generalized, extending over several compositions before and after Op. 30. The limited goal is contrapuntal, the other musical. By this distinction I suggest only that one end is a matter of craft, the other of aesthetics. Certainly there are elements of each in both; the craft of a good composer will be musical, and good music well crafted. The sketches for the second finale to Op. 30, no. 1 reveal unusual aspects about Beethoven's craft—namely, his methods of writing invertible counterpoint—as well as about his aesthetic sensibilities—in this case, his approach to unifying a set of variations. The focus throughout will be on Variation 5. Its evolution is examined in the opening segment of this study, and what that evolution reveals about the genesis of the entire variation movement, in the concluding segment.

This finale, a theme with six variations, is particularly noteworthy in Beethoven's development as a composer of variations, for two reasons that do not at first seem unduly significant because they are common knowledge: First, as Ferdinand Ries wrote in 1838, the original finale for this sonata was discarded and later became the concluding movement of Op. 47, the Kreutzer sonata;[1] and second, this variation movement is the last variation set written by Beethoven before beginning the two ambitious and lengthy sets of variations for piano, Op. 34 and Op. 35, in the spring of 1802.

Apparently all the sketches for the new finale of Op. 30, no. 1 exist in the Kessler sketchbook.[2] Together with the sketches for all three of the Op. 30 violin sonatas, they have been thoroughly and insightfully scrutinized by Richard Kramer in his dissertation. As he has shown, the bulk of Beethoven's work falls between folios 77^v and 81^r, excepting only some earlier jottings, primarily for the theme, which fall in the midst of sketches for the middle movements of the C minor sonata, Op. 30, no. 2.[3] When Beethoven finally reached the point of devoting all his energies to the finale, he commenced by subjecting the theme to a thorough drafting in a full score of three staffs, rather than the customary single-staff sketch. As Kramer noted, the full score "is an anomaly in the sketchbook."[4] In general, when Beethoven resorts to two or more staffs the cause often lies within a passage marked by contrapuntal difficulties, but in this case the extra staffs give him additional room to worry over the inflections of each voice. Painstaking revisions are common in

[1]Wegeler-Ries, p. 83. Gustav Nottebohm later demonstrated on the basis of the sketches that Beethoven wrote the new finale only after completing the other two violin sonatas in Op. 30; see N 1865, pp. 31–32. This observation is then recounted in Thayer-Forbes, p. 317.

[2]The "Kessler" Sketchbook (GdM A 34) has been published in facsimile and transcription by Sieghard Brandenburg; Kesslerisches Skizzenbuch, Veröffentlichungen des Beethovenhauses in Bonn, ser. 1: Skizzen und Entwürfe, vol. v/1-2 (Bonn, 1976, 1978). In the introduction to the volume of transcription (p. 15), Brandenburg for the first time publishes the correct text of Karl van Beethoven's letter to Breitkopf and Härtel of April 22, 1802, showing conclusively that it was the three sonatas for violin and piano (Op. 30) that were then ready for publication, and not the three piano sonatas (Op. 31).

[3]The Sketches for Beethoven's Violin Sonatas, Opus 30: History, Transcription, Analysis (Diss. Princeton University 1973). Kramer examines both finales for Op. 30, no. 1, the second finale in Chapter 11, pp. 496 ff. Beethoven's earliest notation for the new movement appears among sketches for the middle movements of the C minor sonata, Op. 30, no. 2, on folios 62^v, 66^r, 72^r, and 73^v (see pp. 496–99).

[4]Ibid., p. 499.

Beethoven's sketches for variation themes. Joseph Kerman observed this in Beethoven's early variations and it also prevails in the later sets, for obvious reasons: In fashioning a theme capable of supporting a series of variations—whether six or thirty—every nuance, every gesture in the theme must carry the potential for later elaboration.[5]

As a point of departure I would like to recount Kramer's view of the shape and chronology of Beethoven's sketches in Kessler on folios 77^v through 81^r. This will also serve to highlight a difference in our interpretations of these sketches. Kramer's view is this: From the full score of the theme on folio 78, Beethoven momentarily retreated to the bottom of the previous folio to revise further the theme's bass line. Among the changes on folio 77^v that Kramer singles out as "especially important" is a rather telling rewrite of bar six.[6] The revision brings the bass of the theme to its final form, as it stands in example 1. The earlier version (see example 2) spanned two octaves, filling out the upper one by step.

Example 1. Op. 30, no. 1, finale theme

[5]Kerman, "Beethoven's Early Sketches," *The Musical Quarterly*, LVI (1970), 527; see also Lewis Lockwood, "Beethoven's Sketches for *Sehnsucht* (WoO 146)," *Beethoven Studies 1*, ed. Alan Tyson (New York, 1973), pp. 101–2. It would be fruitful to make a systematic study of Beethoven's approaches to sketching variation themes of his own, as opposed to themes appropriated from other composers; see below, p. 145.

[6]Kramer, *op. cit.*, pp. 499–500.

Example 1, continued

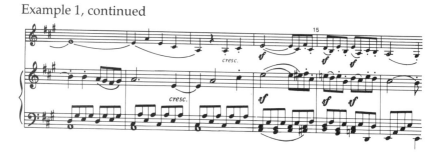

Example 2. Early version of theme; Kessler Sketchbook, folio 78ʳ

Kramer's assessment that the addition of the A♯ has significance is well taken. In a local context it gives the bass a stronger harmonic force; more broadly, the change sets up bar six as a point for chromatic movement

and color in the variations, chiefly in Variation 4, where the A♯ is exploited with particular vehemence.[7] From the full-score sketch of the theme (folio 78^r), back a page for revisions (folio 77^v), Kramer traces Beethoven's path ahead one folio (folio 78^v) to where Beethoven undertakes work on the variations in two stages. The first stage covers little more than a page and a half and comprises initial ideas—sometimes briefly elaborated—for Variations 1, 2, 3, 4, and 6, along with the transition leading into Variation 6.[8]

It is revealing that Beethoven didn't trouble himself to make any notations for Variation 5, the *Minore*. At the very least this is indicative of the straightforward character of some of his previous *Minores,* straightforward in that the point of the variation is the change in mode, so that other features of the theme are little altered. But perhaps more may be inferred in this instance. Perhaps Beethoven's intention was always to render this *Minore* highly contrapuntal, and he realized that in the short space of an incipit there was not sufficient room to wrestle with contrapuntal intricacies. One can observe this same tendency to mix counterpoint and minor mode in several other later variation works of Beethoven: In the variation movement of the Seventh Symphony, in the G major violin sonata, Op. 96, in the Variations for Piano and Flute, Op. 105, no. 1, and in the Variations for Piano Trio, Op. 121a, Beethoven substituted a fugato in the tonic minor for the *Minore* variation.[9]

Finally, the second stage of work delineated by Kramer begins on the bottom staves of folio 79^r with a sketch for Variation 1. No longer is Beethoven satisfied to jot down a telltale idea and then proceed to another. At this stage, having set the order, his purpose is to sketch all of the variations out in full and in succession. The ensuing pages thus present a complete draft of the whole movement, including the coda, and each variation is marked by revisions.[10]

Before advancing my own proposal about Beethoven's methods and objectives it is necessary to understand the genesis of Variation 5 and its

---

[7]*Ibid.*

[8]This type of abbreviated sketching is how Beethoven typically commences work on variations. He aims to settle on a series of ideas to be elaborated in the next stage. In larger variation sets he is not concerned with the order of the ideas at this juncture, only with questions of figuration, contour, rhythm, etc. In the smaller sets order is hardly a problem. As Kramer notes (*op. cit.*, p. 502), "The principal task of the early schematic for the variations seems to have been to draft for each of them an initial proposal, establishing some sort of concertante relationship between violin and piano."

[9]Warren Kirkendale, in *Fugue and Fugato in Rococo and Classical Chamber Music* (Durham, N. C., 1979), p. 243, discusses Beethoven's use of a minor-mode fugato in place of a variation in the tonic minor in Opp. 92, 96, 105, no. 1, and 121a.

[10]The contents of these sketches are discussed in detail by Kramer, *op. cit.,* pp. 504 ff.

special relationship to the theme; for without deciphering Beethoven's layers of activity in this variation, an awareness of his progress in the movement at large proves elusive. To narrow the focus still more, the crux of the matter lies in the first sixteen bars. The theme is given in two eight-measure phrases (see example 1). The first phrase consists of two four-bar segments, the second elaborating the first and extending up the octave in syncopation. Beethoven writes out the repeat of bars 1–8, placing the melody of bars 9–16 in the right hand of the piano, while the violin appropriates what had been the bass line.[11] One may perhaps see an implication of invertible counterpoint in this switch, though no inversion occurs, since the violin still sounds below the theme.

Variation 5 is an exercise in invertible counterpoint at the octave which adheres closely to the details of the theme (see example 3). The theme in its minor mode stands in the bass with few other alterations: In bar 3 the B is flatted, the rhythms dotted, and a trill added; in bar 6 an E♯ is obviously not appropriate in minor, since it would demand a resolution to F♯. What the violin plays at the beginning is taken over note for note by the bass at bar 9, and the bass line shifts up to the right hand. Nothing is feigned or implied. The inversion is strict.

Example 3. Variation 5, final version

---

[11]For the preceding version of the theme (see example 2) the theme's bass remained in the bass, and the violin simply exchanged lines with the right hand of the piano.

Example 3, continued

Beethoven also has the contrapuntal accompaniment mirror the four-bar structure of the theme. Measures 5 and 6 of the violin ornament the first two bars in diminution, reaching up first to the fifth, then to the octave. And in bars 3 and 4 the stepwise descent of the violin (F, E, D, C, B) finds an echo in the bass, measure 6 onward (F, E, D, C, B). Beethoven also thickens the texture with a false stretto in bars 9 and 10.

The sketches for this variation are intimidating, even by Beethoven's standards. As Kramer remarks, "nearly every turn and inflection in either part was to invite a thicket of revision."[12] A tidy version of how they look can be seen in example 4. Curiously, the bass line lies above the treble, above the "Violino solo":[13]

Example 4. Sketches for Variation 5 (mm. 1-16); Kessler Sketchbook, folio 80[r]

[12]Kramer, *op. cit.*, p. 507.

[13]This arrangement is sufficiently strange that Sieghard Brandenburg, in his otherwise commendable transcription of the Kessler sketchbook, printed the bass line on one page (*op. cit.*, transcription, p. 174) and the "Violino solo" line two pages later (p. 176), as if the two lines were independent. Kramer's diplomatic transcription is more accurate in this regard, for the parts definitely interact with each other.

Example 4, continued

The final version of Variation 5 differs only in details. The basic conception, the notion of an invertible counterpoint, is present from the beginning. It is already evident in what I take to be the earliest version of staffs
1 and 3 (see example 5). Looking first at staff 1 (which I have transcribed
below staff 2), we find few departures from the line's ultimate shape. (X's
above the staff in examples 5–7 indicate notes that are changed in a subsequent version.) Staff 3 is in turn only a slightly altered version of staff 1,
placed two octaves higher. The B♭ in measure 3 becomes an A♯ in bar 11
(borrowing the figuration from Variation 2), and bars 6 and 7 cause trouble. Beethoven's first revision of these staffs brings the two lines closer
(see example 6). Gone is the A♯ and double stop in bar 11, and the syncopation in measure 5 is refined; but bar 7 still needs work. Finally, in what
I see as his last major revision, Beethoven irons out the problems at the
end of the phrase (see example 7, bars 7 and 15).

Example 5. Variation 5 (mm. 1-16), first version; Kessler, folio 80^r. Implied counterpoint in brackets.

Example 5, continued

Example 6. Variation 5 (mm. 1-16), second version; Kessler, folio 80^r. Implied counterpoint in brackets.

Example 7. Variation 5, third version; Kessler, folio 80ʳ. Implied counterpoint in brackets.

Example 8. Variation 5, final revisions; other bars as in Example 7. Implied counterpoint in brackets.

But the desire to make these lines correspond more exactly was not the sole, or even always the prime, reason behind the alterations. Beethoven also intended staff 2, the "Violino solo," to invert. His intention was left implicit, but there can be no doubt of its presence. In examples 5 through 8, I have inserted the appropriate version of staff 2 into the counterpoint sketched on staffs 3 and 4, and 5 and 6; that is, I have taken the first eight bars of the violin accompaniment, dropped them down one octave, and positioned them amidst bars 9 to 16, beneath the violin's rendition of the opening bass line. In each example this line is placed in brackets.

Many of the subsequent revisions made in measures 1–8 of example 5 come not from problems of inversion, but from difficulties in bars 9–16 of fitting the inverting lines over the accompanimental bass part.[14] At the same time, other changes in the first eight bars stem from an evolving awareness of the melodic shape of the violin line. As in the final version, the melody divides into two four-bar segments, here even more so than later; bar 5 is slightly more literal in its reuse of material from bars 1 and 2. Measures 3 and 4 of the violin wander a bit aimlessly, as if Beethoven's main concern was simply to find intervals that would invert pleasingly. Clearly, the most significant difference between example 5 and the final version is the transfer of the "Violino solo" from the bass to the right hand of the piano for bars 9 to 16. Beethoven evidently gives himself an initial vote of no-confidence. By buttressing the inverting lines with another bass, he skirts the need to craft a line successful first as melody and then as bass. Any contrapuntal weaknesses in the inversion could be tucked away in an interior voice, smoothed over by a stronger bass line.

Much is improved in the version of example 6. The violin line takes on a sense of direction, and the bass line becomes contrapuntal rather than harmonic. The bass line satisfies Beethoven temporarily, except for the final crucial bars; and the stretto creeps in twice, once in measure 9, more vaguely in measure 13. Because of the stronger bass in bars 11 and 12, Beethoven manages to alter the violin lines to a more quiescent and low-lying figure, which is also more faithful to the bass line it inverts from bar 3. With this change, however, the relative tessituras of the two eight-bar phrases are thrown out of balance. Beethoven thus lowers the altitude of the violin's solo in the next revision.[15] As the "Violino solo" stands in example 6, Beethoven consciously or unconsciously recalls the A minor theme he had written three years earlier for the slow movement to his second violin sonata, Op. 12, no. 2.

With examples 7 and 8 come Beethoven's most significant changes, less for what they show about the growth of this variation in particular than for what they will soon reveal about the evolution of the movement as a whole. The first eight bars arrive at their finished form in example 7, except for the final vexatious bar, while in the next phrase Beethoven struggles with the last three bars, apparently faltering in his calculations

[14]Thus while the counterpoint in bar 2 is acceptable, when placed over the bass in bar 10 the vertical sonorities sound thin because the tonic is doubled on virtually every beat of the bar. The tritone between the lower parts of bar 11 as well as the second inversion dominant are similarly weak. And Beethoven seems likely to have revised the bass of bars 6 and 7 very quickly, since the violin counterpoint of bars 14 and 15 follows more closely the motion of the revision.

[15]The bass line in bars 11 and 12 of example 6 may be a response to the new line Beethoven wrote for the violin in bar 3. Now comes the first glimpse of the descent from the violin's F, emphasizing the scale degrees from F down through B. Note also that there are still parallel fifths crossing from bar 2 to bar 3.

of the inversion in bar 15. In fairness to Beethoven, it should be emphasized that he was laboring on a page that was anything but tidy at this point. Even Beethoven had trouble refining one line on staff 4 against an implied counterpoint transposed from staff 14 at the bottom of the page. All goes well until bar 15. Beethoven can't hammer out an acceptable bass line. Rather than getting closer, he seems to lose ground.

In example 5 there had been a cross-relation and a crude bass. The revisions in example 6 alleviate these problems, but the violin still doesn't achieve an exact transposition of the bass from measures 6 and 7. Beethoven finds the strict transposition in bars 14 to 16 of example 7 by employing a figure in the violin line nearly identical to the same passage in the theme. To support these bars he therefore attempts to fit the earlier version of the theme's bass (that of example 2) to the theme. However, the inverted counterpoint intrudes, and a doubled leading tone ruins an otherwise sensible idea in bar 15. Beethoven drops the bass in midstream. Perhaps his main achievement in this revision is the completion of bar 8, in which he now commits himself to a cadence on G instead of E. In the final modifications (see example 8) the bass lends weight to this tonal emphasis. The notes B-G-A-D of bar 15 stand out clearly on the page, which by now looks more like an ink blotter than a leaf in a sketchbook. Yet if Beethoven were serious about making this bass endure, he would have to relax the strictness of the invertible counterpoint and allow a free ending for the piano right hand in measure 15.[16] As it stands, the cross-relation there testifies to Beethoven's dilemma.

Beethoven may have made the final changes as he wrote the autograph. By comparing example 8 to the final version (example 3), we see that he eventually abandoned the auxiliary bass of bars 9 to 16. The violin part shifts to the right hand of the piano, the contrapuntal line moves to the bass, and the free part becomes a simple filler for the violin.

I would like to raise the possibility that the existence of invertible counterpoint in the sketches is not merely implicit, but actually signaled by the inverted clef arrangement in example 4, and that Beethoven's placement of the bass clef above the treble is a conscious means to a contrapuntal end. There is one pertinent record from Beethoven's early counterpoint studies. Kramer has dated Beethoven's interest in invert-

---

[16]Beethoven certainly allows himself such license in contrapuntal passages of earlier works, but with the sonatas of Op. 30 his resolve to wade through the necessary sketching appears immutable. Kramer comments on this with regard to Beethoven's persistence in sketching the canonic trio of Op. 30, no. 2: On folios 62ᵛ–63 he "assaults the canon from measure 6 (its thorn), seeking to wrest a solution through trial and error as well as through close-up point-counterpoint manipulation" (*op. cit.*, p. 392). Folio 62ᵛ is also where his first notation of the theme for the new finale occurred.

ible counterpoint at c. 1790, the date he assigned to a small half-sheet kept in the Bibliothèque Nationale in Paris (Ms. Autogr. 61). This is the source of Beethoven's earliest known exercise in invertible counterpoint at the octave (see example 9b). Kramer discovered that Beethoven copied this exercise from Johann Mattheson's treatise *Der vollkommene Capellmeister* (Hamburg, 1739), as shown in example 9a.[17]

Example 9(a). Johann Mattheson, *Der vollkommene Capellmeister*, p. 423; invertible counterpoint exercise

Example 9(b). Beethoven's transcription; Paris, BN, Ms. Autograph 61, folio 1ᵛ

Example 9(c). Beethoven's transcription with implied clefs

But Beethoven's copy (example 9b) is not exact. Mattheson's top voice uses a C clef on the bottom line, the tenor a C clef on the fourth line, and both have a key signature of one sharp, placing the exercise in G major. Also, under the second note of the tenor the number 8 indicates that the counterpoint enters an octave above. In Beethoven's copy, on the other hand, there are no clefs or key signatures, but a plethora of numbers. He also preceded the copy with a numbered scale. This I believe was

---

[17]Richard Kramer, "Notes to Beethoven's Education," *Journal of the American Musicological Society*, XXVIII (1975), 92–94. Ms. Autogr. 61 also contains a score fragment for the Piano Concerto in B♭, Op. 19. Three of the four pages of this bifolium are published in facsimile; see Paul Mies, "Ein Menuett von L. van Beethoven für Streichquartett," *Beethoven-Jahrbuch*, V (1966), 85–86.

Beethoven's key, and what he copied was not Mattheson's exercise, but its resolution in the key of C. Over the first note of the tenor he wrote an 8, crossed it out and rewrote it over the second note in emulation of Mattheson. But then the rest of the numbers refer to scale degrees—not intervals as is traditional; moreover, each of these scale degrees is keyed to the preceding ascending octave. The only solution I have found to this puzzle is to place an alto clef on the top staff, a soprano clef on the bottom, and a treble clef in front of the preliminary scale, as shown at the beginning of example 9c.[18] The number 1 thus signifies C, 2 means D, 3 equals E, and so on. In other words, the lower voice is on the top, the upper on the bottom. This is the only other such clef usage of which I am aware, and although it is a curious one at best, it offers an early precedent for how Beethoven approached problems of invertible counterpoint in Op. 30, no. 1.

The extent of the difficulties Beethoven faced in composing Variation 5 probably took him by surprise. He seems to have miscalculated his ability to handle a familiar theme, a theme familiar to him from his contrapuntal studies with Albrechtsberger in 1794–95.[19] As part of those studies Albrechtsberger gave Beethoven thirty-eight fugue subjects, which were to be set first as fugues for two, then three, and finally for four voices. Example 10 provides the beginning of the third setting Beethoven made of an E minor subject. The subdominant answer comes especially close to the theme of Variation 5, even to the trill.[20] If Beethoven did miscalculate his ability to treat contrapuntally a subject upon which he had previously written three fugues, the source of the misjudgment may lie in the course of his studies with Albrechtsberger. The studies commenced with single counterpoint and progressed to imitation and then fugue. After fugue came chorale fugue, and only then did they delve into invertible counterpoint.[21] Thus Beethoven had not written any invertible counterpoint to this theme in his fugal settings.

[18]Kramer's solution differs: "Beethoven transposed the lower voice from tenor to bass clef. Curiously, he added figures above each tone to indicate its scale degree, when he ought to have been figuring intervals" ("Beethoven's Education," p. 92). My solution accounts for the "curiosity" by linking the numbers to the preceding scale. Beethoven didn't copy the exercise; he wrote out a transposed resolution.

[19]On the course of those studies see Gustav Nottebohm, *Beethovens Studien: Beethovens Unterricht bei J. Haydn, Albrechtsberger und Salieri* (Leipzig, 1873), pp. 45 ff., transcriptions on pp. 95–99; and Kirkendale, *op. cit.*, pp. 203–6.

[20]Nottebohm prints Beethoven's settings of this subject for two, three, and four voices, along with Albrechtsberger's corrections. For the two-voice setting see *Beethovens Studien*, pp. 81–82; for the three-voice setting, pp. 93–94; and the four-voice setting, pp. 95–99.

[21]On this chronology see Kirkendale, *op. cit.*, p. 205; and Kramer, "Beethoven's Education," p. 88.

Example 10. Beethoven: Fugue à 4 on theme of Albrechtsberger (beginning)

We turn now to an examination of what the evolution of Variation 5 discloses about Beethoven's strategy in writing the finale as a whole. First of all, the sketches for Variation 5 provide reason to suggest that Beethoven's progress took a different route from that charted by Kramer. To review Kramer's ordering of the sketches: After a full-score sketch of the theme on folio 78^r, Beethoven revised the bass line on the previous page; then came the first stage of work on the variations (a page and a half of incipits) before the more detailed second stage, a complete draft of all the variations and coda in their proper sequence.

But another order seems more probable. The progress indicated by the layers of work on Variation 5 is less direct: First came the full-score sketch of the theme, and then the two stages of work on the variations. Only afterwards did Beethoven return to revise the theme, in light of ideas that first occurred to him in the course of the second stage of variation sketches. One of the main elements of this proposal lies in the irksome revisions of measure 15 found in examples 7 and 8. Example 7 introduces two features of the theme as it stood before Beethoven revised it for the last time: the violin line of example 7, bars 14–16 (except for the last two eighth notes), and the bass, bars 14–15. Out of his efforts to find a smoother approach to the G major cadence in example 8, Beethoven found one of the ingredients for his subsequent revision of the theme. He incorporated the bass of measure 15 (B-G-A-D) into the new bass line for the theme (see example 1, bar 7). Beethoven's handwriting supports my contention that the bass line revisions of the theme came after work on the variations. Beethoven sketched these three lines in a much lighter, quicker, and surer hand than either the earlier sketch of the theme or most of the sketches for the variations.

At the outset of this study, the bass of bars 6 and 7 in example 1 were discussed in reporting Kramer's view of the importance of Beethoven's addition of A♯. I suggest that this too constitutes a retrospective alteration, made only after discovering how much he would utilize the A♯ in the variations, especially in Variation 4.[22] When Beethoven first sketched the theme he was not yet concerned with the A♯ in bar 6, but rather, for reasons stated momentarily, with the E♯ above it in the violin.

To summarize this point: The genesis of the theme was not a question of arduous work that had to be completed before commencing the variations. Instead, the refinements of the theme are products of the variations ostensibly generated by them. What has been thought to be a derivative relationship now should be viewed as reciprocal.

This is as yet only a theory, but one that does much to emphasize how significant this variation movement is in Beethoven's development as a variation composer. The turning point in these sketches occurs in the second stage of work on the variations, the stage devoted to a complete draft of the variations in order. The function of this stage in relationship to the earlier phase of initial jottings now assumes added meaning. Superficially, the purpose of the first stage was to record ideas for each variation, and that of the second stage to elaborate each of the ideas. But on a deeper level—a level at the heart of the differences between the early and late variations—in the first stage, more than merely notating ideas, Beethoven seeks a collection of *heterogeneous* ideas; while in the second stage, more than simply elaborating, he attempts to imbue the divergent ideas with a sense of musical coherence and continuity.

The latter concern is plainly evident in the sketches for the Prometheus Variations, Op. 35. In composing the fifteen variations of this work, Beethoven experiences prolonged uncertainty about how he should order the variations, to the extreme of juggling and shifting cer-

---

[22]Kramer cogently observes how Beethoven's stress of the A♯ continued to grow even after writing the autograph. Beethoven changed the dynamic marking from *forte* to *piano* at the beginning of the autograph copy of Variation 4 to underscore the affect of the A♯ in bar 6 with a sudden *forte*; see *The Sketches for Beethoven's Violin Sonatas*, p. 504.

tain variations as many as five times.[23] One indication of his efforts to sustain a musical continuity comes as a direct result of this juggling, for in order to improve the flow between variations, Beethoven at times recomposes the concluding bars of one to lead into the opening of the next. Another method, with parallels to the methods employed in Op. 30, no. 1, sees Beethoven working on three or four variations grouped together to exploit a specific detail or inflection present in each.[24]

Out of this formula of seeking first diversity and then continuity stems the basic difference between Beethoven's early and late variation sets. It is particularly true of the independent sets of the 1790s that they were conceived as vehicles for Beethoven to enhance his reputation as a concert extemporizer. In the variation movements of more serious works leading up to Op. 30, no. 1, however, he seems to be struggling to find a path away from this improvisatory, ornamental style. The absence of extensive sketching for the early works is thus probably not accidental. They simply didn't require the same degree of revision as did the later sets, when Beethoven grew systematic in his exploitation of individual gestures.

The contrast between early and late variation works can be stated in other terms: Before Op. 30, no. 1, the chief relationship of each variation is generally to the theme; Beethoven's task is to achieve the proper amount of novelty from variation to variation. After Op. 30, no. 1, individual variations relate as much to each other as they do to the theme; the goal is to foster a logical progression from variation to variation. A stark illustration of what the two approaches produce exists in a comparison of the variation movements Beethoven composed in his first and last violin sonatas. The middle movement of Op. 12, no. 1 (written in 1799) is an A major theme with four variations. Although the theme bears a resemblance to that used in Op. 30, no. 1—they both begin with an arpeggiated, tonic $\frac{6}{4}$ chord—the variations are quite pedestrian alongside their Op. 30 counterparts. In the Op. 96 finale, on the other hand, the G major theme and its six variations flow so easily from one to another that Beethoven didn't even number them. It is a testament to what Beethoven wrought in Op. 30, no. 1 that its variations have a much greater affinity with the Op. 96 set written ten years later, in 1812, than with those in his first violin sonata, completed only three years before.

Beethoven may have stumbled onto this more integrated approach to variation composition quite by chance, or rather, through force of cir-

[23]Christopher Reynolds, "Beethoven's Sketches for the Variations in E♭, Op. 35," *Beethoven Studies 3*, ed. Alan Tyson (Cambridge, 1982), pp. 61–63.

[24]*Ibid.*, pp. 72–73. The chief examples of this in Op. 35 are the three introductory variations (*à due, à tre,* and *à quattro*), and the *Minore, Maggiore,* and Coda.

cumstance. Once he decided to replace the original finale to Op. 30, no. 1, his first thought was to replace the old sonata allegro movement with a rondo, but soon the sketches indicate work on a theme and variations.[25] Beethoven thus began writing this new variations set not only with a complete awareness of the other movements, but, more pointedly, with an awareness of the shortcomings of the previous finale. Because that movement had been a sonata allegro movement, Beethoven had had little difficulty sustaining a degree of interrelatedness with the other movements and maintaining an internal coherence not previously expected of variation sets in Beethoven's works. The transferral of these musical expectations to a variation movement constitutes the major breakthrough of the new finale.

Beethoven intended to preserve the good features of the previous finale while eliminating as many of the bad as possible, given the constraints of the new form. Among the problematic aspects of the original movement was the length. Counting the repeat of the exposition, it raced on for 697 bars—this after a first movement of a more modest 331 bars. The replacement finale, also counting repeats, totals just 301 bars. But in addition to length, and perhaps also to form, there is one harmonic turn in the original finale that disturbs the tonal equilibrium; namely, the strong emphasis at the start of the coda on D minor. The middle movement of Op. 30, no. 1, is in D major, but since the one move to this subdominant key in the first movement occurs only briefly at the start of the development, the effect once again is to tip the balance toward the finale. Beethoven evidently felt this imbalance, for when it came time to write the first movement of the Kreutzer sonata, he heavily favored D minor, from the chords of the piano's first entrance to the false recapitulation in that key.[26]

Among the features worth retaining from the original finale of Op. 30, no. 1 was an emphasis on F♯ minor, matching a similar stress in the first movement, and concomitantly, a manipulation of E♯, especially as a

---

[25]The first sketches clearly destined for use as a variation theme are those on folio 73ᵛ. Earlier sketches (in A major and G major) were for a Rondo theme; see Kramer, *The Sketches for Beethoven's Violin Sonatas*, pp. 496–99.

[26]One of the aims of Lewis Lockwood's recent study, "Beethoven's Earliest Sketches for the *Eroica* Symphony" (*The Musical Quarterly*, LXVII [1981], pp. 457–78), was to show that the finale of the Third Symphony, "in content if not in form, was the basic springboard, the essential invariant concept to which the remaining movements of the symphony were then adapted" (p. 461). The extent to which this conclusion is germane to the Kreutzer Sonata is obvious, but not yet fully explored. Thus in addition to the emphasis on D minor in the first movement, the 697 bars (counting the repeat) of the last movement are preceded by 774 bars (counting the repeat) in the first.

passing tone between E♮ and F♯.[27] This motion Beethoven did manage to incorporate from the beginning of his work on the new finale. Less prominently exploited in the old finale was A♯, in keeping with its somewhat weaker position in the first movement. The stress on that degree which then grew as work progressed on the new finale may owe more to the similar emphasis on A♯ (and B♭ as well) found in the middle movement.

One folio after completing the variation finale for Op. 30, no. 1, Beethoven began sketching not one, but two large, independent variation cycles for piano, Op. 34 and Op. 35. In this haste one detects Beethoven's enthusiasm for his achievement in the variation finale just completed. That he then had the two independent variation works published, with opus numbers for the first time, bespeaks Beethoven's own estimation of his success in reapplying his variation techniques on a grand scale. In one of his most quoted letters, Beethoven offered his publisher Breitkopf the two variation sets composed "auf eine wirklich ganz neue Manier."[28] Indeed, the two works represent two different expositions of musical coherence and organization: The premise of Op. 34 is harmonic, with each variation in a different key; and that of Op. 35 is contrapuntal, beginning with cantus firmus variations and ending with a fugue, with a canonic afterthought thrown in for good measure. One of the essential elements of the "neue Manier," present in the finale of Op. 30, no. 1 no less than in Opp. 34 and 35, is an original theme. As Beethoven stated in another letter two months later, "I have included them in the proper numerical series of my great musical works, the more so as the themes have been composed by me."[29] The possibility that Beethoven felt greater license to rework an original theme in light of ideas honed in the attendant variations is an idea worth exploring. While Opp. 34 and 35 were the first to be heralded in this way, they were the products of the "neue Manier," not its source. It was in the means he developed in rewriting the finale to Op. 30, no. 1 that Beethoven found his way to the new ends.

---

[27]On this point see Kramer, *The Sketches for Beethoven's Violin Sonatas*, p. 503.
[28]Anderson no. 62.
[29]Anderson no. 67.

Once Again: On the Question of the Repeat of the Scherzo and Trio in Beethoven's Fifth Symphony*

Sieghard Brandenburg

In recent years a certain type of publication has achieved some accept-ance and market success, one that unites composition and interpretation in a sort of *Gesamtkunstwerk:* the modern study score with commentary. Its model is doubtless the profound, authoritative editions with com-mentary done by Heinrich Schenker at the beginning of this century. Now, however, scores and commentary—each according to the re-sources and commitment of the editor and the various financial consider-ations of the publishers—are adapted to modern research techniques and new analytical methods; they contain more varied material and are geared to a wider audience.

The publishers prudently directed their interest first toward the great masterpieces of our classical composers, for they quite rightly expected a wide public to want to own and understand these works. As a result, within a short time Beethoven's Fifth Symphony was offered three times in this format. In 1971 the edition by Elliot Forbes appeared in the series of Norton Critical Scores—a well-received, didactically oriented aid for those who wished to study the work. This was followed in 1979 by the slightly less commendable "original edition" by Wulf Konold, in cooper-ation with the publishers Goldmann and Schott; and finally, in 1977–79, by Peter Gülke's ambitious two-volume edition from Peters of Leipzig, in a planned series of new editions of the complete Beethoven symphonies.

Some noteworthy differences appear not only in the realization of the three editions but also in their goals. What the first two editions simply touch upon or do not attempt to deal with, the third makes part of its actual mission: the presentation of a correct score based on close study of the authentic sources. With its most important conclusions first an-nounced and demonstrated in practice at the Beethoven Congresses in

---

* The title of this essay refers to that of Egon Voss, "Zur Frage der Wiederholung von Scherzo und Trio in Beethovens fünfter Sinfonie," *Die Musikforschung,* XXXIII (1980), 195–99.

Berlin and Vienna in 1977,[1] this edition drew considerable notice and provoked strong reactions. The most conspicuous difference between Gülke's score and the previous ones is found in the symphony's third movement. Here the editor, employing exactly the same argument raised by Claus Canisius in his little-noticed Heidelberg dissertation,[2] presents a five-section version, as intended in Beethoven's autograph. This decision immediately met with energetic opposition, which the long-delayed volume of commentary could not altogether dispel. In the ensuing discussion there appeared from various parties a series of worthwhile arguments both for and, overwhelmingly, against. But along with these were also made some totally untenable claims, which hinder our efforts to clarify the problem. In this situation we are well advised to reopen the discussion with a careful examination of the sources; this issue seems to have been greatly confused up to now.

*   *   *   *   *

I. AN OVERVIEW OF THE SOURCES

The authentic sources are presented here first in a concise form, preceded by sigla for easy reference. The accompanying tree-diagram indicates the relationships among these sources.

A: Autograph: SPK, Mus. ms. autogr. Beethoven Mendelssohn-Stiftung 8. 153 leaves; probably completed at the beginning of 1808. Also to be grouped with A is SPK, Mus. ms. autogr. Beethoven Mendelssohn-Stiftung 20. 19 leaves.

B: First copy of the score. Until 1945, in the archives of Breitkopf and Härtel, Leipzig; now lost. 321 pages with writing; prepared in September, 1808.

C: Second copy of the score. Lost; to be inferred from entries in the autograph. 277 pages with writing; probably prepared in November–December, 1808, for the premiere.

D: Copy of the parts for the premiere on December 22, 1808.
    a) Narodni Museum, Prague, Lobkowitz-Fond X-Gc-16. 21 parts: a complete set except for the missing alto trombone part.

---

[1] Peter Gülke, "Erfahrungen und Überlegungen bei der Arbeit an einer Neuausgabe der 5. Sinfonie," *Bericht über den internationalen Beethoven-Kongress Berlin 1977* (Leipzig, 1978), pp. 231–36, with discussion on pp. 236–37; see also Gülke, "Überlegungen bei der Beschäftigung mit den Quellen zu einer Beethoven-Symphonie," *Beiträge '76–78; Beethoven-Kolloquium [Wien] 1977* (Kassel, 1978), pp. 76–81.

[2] Claus Canisius, "Quellenstudien und satztechnische Untersuchungen zum dritten Satz aus Beethovens c-Moll-Sinfonie," Diss. Heidelberg University 1966; published only in 1970.

b) GdM, XIII 6149 Fasz. A. 2 parts: No. 1, Viola; No. 2, Violoncelli e Bassi.

E: Copy of the parts from the instrumental parts for the premiere. GdM, XIII 6149 Fasz. B. 3 parts: No. 1, Violino 2do; Viola; No. 3, Violonzelli e Bassi. These were probably prepared shortly before December 22, 1808, and used at the premiere.

F: First edition of the parts. Breitkopf and Härtel, plate number 1329. 22 parts; published April, 1809. The first 100 impressions (F_1) lack the corrections sent by Beethoven on March 28, 1809, which were first accounted for in the subsequent printing (F_2).

G: First edition of the full score. Breitkopf and Härtel, plate number 4302; published March, 1826.

The stemma of these sources may be sketched as follows:

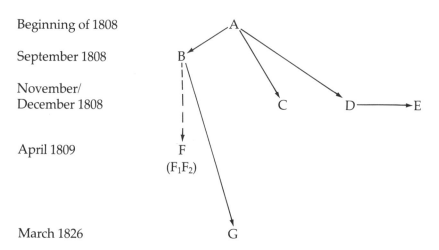

Beginning of 1808	A
September 1808	B
November/ December 1808	C D ——— E
April 1809	F (F_1F_2)
March 1826	G

The following investigation of the sources will provide the basis for some of the claims implied in the overview and the tree-diagram. In particular, it will seek to verify their underlying filiation. In doing so, however, we will limit our discussion to the main problem of this paper, which concerns the third movement of the symphony. We will not ourselves trace the textual problem back to its earliest origins; rather, our investigation should be read in the light of preceding discussions, above all, the works of Canisius, Gülke, Kojima,[3] and Voss.

[3]Shin A. Kojima, "Probleme im Notentext der Pastoralsymphonie op. 68 von Beethoven," *Beethoven-Jahrbuch*, IX (1977), 217–61, especially 231–33.

II. AUTOGRAPH "A"

Canisius gives a very thorough description of the autograph of Op. 67 in his dissertation. If what he presents is not sufficient for us today, the fault lies not with the dissertation's lack of detail, but rather with its point of view: It considers the manuscript only in its present state. Modern methods of describing an autograph go beyond this, attempting to give its original disposition and its later state. These methods enable us to reconstruct the writing process; they provide insights into the stages of the compositional process and shed light on the transmission of different versions of the text, both in the autograph and elsewhere.

Canisius correctly described the structure of the manuscript as a series of fascicles, primarily consisting of three nested double-leaves each. This, however, is not the original structure, but rather the result of bookbinding by the Preußische Staatsbibliothek in the mid-1930s. The original structure is the same as in many other Beethoven autographs: a series of consecutive bifolia, with disruptions in a few places. Where such irregularities occur, one can infer corrections or later additions. Unusual paper types can be similarly interpreted.

Current Structure of Mendelssohn-Stiftung 8 (Autograph of Op. 67)

Pages	Paper type (see below)	Watermark quadrant and mold	
1/2	I	3B	
3/4	"	2B	
5/6	"	4B	
7/8	"	1B	
9/10	"	4B	
11/12	"	1B	
13/14	II	2A	glued onto page 11
15/16	I	3B	
17/18	"	2B	
19/20	"	1A	
21/22	"	4A	
23/24	"	4A	
25/26	"	1A	from here on, follows original structure

Structure of Mendelssohn-Stiftung 8 before 1930
1st movement: Allegro con brio

⌈1/2	I	3B	
⌊3/4	"	2B	
⌈5/6	"	4B	
⌊7/8	"	1B	
⌈ 9/10	"	4B	
⌊ 11/12	"	1B	
⟍13/14	II	2A	glued to page 11; page 14 blank
⌈15/16	I	3B	
⌊17/18	"	2B	
⌈19/20	"	1A	
⌊21/22	"	4A	
⌈23/24	"	4A	
⌊25/26	"	1A	
–27/28	"	3A	
–29/30	"	1B	
⌈31/32	"	3B	
⌊33/34	"	2B	
⌈35/36	"	4B	
⌊37/38	"	1B	
⌈39/40	"	3B	
⌊41/42	"	2B	
⌈43/44	"	4B	
⌊45/46	"	1B	
⌈47/48	"	3B	
⌊49/50	"	2B	
⌈51/52	III	3B	
⌊53/54	"	2B	
⌈55/56	II	1A	
⌊57/58	"	4A	
⌈59/60	"	2A	
⌊61/62	"	3A	
⌈63/64	III	4B	
⌊65/66	"	1B	

| ⌐67/68 | II | 3B |
| └69/70 | " | 2B |

| ⌐71/72 | " | 3A |
| └73/74 | " | 2A |

| ⌐75/76 | " | 4A |
| └77/78 | " | 1A |

| ⌐79/80 | IV | 2B |
| └81/82 | " | 3B |

| ⌐83/84 | " | 1B |
| └85/86 | " | 4B |

2nd movement: Andante con moto

| ⌐87/88 | IV | 2B |
| └89/90 | " | 3B |

| ⌐91/92 | " | 4B |
| └93/94 | " | 1B |

| ⌐95/96 | " | 4B |
| └97/98 | " | 1B |

| ⌐ 99/100 | " | 1B |
| └101/102 | " | 4B |

| ⌐103/104 | " | 3B |
| └105/106 | " | 2B |

| ⌐107/108 | " | 4B |
| └109/110 | " | 1B |

| –111/112 | " | 3B |
| –113/114 | " | 1B |

| ⌐115/116 | " | 2B |
| └117/118 | " | 3B |

| ⌐119/120 | " | 1B |
| └121/122 | " | 4B |

| –123/124 | " | 2B |

| ⌐125/126 | " | 4B |
| └127/128 | " | 1B |

| ⌐129/130 | " | 3B |
| └131/132 | " | 2B |

⌈133/134	IV	3A
⌊135/136	"	2A
⌈137/138	"	1B
⌊139/140	"	4B
−141/142	"	1A
−143/144	"	1B

3rd movement: Allegro

⌈145/146	V	1B
⌊147/148	"	4B
⌈149/150	IV	3B
⌊151/152	"	2B
⌈153/154	"	2A
⌊155/156	"	3A
⌈157/158	"	4B
⌊159/160	"	1B
⌈161/162	"	1A
⌊163/164	"	4A
⌈165/166	"	3A
⌊167/168	"	2A
⌈169/170	"	2A
⌊171/172	"	3A
⌈173/174	"	1A
⌊175/176	"	4A
⌈177/178	"	3B
⌊179/180	"	2B
⌈181/182	"	4B
⌊183/184	"	1B
⌈ 185/186	"	3B
−188/187	"	3A
⌊ 189/190	"	2B
⌈191/192	"	4B
⌊193/194	"	1B
⌈195/196	"	4A
⌊197/198	"	1A

⌈199/200	IV	3A	
⌊201/202	"	2A	
⌈203/204	"	1B	
⌊205/206	"	4B	
⌈207/208	"	2A	
⌊209/210	"	3A	

4th movement: Allegro

⌈211/212	IV	1B	1
⌊213/214	"	4B	
⌈215/216	"	2B	2
⌊217/218	"	3B	
⌈219/220	"	1B	3
⌊221/222	"	4B	
⌈223/224	"	2B	4
⌊225/226	"	3B	
⌈227/228	"	4A	5
⌊229/230	"	1A	
–231/232	"	3A	6
–233/234	"	2A	7

Pages 235/236 originally sewn over page 234; page 235 blank

–235/236	IV	1A	
⌈237/238	"	2A	8
⌊239/240	"	3A	
–241/242	"	4A	9
⌈243/244	"	4B	10
⌊245/246	"	1B	
–247/248	"	4B	11
–249/250	"	2A	12
⌈251/252	"	3B	13
⌊253/254	"	2B	14
⌈255/256	"	3A	15
⌊257/258	"	2A	16
–259/260	"	3A	17

⌐261/262	IV	4A	18
⌊263/264	"	1A	
⌐265/266	"	4A	19
⌊267/268	"	1A	
⌐269/270	"	3A	20
⌊271/272	"	2A	
⌐273/274	"	1B	21
⌊275/276	"	4B	
⌐277/278	"	2B	22
⌊279/280	"	3B	
⌐281/282	"	1B	23
⌊283/284	"	4B	
⌐285/286	"	2B	24
⌊287/288	"	3B	
–289/290	"	3B	25
⌐291/292	"	1A	26
⌊293/294	"	4A	
⌐295/296	"	1A	27
⌊297/298	"	4A	
⌐299/300	"	2A	28
⌊301/302	"	3A	
⌐303/304	"	4B	29
⌊305/306	"	1B	

Paper types

I: 16-staff oblong: TS (total span) = 195 millimeters; watermark mold A: eagle/GFA—3 halfmoons; mold B: mirror image of A

II: 16-staff oblong; TS = 196 millimeters; watermark mold A: crossbow/AM—3 half-moons; mold B: mirror image of A

III: 16-staff oblong; TS = 195 millimeters; watermark mold B: eagle/GFA—one moon, in mirror image

IV: 16-staff oblong; TS = 195.5–196 millimeters; watermark mold A: lily/shield with bar—KOTENSCHLOS; mold B: mirror image of A

V: 16-staff oblong; TS = 197 millimeters; watermark mold B: six-pointed star—one half-moon with face looking outward

The fourth column (in the fourth movement) represents an old inconsistent numbering system of the gatherings in the autograph. Between pages 251/252 and 257/258 it changes over to a foliation. Presumably this numbering was given because the movement went to the copyist unbound. A system of older stitch holes encroaches so much on the musical notation that it would not have been completely readable with the stitching in place. The first three movements display similar older stitch holes. Judging from the differences in the number and order of these holes, each movement must have been bound separately and sent individually to the copyist.

The schematic representation of the manuscript's structure at once reveals a peculiarity of the autograph. The first movement is written almost exclusively on Italian paper (paper types I-III). Only at the end does a Bohemian paper appear (paper type IV), a type which predominates in the last three movements. These two bifolia at the end of the first movement (pages 79–86) represent a correction. Possibly they replace an earlier version on Italian paper. It may therefore be assumed that aside from the above-mentioned correction, the first movement was finished quite some time before the rest of the symphony. Evidence from the sketches supports this conclusion.[4]

The remaining three movements, with the exception of a single bifolium at the beginning of the third movement (pages 145–48), are written on the Bohemian KotenSchlos paper. Among Beethoven's manuscripts, this paper first appears toward the middle of 1807, to be used primarily for about a year. (We come across a little of it many years later, even in 1825.) This leads to the conclusion that the movements were written consecutively into the score. (To be sure, the sketches contain a few interruptions for work on the Op. 69 cello sonata and a few smaller pieces.) In his well-known letter of March, 1808, to Count Oppersdorff,[5] Beethoven said the symphony had been ready for a while, and thus we can conclude that the autograph was finished toward the beginning of 1808. A few final touches and corrections naturally would have been added later during copying and rehearsing.

Let us now focus our attention on the third movement. There appears at the beginning a bifolium of paper type V, the only one of its type in the autograph. Its uniqueness has convinced other scholars that it is a replacement for a discarded bifolium of KotenSchlos paper.[6] It also differentiates itself from the surrounding leaves by the manner of its division into measures. Almost without exception, the other leaves were initially ruled into three widely spaced measures per page by three barlines drawn with a straightedge; during the writing process, these were further divided freehand as needed. On this double-leaf, however, all of the barlines were drawn freehand. In addition, the text appears strikingly clean, which could mean it is a second or "fair" copy. The crosshatchings in the bass (measures 5-8) are apparently due to a copying error.

---

[4]The sketches for movements 2–4 are mainly found in a sketchbook from the second half of 1807; see Alan Tyson, "Beethoven's Home-made Sketchbook of 1807–08," *Beethoven-Jahrbuch*, X (1983), 185–200. Most of the more advanced sketches for the first movement are found on single leaves from the period before the autumn of 1807.

[5]Anderson no. 166.

[6]See Alan Tyson, "Sketches and Autographs," in *The Beethoven Companion*, ed. Denis Arnold and Nigel Fortune (London, 1971), p. 455; also Tyson, "The Problem of Beethoven's 'First' Leonore Overture," *Journal of the American Musicological Society*, XXVIII (1975), 316.

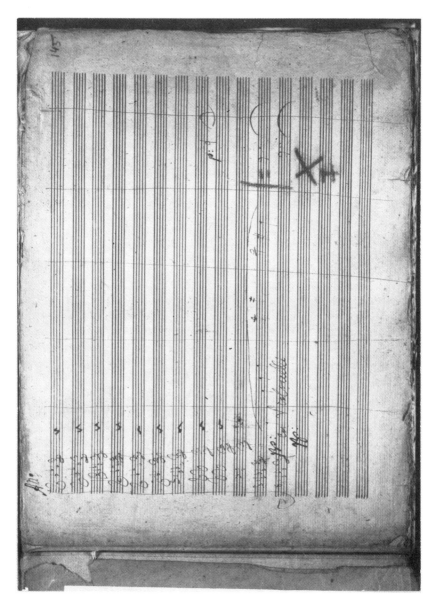

Plate V. Autograph of Symphony No. 5, Op. 67 (Berlin, Staatsbibliothek Preussischer Kulturbesitz, Mendelssohn-Stiftung 8), p. 145

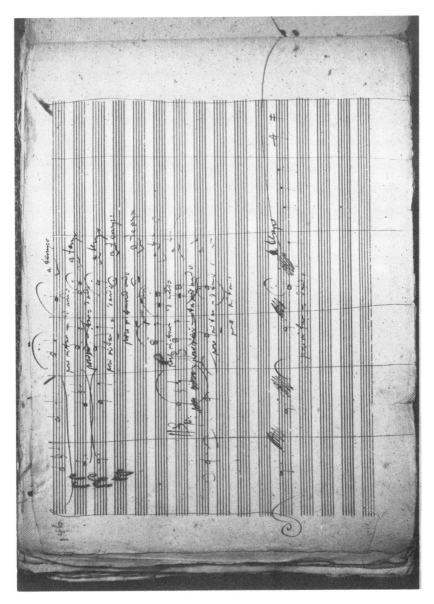

Plate VI. Autograph of Op. 67 (SPK, Mendelssohn 8), p. 146

Only vague guesses are possible about the discarded original version of these pages. Perhaps the movement once opened with two or more introductory measures, as it does in the latest sketches:[7]

Example 1(a). Landsberg 10, p. 73, st. 3

Example 1(b). Landsberg 10, p. 74, st. 1

Example 1(c). Landsberg 10, p. 74, st. 8

The suppression of these bars perhaps explains why so few measures appear on the first page (page 145); the text is written in an unusually spacious manner. We must also not exclude the possibility that Beethoven was allowing for a change in instrumentation. Finally, we may hypothesize a connection between the new formulation of the movement's beginning and the numerous efforts to introduce a da capo on page 185 f., which will be discussed below.

The next apparent irregularity in the structure of the autograph occurs at pages 185–90. Here, inside a bifolium (pages 185/186–189/190), lies a single leaf—incorrectly bound in today—which proves to be a replacement for page 186 and measure 1 of page 189. The cancelled text on pages 186 and 189, worked over many times, can be clearly read in its final version: It is almost identical with the text on the substitute leaf 188/187.

Are we simply dealing here with a fair copy? This does not seem likely; Beethoven left quite a few other labyrinths for his copyist to work

[7]SPK, Mus. ms. autogr. Beethoven Landsberg 10, pp. 73 and 74.

through. We must seek another explanation. Perhaps we can achieve some clarification if first we dissect and enumerate the individual stages of composition of this passage.[8]

1. The difficulties in notation first become obvious with the last measures leading back to C minor (measures 231–37) on pages 184 and 185 (see plates VII-VIII). Beethoven first set the leading voice in the bassoon. The manner of bar divisions in this voice (staff 7) clearly indicates that the last two measures on page 185 (measures 238a/239a), as well as the final two barlines, were added in a later phase of reworking.

2. In the next step, the main voice was given to the basses (staff 12) and stricken from the bassoon. At the end of the bass phrase (measures 237) one can detect a sign 𝆓 (later canceled), and underneath this the abbreviation D.S. (dal segno). Perhaps both signs were entered when the bass was written down. This would explain the slight expansion of the notes in measure 237. They could have taken up the complete space—as the bassoon line had before—since the first-ending measures (238a/239a) and their closing barlines were not yet there.

The symbol 𝆓 and the abbreviation D.S. doubtless indicate a verbatim repeat starting from measure 2 of the scherzo. At that spot, on page 145 (see plate V), we find no corresponding indication, but even without this Beethoven's intention is clear enough. What remains unclear, however, is how far the repeat should extend. The note-for-note repetition indicated by the D.S. could, but does not necessarily, imply a repeat of the trio—which would make an overall five-part movement. Beethoven could simply have intended a recapitulation of the scherzo, leading directly into the coda.

Such a plan fully matches the concept held in the sketches. All of these, from the earliest sketch in the Eroica Sketchbook (Landsberg 6, pages 155/156) to the latest continuity drafts from the winter of 1807 (especially Landsberg 10, pages 74–76 and Landsberg 12, page 1) show the "normal" three-part construction of scherzo—trio—scherzo da capo. In the sketches from 1807 there also appears a relatively brief coda leading to the fourth movement. The da capo is always meant literally: It is designated by the customary abbreviation D.C., never written out, in the extant sketches. If Beethoven meant to use this three-part form in the autograph as well, the cancellation of the symbol 𝆓 and the abbreviation D.S., if it actually took place at stage 2, would indicate a rejection of the literal repeat of the scherzo and suggest a new alternative: A B A' through variation + Coda.

[8]Canisius has already taken this approach, although without sufficiently exploring its consequences. See Canisius, *op. cit.*, pp. 81–101.

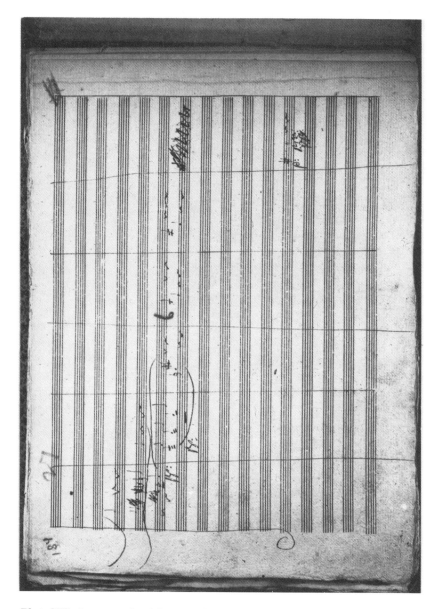

Plate VII. Autograph of Op. 67 (SPK, Mendelssohn 8), p. 184

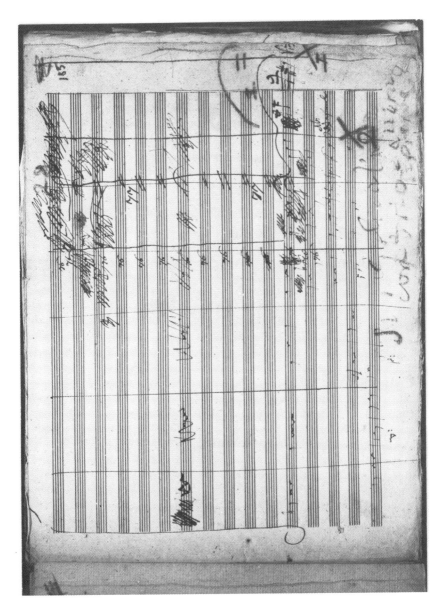

Plate VIII. Autograph of Op. 67 (SPK, Mendelssohn 8), p. 185

In fact, the varied scherzo (measures 238b–323), as we know, follows immediately on the next page (page 186). On the other hand, it should be stressed that the mark ♯♯ and the indication D.S. do not preclude the *intention,* at some earlier point, to have a five-part structure. If so, it seems very likely that the cancellation of the ♯♯ and the D.S. occurred at a later stage than this.

3. The next step in the formation of the autograph was doubtless the writing of the varied scherzo from page 186 on (measures 238b–323). It may remain an open question whether only the main voice was notated, and how far the notation goes; what interests us here are only pages 186 and 189. It is not difficult to detect the original version of the bass voice in measures 238b–244:

Example 2. Autograph, p. 186/189, mvt. 3, mm. 238b-244; bass voice, first version

The bass joins directly to measures 236/237 on the previous page. (This is another indication that measures 238a/239a on page 185 were not yet present at this point.) The more recent writing of measures 236/237 and 238b/239b at the beginning of page 186 (see plate IX) took place at a later stage of composition, as the different layers of writing and extremely narrow bar divisions prove (see step 5 below).

4. The next phase is revealed through the attempt to make the insertion of the "reprise" more effective by using more refined voice-leading in the bass and a short imitative play with the headmotive in the strings. Beethoven tried out this thoroughly attractive, witty idea in various forms on staffs 1, 2, 3, and 12 (violin I, violin II, viola, and bass) and in sketches under staff 12 at the bottom of page 185—all, however, without arriving at a definite solution:

Example 3(a). Autograph, p. 185, st. 1-3, 12; first version

Example 3(a), second version

Example 3(a), third version

Example 3(b). Autograph, p. 185, st. 13–16; sketches

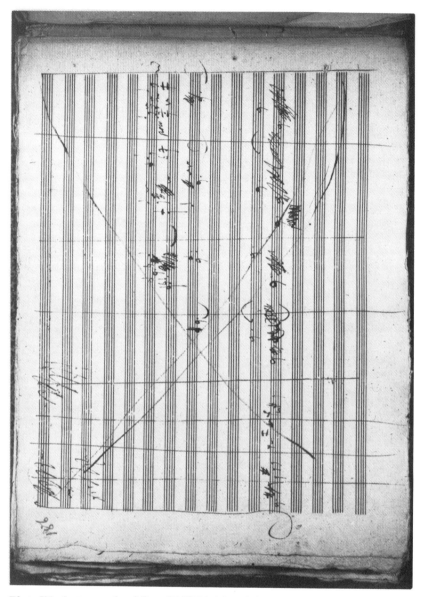

Plate IX. Autograph of Op. 67 (SPK, Mendelssohn 8), p. 186

Even the continuation (measures 238b–244) on page 186/189 seems affected by this rewriting. In the new version, the bass plays:

Example 4. Autograph, p. 186-189; altered bass line, mm. 238b-244

5. The numerous efforts on page 185 at realizing this new idea resulted in an exceptionally confusing score (see plates VIII and IX). Probably Beethoven now felt compelled to write out the two central measures 236/237—up to now the last on this page—in a more legible form. He copied them on the following page (186), again subdividing the two measures (238b/239b) that were already there, and repeatedly wrote over the earlier text. The violins and violas thus gained a new variant, which had been sketched earlier on page 185 (staff 14):

Example 5. Autograph, p. 186; string parts, mm. 236-42

6. In the following stage—whether it was a new idea or an earlier one—Beethoven decided to write out the entire five-part form of the movement. Now the sign 𝄋 and the abbreviation D.S. had to be crossed out, if this had not been done before. Evidence for this new step may be found in the nineteen leaves of Mendelssohn 20. It can be demonstrated convincingly that these were originally part of the autograph, lying between leaves 185/186 and 188/189:

a) The pattern of the stitch holes in Mendelssohn 20 matches exactly those of the third movement in the autograph.

b) The cross $\overset{X}{1}$, written with red crayon (Beethoven's famous *Rötel)* in the right-hand margin of page 185, has been partially transferred to page 1 of Mendelssohn 20. The first leaf of Mendelssohn 20, therefore, must already have lain under leaf 185/186 when Beethoven indicated the first-ending measures 238a/239a with this sign.

c) The designation for the second-ending measures 238b/239b on page 188 of the autograph—also written with red crayon—has left a mirror impression on the last page of Mendelssohn 20 (page 38). The last leaf of Mendelssohn 20, therefore, must at one time have been positioned next to leaf 188/187.

d) Two holes in leaf 185/186 at the far margin of staff 13 match, in form and position, similar holes in all nineteen leaves of Mendelssohn 20. Apparently, leaf 185/186 of the autograph and the leaves of Mendelssohn 20 were sewn together at some later point, no doubt with the intention of covering the text of the repeat of the scherzo and trio, which had been sporadically copied out in Mendelssohn 20.

The contents of Mendelssohn 20 and the autograph support the bibliographical evidence for their union. Mendelssohn 20 begins with measures 238a/239a and ends directly with measure 237, the last (at that stage) bar of page 185. On both musical and logical grounds, Beethoven probably then decided to write the two first-ending measures (238a/239a) on page 185. They were thus added on the outer margin and were struck from the first page of Mendelssohn 20. The continuity of the musical text was assured by Beethoven's instruction *Vi-* (page 185, level with staff 12) and *-de* on page 1 of Mendelssohn 20 (staff 12, before measure 240a).

In all likelihood, the single leaf 188/187 also belongs with the leaves of Mendelssohn 20. It was earlier established that its text, with only a very few differences, matches that of the last version of page 186 and measure 1 of page 189. With the insertion of Mendelssohn 20, in any event, page 186 had to be canceled in order to guarantee the proper continuity. This also produced the necessity of writing the stricken measures anew in their correct place, that is, at the end of Mendelssohn 20, on leaf 188/187. (Perhaps notational technicalities led to the striking of the first measure from page 189 and its transfer to page 187, even though its position did not in itself necessitate its cancellation.)[9]

Probably because of its fragmentary character, Mendelssohn 20 is consistently referred to in the literature as a sketch. Our investigations do not support this view. It is better thought of as an incompletely written-out portion of the autograph score, dealing precisely with the repetition of the scherzo and trio in the framework of the five-part structure A B A B A' + Coda.

[9]It is not entirely clear when the two manuscripts were separated from one another. Apparently this happened quite late, after both manuscripts had come to the Berlin Royal Library (through the Mendelssohn Stiftung) in 1908, but before Mendelssohn 20 was examined by Schünemann in 1910 (he dated his entries "1.IV.1910"). Mendelssohn 20 still bears an old label with the same shelf mark, "Mendelssohn 8," as the autograph. The number "8" was only recently changed to "20" in pencil. The binding of Mendelssohn 20 dates from the 1930s.

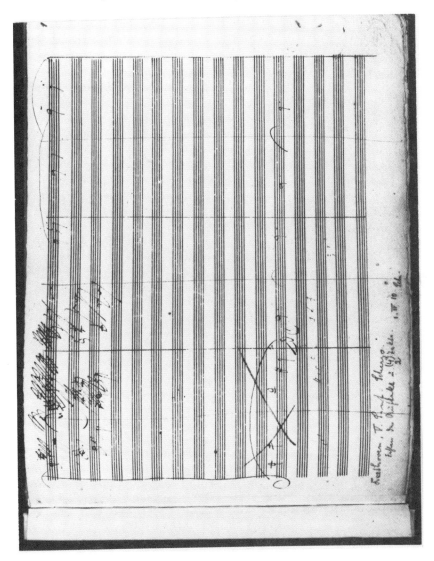

Plate X. SPK, Mendelssohn-Stiftung 20, p. 1

The question arises as to why Beethoven bothered to write out this repeat when he could have accomplished the same end—as in fact happened later—at much less expense by using first-ending and second-ending measures and the corresponding repeat signs. Perhaps an answer to this can be found by taking a look at the structure of the manuscript Mendelssohn 20.

Structure of Mendelssohn 20

Pages	Paper type	Watermark quadrant and mold
⌈1/2	IV	3A
⌊3/4	"	2A
⌈5/6	"	1B
⌊7/8	"	4B
9/10	"	2B
⌈11/12	"	1A
⌊13/14	"	4A
−15/16	"	2A
17/18	"	3B
⌈19/20	"	4A
⌊21/22	"	1A
⌈23/24	"	1B
⌊25/26	"	4B
⌈27/28	"	2B
⌊29/30	"	3B
⌈31/32	"	1A
⌊33/34	"	4A
⌈35/36	"	3B
⌊37/38	"	2B

The paper is the same KOTENSCHLOS type as the autograph. As in that case, the pages were preruled into three measures with the aid of a straightedge.

Corresponding to the noticeable irregularity in the structure between leaf 9/10 and leaf 17/18 are unusual breaks in the musical text, which, one can quickly ascertain, are not the result of faulty binding of the leaves. On

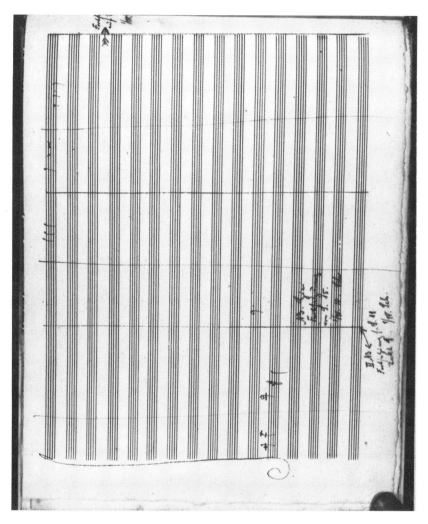

Plate XI. SPK, Mendelssohn 20, p. 10

page 10, measures 100–103 immediately follow measure 59 of the scherzo. Page 11 presents two versions: The older, canceled, repeats measures 100–103; the second begins with measures 60 ff., which had been dropped from page 10. However, the four displaced measures (100–103) on page 13 are not struck out.

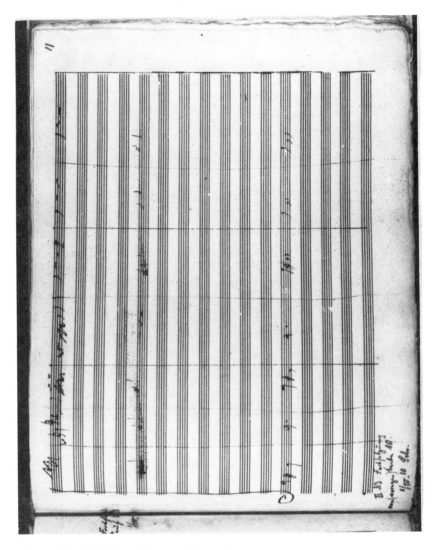

Plate XII. SPK, Mendelssohn 20, p. 11

Example 6. Mendelssohn 20, pp. 10-11

These unquestionable mistakes in notation could, on the one hand, be explained by a momentary lapse in concentration during the transcription, hence a simple oversight by Beethoven; the concluding passages of measures 100 ff. and measures 60 ff. are, in fact, very similar and can be easily interchanged if one is not careful. On the other hand, these methods of notation could hark back to a plan (later abandoned) for shortening the repeat. The irregularity of the manuscript's structure suggests that leaves 11/12, 13/14, and 15/16 are later interpolations. In fact, if one sets aside the three leaves mentioned above, the text beginning on page 10 with measures 100–103 continues directly on page 17 with measures 104 ff. So perhaps Beethoven consciously tried to eliminate measures 61–99 in the repeat; similar cuts within the scherzo are already found in the sketches.[10] Possibly he also planned a different instrumentation for one

[10]The scherzo was significantly more broadly planned in the later sketches (e.g., GdM, Ms. 38A) and contained segments in E♭ minor and F minor.

place or another, and thus a more definitely varied five-part form: A B A' B' A" + Coda. This could have been the reason for writing out the da capo in Mendelssohn 20.

The addition of the three leaves 11/12, 13/14, and 15/16, comprising measures 61–103, again restores the scherzo to its original form during the repeat. The incomplete nature of the score in Mendelssohn 20 perhaps implies the same intention. It does not revoke the repeat, but rather confirms its literalness, which can now be achieved by the first-ending and second-ending measures with the corresponding repeat signs. Along with this incompleteness of Mendelssohn 20, we should consider another point: the imitation of the theme in the violins and violas at the boundary measures 235–37, 238a/239a, and 238b/239b–240. This was consequently struck from pages 185 and 186 in the autograph and pages 1 and 38 in Mendelssohn 20:

Example 7. Mendelssohn 20, p. 1;   Mendelssohn 20, p. 38;
string parts, mm. 238a-240a   string parts, mm.
                                                          234b-235b

7. The designation of the first-ending and second-ending measures was accomplished in two stages. In the first phase, Beethoven was satisfied to write in ink: "Nb: das erstemal" under measure 238a on page 185 (staff 14). (Perhaps there was a corresponding sign on the first of the two discarded leaves at the beginning of the movement. Since these leaves were not preserved, however, this speculation cannot be further pursued.)

8. In the second phase, Beethoven used red crayon. In measure 4 on page 145—the two discarded leaves having already been replaced—he marked the insertion of the repeat, and indicated the first-ending measures on page 185 accordingly. He further clarified his intention with the

instruction: "Si replica l'all[egr]o/con trio e allora/si prende 2."[11] Finally, on page 188 there followed the sign for the second-ending measures.

9. At a later date—perhaps done by Beethoven himself—leaves 185/186 in the autograph and 1/2 through 37/38 in Mendelssohn 20 were sewn together with two stitches in the outer margin (level with staff 13). This must have been done later than step 8, because otherwise the red-crayon marking on page 1 of Mendelssohn 20 (see step 6b) would have appeared elsewhere; its position relative to the stitching holes cannot be reconciled with a prior stitching-together of the leaves. With this sewing, the fragmentarily written-out repeat of the scherzo and trio was hidden. The meaning of this step is not completely clear. If it was meant to cancel the repeat, it did so only imprecisely and in contradiction to the red-crayon markings on page 185, which were still valid.

Apparently, at one point Beethoven intended a comprehensive change at the end of the movement, encompassing at least pages 203–10. The structure of the manuscript here does not show any irregularity; Beethoven apparently replaced several bifolia. What betrays the change is the preservation of one of the discarded bifolia in the sketch miscellany Landsberg 12.[12] Since the transformation of the movement's conclusion has no bearing on our present subject, we shall not investigate it further here.

*   *   *   *   *

III. SCORE-COPY "B"

In his letter of March, 1808, Beethoven offered a copy of the Fifth Symphony to Count Oppersdorff, for whom the work was composed. The unusual, perhaps deceptively phrased, grammatically and logically incorrect expression, "da die Copiaturen welche ich für sie machen lassen, billigstens 50 fl. ausmacht" ("for the copies which I having made for you come to at least fifty florins"), leads one to believe that the copy in question was not yet ready; otherwise Beethoven could have quoted an exact price. The Count had already paid 200 florins for the symphony in June,

---

[11]Canisius (*op. cit.*, pp. 73–74) and Gülke, following him, incorrectly read this as "Si replica al' [legro] con trio e allora 2 se piace," and thus are in the predicament of interpreting the "se piace" as binding.

[12]DSB, Mus. ms. autogr. Beethoven Landsberg 12, pp. 69/70–67/68. It was Nottebohm who first pointed this out. See Nottebohm, "Skizzen zur Symphonie in C-moll und zu einigen anderen Werken (Op. 61, 69)," N II, p. 531. Canisius, *op. cit.*, p. 153, states that the bifolium originally belonged to Mendelssohn 20. I cannot agree with this view, as it fails to take into account the function of Mendelssohn 20.

1807, and then he came up with another 150 florins on March 29, 1808;[13] possibly, even these payments did not yet cover the total price for the work.

A note on the final receipt, however, shows that the promised copy had still not arrived on the 25th of November, 1808. Beethoven's correspondence reveals that he had sold the Fifth Symphony, together with the Sixth, to the publishing house of Breitkopf and Härtel in September, 1808.[14] On November 1, 1808, he apologized to the Count, referring to his financial situation: "Necessity drove me to hand over to someone else the symphony which I composed for you, and another one as well."[15] In compensation, Beethoven then dedicated the Fourth Symphony to the Count. It can be inferred from these events that the Count never received a copy of Op. 67; but then, other of Beethoven's Maecenases fared little better.

The exact number of copies of the Fifth Symphony that Beethoven prepared before the work's appearance must, naturally, remain speculative. If only because of Beethoven's desire to maintain a claim of ownership to the piece, there could not have been many. The autograph itself nevertheless shows evidence of having been copied three times. Two of these copies (B and C) were clearly full scores. The pagination of these copies allows us to reconstruct them completely, for the copyist (in both cases the one Tyson calls "Copyist D") numbered the pages above the first staff, and, in the final movement, occasionally also below the sixteenth staff. The third copy (D) was a copy of the parts, as can be seen from the numbering of the sections and other pertinent markings.

The first of the two copies of the full score, B, corresponds to the following markings in the autograph:

1st mvt.: Pagination from 1 to 99 in ink, over the first staff
2nd mvt.: Pagination from 1 to 52 in lead pencil, over the first staff
3rd mvt.: Pagination from 1 to 64 in lead pencil, over the first staff
4th mvt.: Pagination from 1 to 106 in red crayon, over the first staff

All in all, B comprised 321 written pages. The copy was written very spaciously. This leads one to hypothesize that it was not prepared for Beethoven's own use, but for a solvent purchaser; copying rates were calculated by the number of sheets in the copy, rather than in the model.

---

[13]Anderson, Appendix G, no. 3, after Thayer-Deiters-Riemann III, pp. 12–13. Anderson's translation grossly distorts the meaning of the original text.

[14]Anderson no. 174 and Appendix G, no. 5.

[15]Anderson no. 178: "Noth zwang mich die Sinfonie, die ich für sie geschrieben, und noch eine andere dazu an jemanden anderen zu veräussern."

The markings in the autograph are sufficient to identify B as the copy that was preserved in the archives of Breitkopf and Härtel in Leipzig until the end of the Second World War. This copy was presumably destroyed in the war; in any case, it is missing today. However, a large number of pages (a title page and 115 pages of musical text) are preserved as photocopies in the Beethoven-Archiv in Bonn. These match exactly the sectional divisions of B found in the autograph. Since the Leipzig copy was paginated at the publishers', its makeup can be reconstructed precisely: page 1, title; pages 2–100, first movement; pages 101–2, blank; pages 103–54, second movement; pages 155–218, third movement (the 64-page span indicates that the repeat of the scherzo and trio was not written out); pages 219–324, fourth movement. Possibly there were some blank pages at the end.

The loss of copy B is ameliorated only slightly by the presence of the Beethoven-Archiv photocopies. Unfortunately, exactly those pages which are of special interest to us here are missing—page 155 with measures 1–4 of the scherzo, page 195 with measures 232–238a/239a, and page 196 with measures 238b/239b–244. These were not photocopied because they apparently contained no markings in Beethoven's own hand. A substitute of sorts is found in the testimony of Georg Schünemann, who, in preparing the 1942 facsimile of the autograph, studied and described copy B. According to him, measures 238a/239a and 238b/239b follow each other immediately, as in the original edition (F) and the first edition of the full score (G); they are not marked as first-ending and second-ending measures. Nor is there a repeat sign or any corresponding verbal direction. Schünemann reports: "In the copy which Beethoven reviewed and corrected, this error is *not* improved. A later hand has added 'concerning this passage see Lenz: *Beethoven,* Part 2, page 30' ['wegen dieser Stelle s. Lenz: Beethoven 2ter Theil, pag. 30'].”[16]

By contrast, Canisius, influenced by the famous "Berichtigung" published by Breitkopf and Härtel in the *Allgemeine Musikalische Zeitung* of 1846, claims that measures 238a/239a and 238b/239b are clearly marked "1" and "2" in the copy, and that there also appears the direction: "Si replica con Trio allora 2.”[17] The publishers, however, do not speak of the "autograph" or the "copy" in their communication. They mention the "original manuscript of the full score," which is marked "mit Rothstift" ("with red pencil").[18] Canisius is doubtless wrong to connect this expression with copy B. At that time, the phrase was much more the going syn-

---

[16]Georg Schünemann, ed., *Beethoven. Fünfte Symphonie. Nach der Handschrift im Besitz der Preussischen Staatsbibliothek* (Berlin [1942]), p. 38.

[17]Canisius, *op. cit.*, pp. 17–23 and p. 99, n. 1.

[18]*Allgemeine Musikalische Zeitung*, XLVIII (1846), columns 461–62.

onym for "autograph." So there is no reason to doubt Schünemann's assertions.

Schünemann passes over in silence the other critical passage in the Leipzig copy, measure 4 on page 155. Perhaps one can conclude from this that there was no indication of a repeat here. Our investigation of the first edition (F) will later provide us with further evidence in support of this assumption.

The dating of B is of great importance in ranking the sources. It used to be unanimously accepted by Beethoven scholars that B was the engraver's model that was given to the publisher, Gottfried Christoph Härtel, in Vienna around mid-September, 1808. (Härtel's receipt for the works purchased at that time, including Op. 67, is dated September 14.) The late Shin A. Kojima, in his article on the sources of the *Pastoral* Symphony,[19] took the strongly opposing view that Härtel received not B, but an unknown copy X as the printer's source for the original edition F. Copy B, on the other hand, would first have been sent to Leipzig on March 28, 1809. According to Kojima, B would have served the function of informing the publisher of those "little improvements" which Beethoven, by his own testimony, undertook in the wake of the premiere performance in December, 1808, and which the composer mentioned in his letter of March 4, 1809. Kojima was convinced that Beethoven did not send a list of corrections (as we know he did in other cases), but rather a new full score of the symphony, namely, copy B. As for the whereabouts of the missing engraver's copy X, the author, on the evidence of a report by Friedrich Rochlitz,[20] speculated that after engraving, it was sent to E. T. A. Hoffmann for review and eventually passed into his possession.[21]

---

[19]See note 3.

[20]*Allgemeine Musikalische Zeitung*, XXIV (1822), column 666: "Zugleich sandte man ihm [Hoffmann] die, eben in den Händen der Notenstecher befindliche, grosse, herrliche Symphonie von Beethoven aus C moll, in Partitur; mit dem Gesuch darüber zu schreiben."

[21]According to E. T. A. Hoffmann's letters (*E. T. A. Hoffmanns Briefwechsel*, ed. F. Schnapp [Munich, 1967–69], Vol. 1, no. 276), Hoffmann received the request to review the two symphonies, Op. 67 and Op. 68, only in June, 1809, that is, two months after the appearance of the first edition F. His agreement (Hoffmann letter no. 278) dates from July 1, 1809. In mid-July, 1809 he received a score-copy of Op. 67, the original edition F, and the four-hand arrangement of the symphony that Breitkopf and Härtel had just published. He sent these items back to the publisher on May 30, 1810 (Hoffmann letter no. 318). When Härtel mistakenly reminded him about these items on July 23, 1812, Hoffmann answered: "I also most humbly request you to see whether in my last reckoning, of July 23, 1812, by mistake the Beethoven Symphony No. 6 in C minor [Hoffmann follows the numbering system used at the premiere of Op. 67 on December 22, 1808; the *Pastoral* Symphony, as No. 5, was also performed] and the same work arranged for four hands were entered as not yet having been returned. For according to my own notes, I certainly

Kojima's thesis is accepted without question by Gülke, and with certain reservations by Voss—yet probably in both cases without recognition of its relevance for the text of the symphony. For, if copy B first appeared in March, 1809, as Kojima would have it, and did in fact contain those "little improvements," then to a certain extent it represents the final version ("Fassung letzter Hand"). The absence of repeat signs in measures 4 and 238/239 of the third movement could then be interpreted as Beethoven's rejection of the five-part form in favor of the three-part form of the scherzo. (The presence of the two unnecessary first-ending measures would then be explained as a copyist's mistake, which Beethoven did not notice and thus did not correct.)

Kojima's theory, however, does not stand up under examination. Certain inconsistencies catch our eye right away. Is it not an unusual luxury to send a full copy of the score—especially one written so spaciously—instead of a brief list of corrections? This copy, as we have seen, would have cost Count Oppersdorff at least fifty florins. Never in later years did Beethoven claim such a great expense from Breitkopf and Härtel.

Furthermore, it can be shown that B never contained the "little improvements" for whose sake the copy was supposedly prepared. In the first place, it is not certain that the publishers paid attention to all of Beethoven's suggested corrections, and so we cannot know their full extent. Those which the publishers did make, however, are easily detected through a comparison of the first, uncorrected printing F_1 with the second, corrected printing of the original edition F_2, in which the fermatas in the first movement were lengthened by the addition of measures 4, 23, 127, 251, and 481. It is known that these alterations did not appear in the autograph, which remained in the state it had been in before the premiere performance on December 22, 1808. Thus B as copied from the autograph also did not contain them. In fact, Schünemann assures us several times that the added measures were first inserted into B with red ink by a proofreader *at the publishers'*.[22] This apparently happened only in 1825–26, when B was being prepared as a *Stichvorlage* for the first printing of the full score G (see discussion below). In this case, what sense would there have been in preparing such an incomplete, outdated copy in March, 1809 and sending it to the publishers?

A final observation fully destroys Kojima's thesis. In the autograph, most of the page numbers corresponding to B are crossed out and written

---

sent back both of them together with the copied-out score that had accompanied them" (Hoffmann letter no. 375).

[22]Schünemann, *op. cit.*, p. 12, and frequently.

over with the page numbers corresponding to C. Therefore, of the two copies of the full score, B is earlier than C. Since C appeared before the premiere performance of the symphony on December 22, 1808 (see below), B must also have been prepared before this date. But how else could B have come into the possession of the Leipzig publishers if it was not the *Stichvorlage* purchased in September, 1808? We must conclude that the unknown copy X and copy B are identical. On March 28, 1809, Beethoven did not send a new, complete full score to his publishers, but instead simply a list of corrections, which is undoubtedly now lost.

The absence of repeat signs and of first-ending and second-ending markings in B (measures 4, 238a/239a, and 238b/239b) cannot be seen now as an intended tripartite form, and certainly not as a return to such a form. As the page entries tell us, the copyist found the autograph at least in the condition described above as stage 6, that is, with the leaves from Mendelssohn 20 inserted and measures 238a/239a added to page 185 of the autograph. In this state, there was no question about the five-part form of the movement. Perhaps Beethoven had already marked the first-ending measures 238a/239a: "Nb: das erstemal," as mentioned in stage 7. It is possible, however, that the red-crayon markings (stage 8) were not yet present in the autograph;[23] the copyist, otherwise so careful, would not have overlooked them so consistently at all the places where they appear (measures 4, 238a/239a, and 238b/239b). So he must have had to find his way through the incompletely marked autograph on his own. Mendelssohn 20 was probably recognizable to the copyist as a repeat of the scherzo and trio, although in its fragmentary state it certainly wasn't reproducible. The fully written-out text picked up again at page 38 in Mendelssohn 20 and page 188/187 in the autograph. Here he correctly chose the measures that he thought must represent "das zweitemal" ("the second time"), bars 238b/239b. But as a mere copyist, he could not have dared to add his own repeat signs and first-ending or second-ending markings.

However the musical text of B may have come into being, Beethoven did not review or correct it adequately. The text of the original edition F, identical with B, is not based on a printer's error, but rather on an error in the *Stichvorlage*—B itself—of which Beethoven was not aware.[24]

IV. SCORE-COPY "C"

The following markings in the autograph correspond to score-copy C:

---

[23]This was already surmised by Kojima; see *Beiträge '76–78, Beethoven-Kolloquium [Wien] 1977* (Kassel, 1978), p. 81.

[24]Voss, though he was working from other basic premises, arrived at the same conclusion himself.

1st movement: Pagination from 1 to 73 in thick lead pencil, over the first staff. At the end of the movement, on page 86, the copyist noted in ink the size of the copy: "18 1/2 Bögen." (A Bogen is to be understood here as one bifolium, equal to four pages.) The movement would thus run to seventy-four pages, the first page presumably for the title and the following seventy-three for the music.

2nd movement: Pagination from 1 to 50 in thick lead pencil, over the first staff. The copyist noted in ink the length of the copy on page 143, at the end of the movement: "12 1/2 Bögen." This exactly corresponds to the fifty numbered pages of text; the copy, then, contained no blank pages.

3rd movement: Pagination from 1 to 42 in thick lead pencil, over the first staff. The size of the copy is noted in ink by the copyist at the end of the movement, on page 209: "17 1/2 Bögen." This comes to a total of seventy pages, which leaves a discrepancy of twenty-eight pages with the number given in the pagination. The copyist had obviously written out the repeat of the scherzo and trio. Together, these two sections (measures 1–236) encompass exactly twenty-eight pages. Added to the forty-two numbered pages given, they make a total of seventeen-and-a-half bifolia, or seventy pages. So in the third movement also, the copy apparently had no blank pages.

4th movement: Pagination from 1 to 83 in thick lead pencil, some over the first staff and some under the sixteenth. The copyist wrote out the beginning of the reprise (measures 207–31), which was not written out in the autograph but was indicated instead by a reference to the relevant measures in the exposition. (The pagination of this section, 40–45, is found under the sixteenth staff in the exposition.) The size of the copy is entered in ink on page 305: "21 Bögen," totaling eighty-four pages. The last page was probably blank.

The copyist of copy C is the same as for B, namely the one Tyson calls Copyist D. It has already been shown that C was prepared later than B. The numbers for B were crossed out in troublesome places and made unrecognizable, then replaced with the pagination for C. As we have advocated mid-September as a date of appearance for B, this must present a *terminus ante quem non* for C. As a copy of the autograph, C most certainly did not originally contain the five measures that were added to the first movement during the rehearsals before the premiere on December 22, 1808. This date must therefore be the *terminus post quem non* for C. After this point, a copy of the autograph would have been meaningless.

Despite the repeat of the scherzo and trio in the third movement, C is materially shorter than B; 277 pages in C, compared with 321 in B. Perhaps the composer instructed the copyist to write more narrowly. (His constant complaint about copyists who sought higher fees by writing spaciously is only too well known.)[25] This crowding suggests that C was probably prepared for Beethoven's *personal* use—indeed, for the premiere of the symphony. The confusing appearance of the autograph certainly would have made it unusable as a rehearsal or conducting score. The writing-out of the repeat in the third movement may likewise have resulted from practical considerations. We propose, then, November or the beginning of December, 1808 as the time of origin of copy C.

The most meaningful difference between C and B is the writing-out of the repeat in the third movement. Here in C the intended five-part form of the movement is clearly made manifest. Probably the copyist came upon the red-crayon markings (mentioned above in our discussion of step 8 of the autograph), in particular the direction "si replica l'all[egr]o con trio e allora/si prende 2," and carried out their intent. (Conversely, this discrepancy is a further indication that the copyist did not yet have this instruction before him as he was preparing score B.) Perhaps he also received additional oral instructions from Beethoven. If copy C was in fact prepared and used for the rehearsals of the symphony in November–December, 1808, then it is likely that all the small improvements "during" the first performance—which Beethoven refers to on the 4th and 28th of March, 1809[26]—were added here in C and not in the autograph.

To a certain extent, it is copy C of the score that represents the final version ("Fassung letzter Hand"). Its loss is therefore the more regrettable. No trace remains of its location. If Beethoven himself canceled the repeat of the scherzo and trio, the evidence would presumably appear in C. Copy D of the parts, which, because of its intended use for the premiere performance, stands on the same level as C, cannot completely compensate us for this loss, as will be shown in the following section.

V. THE COPIED PARTS "D"

The third copy prepared from the autograph was a set of parts. This set too has left its traces in the autograph, in the form of various copyists' entries. The most important of these is a sectional division. The copyist, again the one Tyson named Copyist D, divided each movement into several sections of varying length, which he indicated at the end of each section by means of measure numbers. In this way he could more quickly

---

[25]J. F. Reichardt, on the occasion of the premiere performance of the Fifth Symphony, made the remark: "A nobleman near us assured me that during the rehearsal he had seen that the violoncello part, which was very busy throughout, was made up of thirty-four bifolia. The copyists here know how to spin things out just as much as, with us, the court and legal scribes do." See J. F. Reichardt, *Briefe die Musik betreffend . . .* , ed. G. Herre and W. Siegmund-Schultze (Leipzig, 1976), p. 277.

[26]Anderson no. 199 and 204.

recognize omissions, duplications, or miscounted rests, and keep the parts in alignment. The first movement was divided into six segments of 22, 100, 62, 80, 102, and 131 measures; the second, into three segments of 123, 35, and 89 measures; the third, into five segments of 52, 88, 20 (first-ending and second-ending measures in the trio were numbered separately), 77, and 133 measures (the remaining four measures were not expressly marked). Finally, the fourth movement contained six segments of 86, 68 (first-ending and second-ending measures were numbered separately), 54, 110, 45, and 83 measures.

The copy made with the aid of the sectional divisions comprised at least twenty-two parts, counting one for each participating instrument. For performing purposes this number was insufficient, and the string parts had to be "duplirt" (duplicated). Generally this was done by having the first string part, once it had been looked over by the composer and corrected by the copyist, recopied again and again as needed. These first string parts, and the "Duplir," or duplicate, parts are here collectively labeled "D." Theoretically, the first string parts and the duplicate parts do not stand on a comparable level of importance as sources; but with regard to the issues we are raising there would be no point in differentiating between them.

Without a doubt D is the set of parts that was prepared for the premiere performance of the symphony and was used at that performance. Accordingly, it must have been prepared not too long before the terminal date of December 22, 1808; perhaps in November, but at the latest in early December of that year. It is entirely possible that D was prepared even before score-copy C, which, it was earlier suggested, was also used at the premiere. For if C had already been available, it would have been more sensible to copy the parts from C, which was a corrected score. In view of the legibility problems of the autograph, this procedure would have been less likely to give rise to errors, significantly quicker, and cheaper as well (from later documents it is clear that copyists demanded higher fees for copying from autographs). The dates of C and D may not, however, lie too far apart. Both were dependent on the point at which Beethoven would definitely have been able to count on having an "Akademie" in the winter season of 1808. Without a firm commitment he would hardly have taken on the cost of such an extensive copying job. The letters that Beethoven wrote in connection with the concert of December 22, 1808 are for the most part undated and not available in the original. Accordingly, one can estimate the dates of C and D only in light of the normal procedures of concert management. Since minimal rehearsals were held, the performance materials were needed only a short time before the concert. Surely C originated after B, and D was ready by December, 1808.

We possess a substantial number of the instrumental parts of D, far more than were known to Nottebohm, Canisius, or originally even Gülke. A nearly complete set, consisting of twenty-one parts, is preserved in the Narodni Museum in Prague. A penciled notation by an early hand on the title page of the first violin part reports that the only missing part is the one for the alto trombone. Two other parts (Viola and Violonzelli e Bassi) are found in the Archive of the GdM. There can be no doubt that the Prague and Vienna parts originally belonged together and were actually used for the first performance. They are entirely in the hand of Copyist D, who was also responsible for the entries in the autograph relating to the original performance parts. This copyist (unlike the copyists Schlemmer and Rampel) worked for Beethoven only a relatively short time, from the end of 1805 to the end of 1808.[27] In the entire set of wind parts, in the timpani, and in the Vienna viola part we find that same sectional division that we have met in the autograph. The Prague string parts (Violino I and II, Viola, Violoncelli e Bassi) show another division in the first, second, and fourth movements; this might be an indication that they were copied from another source. The Vienna part for the cellos and basses contains no sectional division; it is certainly one of the last of the duplicate parts.

All of the parts in both the Vienna and Prague collections are made on paper that can be dated 1808–09, as we can determine from their use in other Beethoven manuscripts. Thus they all fall into the period under discussion. The oft-mentioned five measures that were added to the first movement in the wake of the first performance (measures 4, 23, 127, 251, and 481), were not originally present in any of the parts. Clearly, they were added later—probably by Copyist D—in a somewhat lighter ink. Further evidence that the parts belonged together is provided by the title pages of the individual parts. At first they bore only the name of the appropriate instrument and, written very small in the upper left-hand corner, the genre indication "Sinfonia." An unknown hand, here called "P," has added on all the title pages the more specific indication "Sinfonia in C m" or "Sinf. in C m" in large strokes (see plate XIII). (P is also met with on the title pages of the set of parts known as copy "E"; see below.)

On the title page of the first violin part (in the Prague copy), which also names the composer, another anonymous hand has made the notation "Parti 23"; that is, two more than now survive. It is plausible to identify the two lacking parts with the two Vienna parts. Perhaps they (along with copy E) were discarded as duplicates, and then came directly or in-

[27]See Alan Tyson, "Notes on Five of Beethoven's Copyists," *Journal of the American Musicological Society,* XXIII (1970), 439–71, especially 456–60.

Plate XIII. First violin part used at the premiere of Op. 67 (Prague, Narodni Museum)

directly through another owner to the Musikverein in Vienna. The remaining parts were kept in the possession of a collector. The opposite hypothesis, that the parts which ended up in Prague came from the music collection of the Vienna Gesellschaft, is less probable but certainly not to be entirely excluded. (After all, we should keep in mind that many valuable Beethoven manuscripts were separated from the Gesellschaft archives, for example the cadenzas to the piano concertos, which were split off from the Archduke Rudolph collection, and the second and third movements of the Piano Sonata in E♭, Op. 81a.) The separation of the parts probably took place before 1830, when a flood took place in the Archive;[28] like many other older manuscripts in the GdM, the Vienna parts show extensive water stains, but no such damage appears in the Prague parts.

Although it may appear tedious to pursue such questions of the identity and matching of the two sets of parts (more will be said about this in the discussion of the musical text), they are of great importance for the evaluation of the sources as well as for the problem of distinguishing other sources. For example, the instrumental parts signed by Ferdinand Piringer (GdM, 6149 Fascicle B, Nos. 4–6), which Gülke mentions in passing, are from a considerably later date (about 1826) and can have no claim to authenticity. On the other hand, the Prague parts for piccolo and second and third trombone, which of course pertain only to the finale, belong without a doubt to the parts used for the first performance—Gülke's opinion to the contrary.

Owing to the many scribal errors and discrepancies in Copy D, Gülke ascribed a very low value to it. He apparently overlooked the fact that the two Vienna parts and all the wind and timpani parts in the Prague collection contain numerous autograph corrections by Beethoven. Unusual readings such as those of the trumpets and timpani in the first movement (measures 282–86) are not simply to be explained as errors in copying; rather, they deserve careful consideration.

The five measures added to the first movement, as noted earlier, were entered not by Beethoven but by a copyist. He in turn must have had a source to work from, which could not have been the autograph. He used either a list of corrections or else score-copy C, into which Beethoven may earlier have entered the "little improvements." A comprehensive, thorough-going revision was undertaken chiefly in the two Vienna parts (and also in the three parts designated copy E, but only sporadically in the Prague parts) by an unknown hand, here indicated as "Q." For this

---

[28]For this information I am indebted to a friendly communication from Mr. Peter Riethus of the Gesellschaft der Musikfreunde, Vienna.

too a score other than the autograph, possibly C, could have served as a source. The first performance parts thus constitute a valuable, if not completely satisfactory, substitute for C and the similarly lost correction list for Breitkopf and Härtel of March 28, 1809.

The first performance parts require the closest attention with regard to the problem of the repetition of the scherzo and trio. The repeat is written out completely; the copyist apparently took Beethoven's direction on page 185 of the autograph ("si replica l'all[egr]o con trio e allora si prende 2") in the same sense as during the preparation of C. At the point of origin of C and D, the five-part division of the movement doubtless stood firm. But now, however, as can be seen in all parts of D (not, of course, in those parts which first appear in the finale), the repetition was canceled. This appears to have taken place in two stages:

1. As a first step, an unknown hand (here called "R") indicated in pencil the added measures 237 and 238b by means of the signs *Vi-de* and ⊘, and boldly crossed out measures 238a through 237b, which lay between them. Probably at the same time, the leaves that stood between the added passages were sewn together at the outer margin with two stitches, as had been done in the autograph and Mendelssohn 20; there, however, the purpose of this procedure had not been entirely clear. In the present case the intent was obvious to cancel the repetition and facilitate the turning of the pages. Due to the page breaks, a portion of the canceled repetition—namely, some measures near the added passages—remained visible. It is worth noting that in some parts this first step of revision was itself canceled and then re-established. Thus the composer provided no definitive instruction for the shortening of the movement.

2. The second step, carried out by another unknown hand ("S"), completes the work of the first. To ease the page turns further, some passages were rewritten, in ink, so that a few measures of rest fell between the pages. The new version was made up on odd slips of paper that were pinned over the old reading and partially pasted down. The still-visible remains of the canceled repetition were then covered up with pieces of plain unlined paper, which were pasted over them. Here and there the leaves standing between were gathered together with a few stitches. In the Prague parts the stitching and gluing are still largely intact; in the Vienna parts, thanks to the curiosity of scholars, some of the pasted and sewn-down strips have unfortunately been lost.

The evaluation of these two steps depends on our view as to when and by whom the revisions were made. Not a single instance reveals Beethoven's hand, so far as we can tell from the paste-downs. Yet this does not mean that these changes were not made with his knowledge and approval. He himself could have written them into score-copy C, or

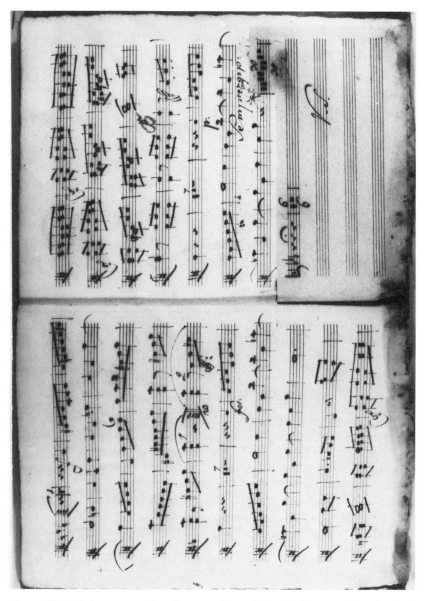

Plate XIV. Viola part used at the premiere of Op. 67 (Vienna, Gesellschaft der Musikfreunde)

Plate XV. Viola part used at the premiere of Op. 67 (Vienna, GdM)

at least indicated them there, and then left it to a friend to enter them into the parts we call D. On the other hand, the possibility must be considered that the coincidence of the D parts with those of the first edition, F, which was ultimately unavoidable, could have come about through the intervention of any well-educated musician, who might have arrived at the same revision independently of the composer. In fact, in another place in the Prague second violin part there is a strip bearing the text of the first edition, F; a similar situation is demonstrated by Kojima at several places in the first performance parts of the *Pastoral* Symphony. (Indeed, the hands of these strips for Op. 67 and Op. 68 appear to be identical.) The authenticity of the revision is thus dependent on these factors: a) the dates of the two revision stages; b) the identity of the two hands that undertook them; and c) the provenance of the first performance parts.

We turn first to the problem of dating. Gülke, perhaps rendered uncertain by earlier criticism, regards as a possibility an early cancellation of the repetition, and thus in effect argues against his own editorial decision. The repetition seems to have been canceled at an early stage, writes Gülke, "for, in the greater number of the parts the handwriting and ink of the correction material and the paper used for the pasted-down corrections are the same as in the parts themselves. This would argue for a very early revision of the repetition, and thus also, that the lost letter [?] to Härtel, in which Beethoven, among other things, specified the addition of the extra measure before the second measure in the first theme of the first movement, must also have informed him of the cancellation of the repetition. Thus it would have arisen as a nearly spontaneous reaction to the not very successful first performance."[29]

Gülke's views, however, are based on certain incorrect assumptions. It is not true that the handwriting and ink of the corrections are the same as in the parts themselves; Copyist S of the pasted-down (and pinned-on) strips of notation is not identical with Copyist D. The papers used are also of different places of origin; accordingly, no conclusions about their chronology can be drawn from them. Nevertheless, the correction strips have preserved a valuable clue to the date of the second stage of revision. As Nottebohm has already observed, on the back of one of the notational strips in the Vienna viola part there is a fragment of an arrangement of the finale of Beethoven's Seventh Symphony;[30] moreover, it too is in the hand of Copyist S. The second revision step thus could not have taken place before the composition of Op. 92—that is, 1812.

[29]Gülke, *op. cit.*, p. 44.
[30]Nottebohm, "Die ausgeschossenen zwei Takte in dritten Satz der C-moll-Symphonie," N I, pp. 17–20.

Canisius argues for a still later date, claiming (probably correctly) that a revision such as this probably came into being only after the publication of the symphony in December, 1816.[31] Since the second revision stage must have taken place before the separation of the Vienna and Prague parts from one another, the date of its execution can be narrowed down to between 1816 and 1830.

The first stage of revision, done in pencil and with several layers of over-writing, cannot be confined to the same dating limits as the second. It could have been carried out before 1816, or even before 1812. The very fact that it was made neither by Beethoven nor by Copyist D, who otherwise corrected the parts, allows the supposition that the abridgment of the movement does *not* belong among these "little improvements" made "during" the first performance. Some further light in this regard arises from the parts here designated "E," which by virtue of their strong resemblance to D must now be brought into the discussion.

VI. THE COPIED PARTS "E"

The GdM possesses, aside from the parts for the first performance, much other relevant manuscript material. Most of this can be traced back, directly or through various intermediate stages, to the first edition "F." However, three parts, here called "E," do not belong to this transmission line (XIII 6149 Fasz. B: No. 1, Violino 2do; No. 2, Viola; No. 3, Violonzelli e Bassi). In these, as in the first performance parts, the repeat in the third movement is fully written out, and later, in the same way and by the same hands, R and S, canceled in two stages of revision. As in D, the title pages are completed by Hand P ("Sinf. in C m"), and revisions by Q appear in E as well. E and D therefore certainly belonged together for some time. Since E shows the same water stains as the two Vienna parts of D, it must have been separated from the Prague parts and present in the Vienna Archive before 1830.

What distinguishes E from D is the absence of any autograph corrections by Beethoven. Another significant distinction is the employment in E of a very unusual double-pressed paper. In the preparation of this type of paper, two freshly made sheets are laid one upon another without felt interleaving, so that they bind together. The purpose of this somewhat old-fashioned procedure is to achieve a heavier quality of paper. As a rule, sheets from two different sieves are placed upon one another, with the result that the watermarks are often difficult to read. In this case they consist of: 1) a posthorn emblem with crown above and bell below, such as is found in many letter papers; and 2) a type of anchor. Both signs are

[31]Canisius, *op. cit.*, p. 43.

widely disseminated, so that a determination of their point of origin is not possible without further evidence. The three copyists of E show a Viennese style of writing, and thus the paper may stem from a small Lower Austrian mill.

The paper used in E is also found in a copy of the first violin part from the Choral Fantasy, Op. 80 in the Gesellschaft der Musikfreunde (Ms. A 30). It appears to be the only part that survives from the first performance of the work, which took place on December 22, 1808. The twenty-five bars of the keyboard introduction are still lacking here. Beethoven originally improvised them and only wrote them out a year later, in 1809, in connection with the publication of the work, as is shown by the sketches in Landsberg 5. As is well known, the Choral Fantasy, which was intended to be the crowning final work in this *Akademie*, was finished only shortly before the event itself. According to Beethoven's own admission, time was so short that he could not even copy out a score (he probably meant that he could not have a copy of the score prepared from his autograph). According to Seyfried, the parts were still wet when they were used for a hasty rehearsal. It may thus be assumed that the violin part, Ms. A 30, was made just a few days before the concert.

In view of the rarity of the paper, we can assume the same dating for the three parts of source E of Op. 67 as for GdM, Ms. A 30. They may well be parts that were needed at the last minute for newly added orchestra members. They too were probably used for the first performance on December 22, 1808.[32] The sources used for E were probably some parts from D—not autograph A, and probably not copy C, either. Curiously, E already contains the measures added to the first movement in D (measures 4, 23, 127, 251, and 481). The fermata extensions were therefore added not *after* the first performance (as is often stated) but were already in existence earlier, during the rehearsals. Assuming that our dating of E is correct, the work was performed on December 22, 1808 in the form in which we know it. Beethoven's foundation in his letter to Breitkopf and Härtel of March 4, 1809—"some small corrections which I made *during* the performance"—must therefore be read with some reservations.

In E, as in D, the repetition of the scherzo and trio in the third movement is fully written out. Thus, at the time E was prepared, a few days before the *Akademie*, it still possessed full validity. This also must be taken as an indication that the abbreviation of the movement did not belong among the "little improvements." Both E and the Vienna parts for the premiere show especially numerous entries by the corrector Q, who

---

[32]See Shin A. Kojima, "Zur Quellenkritik von Beethovens Chorfantasie Opus 80," *Musik. Edition, Interpretation, Gedenkschrift Günter Henle,* ed. M. Bente (Munich, 1980), pp. 264–81, especially p. 270.

probably worked from a score. Q includes the repetition in the third movement in his revision; for him it was still valid.

It is rather difficult to date Q's work exactly, and the following indications can only be a vague approximation. The five parts so carefully scrutinized by Q[33] are marked at the end of the last movement with the word "revid." ("revised"). It seems permissible to link Q with the word's appearance. The same indications, "revid." and "revidirt," apparently by the same strange hand, are found on the title pages of two parts used for the first performance of the Seventh Symphony.[34] Does this mean that Q's work can be dated after the writing of those parts—that is, after 1813? If this were true, then the revision carried out by R, in which the repetition was canceled for the first time, would date from after 1813 but before 1830, when the separation of the Vienna parts from the Prague parts took place.

The authenticity of the two revision stages basically depends not on when, but by whom they were undertaken. Unfortunately, the entries made by Hand R are not idiosyncratic enough to permit its identification. By contrast, the features of Hand S in the second revision stage are much more easily grasped. We find it not only here but also as a correcting and supplementary hand in many other places in D and E. S was probably a capable, practicing musician, and not a mere copyist dependent upon instruction. His other entries in D and E are everywhere careful and noteworthy. He most likely worked from a score, perhaps from copy C. The arrangement of Op. 92 in the Vienna viola part from D may be his own work. The viola part in E contains a strip of notation on the back of which is found, also in S's hand, an incomplete effort at an arrangement of the "Kreutzer" Sonata, Op. 47, for string ensemble. All this indicates that S was to some degree autonomous in both his musical and his compositional activities.

Up to now it has not been possible to identify S. He is certainly not Ferdinand Piringer, Director of the Concert Spirituel, whom we shall discuss shortly; neither is he to be identified with Franz Xaver Gebauer, Piringer's predecessor, nor his successor, Karl Holz. Handwriting samples by other musicians from Beethoven's circle—for example, Ignaz Schuppanzigh—are not presently available to me. It is therefore necessary to go more deeply into the question of the provenance of D and E. If even a part of these were from Beethoven's personal estate, this would be an important clue to the authenticity of the revision stages R and S.

The view is widely held that the extant first performance parts for Beethoven's orchestral works come directly from among his own per-

[33]The two Vienna first-performance parts from D and the three parts labeled E.
[34]GdM, XIII 1399: Violino 1mo No. 4 and Violino 1mo No. 5.

sonal papers.[35] However, the evidence for this is in most cases hard to establish. The orchestral parts for the Fourth and Fifth Symphonies may have already left his possession within his lifetime. On May 27, 1813 Beethoven wrote to Joseph von Varena in Graz: "Instead of one symphony you are getting two, firstly, the one you asked for written out and duplicated—and, secondly, another which, I believe, has not yet been performed at G[raz]. The latter is also written out. . . ."[36] Some weeks later, on July 4, 1813, he requested that Varena "return immediately, since they do not belong to me, . . . the C minor symphony [and] the B♭ symphony. . . ."[37] The posthumous list of Beethoven's possessions contains a heading "copied-out parts for Beethoven's works," but neither here nor anywhere else is there a specific listing of the material for Op. 67. This of course does not preclude the possibility that at least some parts of Op. 67 were in Beethoven's posthumous papers, in which case they could have been auctioned off on November 5, 1827. The list is very imprecise, and the contents of the individual lots were not very carefully sorted out. The Gesellschaft Archive in Vienna contains a list of the musical contents of Beethoven's estate acquired from Ferdinand Piringer, executed in duplicate and dated November 9, 1827.[38] Item 6 on the list, "Beethovens Sinfonie in C mol—Orchesterstimmen," is priced at three florins. According to the same source, the Gesellschaft also obtained from Piringer a score (probably Estate Lot 209) and corrected "Auflagstimmen," or "copied parts" (not named in the estate list), for the Fourth Symphony, for a total of ten florins; also complete orchestra parts ("vollständige Orchesterstimmen") of the Seventh Symphony (Estate Lot 192) for four florins, and a score of the *Pastoral* Symphony (not mentioned in the estate list), also for four florins.

Piringer's transaction was not, it seems, entirely selfless. He held back some of the material he had obtained at the auction (presumably for his own impressive collection); other items he raised in price, so that he received more money for the items he sold to the Gesellschaft than he had spent altogether himself at the auction on November 5. He may not have actually bought at auction all of the musical material that he sold to the

---

[35]See Nottebohm, "Die ausgeschossenen zwei Takte . . . ," N I, p. 18: "The whole collection was in Beethoven's possession and at the time of the auction of his estate was purchased by the Gesellschaft der Musikfreunde." However, the Gesellschaft is not listed as the direct purchaser in the various surviving auction catalogs, nor in Hotschevar's list of purchasers.

[36]Anderson no. 424.

[37]Anderson no. 428.

[38]For knowledge of this document I am indebted to Dr. Otto Biba of the Gesellschaft der Musikfreunde.

Gesellschaft, but rather acquired some of it at about the same time through purchase or exchange. In any case the material changed hands very quickly.

Another purchaser at the auction of November 5 who was exclusively interested in orchestral material was a certain Fischer, perhaps to be identified with Johann Fischer, an adjunct member of the Royal Lower Austrian Civil Building Authority ("k.k. niederösterreichischen Civil-Baudirektion"), a supporting member of the Gesellschaft der Musikfreunde, a practicing violinist, and an amateur conductor.[39] Among other items, he obtained as Estate Lot 197 two packets of the parts to two unspecified symphonies. Piringer and Fischer could have made a prior arrangement to acquire their material in collaboration. From the relatively low price that Piringer demanded for the parts to Op. 67 (three florins, compared with four florins for Op. 92 and ten florins for Op. 60), we may assume that the Op. 67 parts were not fully complete. Perhaps the transaction was limited to duplicate parts. In any event, chances are that the two Vienna parts from D and the three parts of E belong to the material that Piringer deposited on November 9, 1827, and that they actually do come from Beethoven's estate. The three revision stages Q, R, and S would, accordingly, have been accomplished during his lifetime, and if they were not carried out by the composer, could well have been done with his knowledge and, ultimately, his approval.

The other parts comprising D, as noted earlier, probably came somehow into the hands of a collector (perhaps a Viennese?) before 1830. This man was in the habit of marking, in ink, his pieces with the initial "W," occasionally only on the title page of the first violin part. (The "W" looks very similar to the abbreviation for "Violini" used by Schubert.) A considerable part of the Beethoveniana in the Lobkowitz Collection in the Narodni Museum in Prague—including almost all of it that has high value as a source—is marked in this way (see plate XIII). The collection of "W" apparently passed later to another collector, who now marked the title pages of all the parts with the initial "L," written in red crayon. This initial is found in all the manuscripts that had formerly belonged to W. (Many of the parts also show an initial "S:," written in lead pencil, on the top of the title pages.) However, the entire collection of W-L did not go into the Lobkowitz Collection. The first performance parts of the *Pastoral Symphony*, which have the same provenance (W, L, and S), ended up—probably after 1830—in the Archive of the GdM.

---

[39]See Anton Ziegler, *Addressen-Buch von Tonkünstlern, Dilettanten . . . in Wien*, (Vienna, 1823), pp. 135 and 162.

VII. THE FIRST EDITION "F" AND THE PRINTED SCORE "G"

Sources F and G require far less attention than the preceding ones, for they are highly dependent on the other sources and could not have been nearly so strongly influenced by Beethoven. It was established earlier that score-copy B, and not any other manuscript copy X, was the manuscript that Härtel acquired in mid-September, 1808. The adjustment of the first violin part as a conducting part for the concertmaster doubtless necessitated certain written preparations; B could not be printed from without these alterations. The other parts too presumably do not stem directly from B, but were printed from copied parts which had been prepared earlier from B. B possesses (according to the photocopies preserved in the Beethoven-Archiv) a characteristic sectional division by means of measure numbers, similar to that seen in the autograph.

The parts copied from B in all likelihood served first of all the practical purpose of trying out the new work. As is well known, the symphony was performed twice "from the manuscript" before the appearance of the printed parts in Leipzig: the first time at a "guest concert" (*Gastkonzert*) of the Dresden chamber musician Tietz, on January 23, 1809; the second time, a little later at one of the weekly concerts at the Gewandhaus. Brief notices of both concerts appeared in the *Allgemeine Musikalische Zeitung*.[40] Some uncertainty about the text of the third movement must already have arisen at one of these concerts, with a question directed to Beethoven. This is doubtless what prompted his letter of March 28, 1809 to Breitkopf and Härtel: "You stated that you had found another mistake in the third movement of the symphony in C minor—I don't remember what kind of mistake it can be—It is always best to send me the proofs with the score which you have received."[41] Since Beethoven did not know what precisely had been referred to, he could not reply more exactly. A clarification of the problematic passage could not be made.

The main business of the letter of March 28 was to transmit those "little improvements" which, according to Beethoven's own testimony, he had decided upon "during" the first performance of the Symphony. We know, however, that before the arrival of the list a press run of one hundred copies (F_1) had been prepared (apparently, only one example has been preserved).[42] Thus Beethoven's revisions could only be accommo-

---

[40]Volume XI (1809), columns 280–81 and 433–35.

[41]Anderson no. 204.

[42]British Library, London, Hirsch Collection. The GdM possesses a score-copy from the 1820s in the hand of the amateur Friedrich Klemm, which likewise does not contain the "little improvements" of March 28, 1809; perhaps it was prepared from a copy of the first edition F_1. In this copy the two superfluous measures 238a/239a are also included. A repetition of the scherzo and trio is not indicated.

dated in the following press run. Whether the publishers took care of all the desired changes, as we enquired earlier, cannot be determined, since the correction list that was sent is lost. It would have been highly remarkable, however, if corrections had not been made in the third movement, inasmuch as the composer had already requested that they be entered. According to a "printing book" (*Stichbuch*) that was formerly in the publishers' archive, both press runs, F_1 and F_2, were prepared as early as April, 1809.[43]

That Härtel's query had in fact dealt with the two extra measures, 238a and 239a, is clear from the ensuing correspondence. When Beethoven first saw a copy of the first edition, F_1, in the autumn of 1809, he was infuriated over the large number of errors it contained.[44] At once he sent another list of corrections; but this too, like the first one, is lost. Besides, it is doubtful that it was heeded. Probably the critical passage in the third movement was not even now recognized, let alone set straight. Beethoven came back to this point for the first time in the famous letter of August 21, 1810,[45] in which he ordered that the two superfluous measures, 238a and 239a, be eliminated. His wording, "I have found the following additional mistake in the C minor Symphony," makes it clear that only now was he aware of this problem. In his letter of October 15, 1810 he "has a vague recollection" that the publisher had already asked him about this very point. At that time, however, "perhaps I forgot to send you a reply about it at once; and the bars may be there still—."[46] From all these remarks by Beethoven, it is once again to be concluded that the cancellation of the repetition in the scherzo and trio, which is indirectly connected with the elimination of measures 238a and 239a, was not an immediate consequence of the unfortunate concert of December 22, 1808. The publishers may have entered the later corrections of 1810 by hand in isolated copies of the work that they had in stock; but they were not made in the plates of the first edition F.

The corrections were overlooked as well in the preparation of the first printed score "G," which certainly originated without Beethoven's collaboration. The score, which appeared in 1826, goes back directly to score-copy B; accordingly, it has no value of its own as a source, but can be of use in the reconstruction of B. Schmieder proposed the view that the printer's source for G was another manuscript that had been pre-

---

[43]See Wolfgang Schmieder, "Nochmals: Originalhandschrift oder Erstdruck," *Allgemeine Musikzeitung*, LXVII (1940), 259, n. 44.

[44]See Beethoven's letter to Breitkopf and Härtel of November 2, 1809 (Anderson no. 228).

[45]Anderson no. 272.

[46]Anderson no. 281.

pared from B. In support of this view he adduced a copyist's payment in the Breitkopf and Härtel archive, along with the incorrect assumption that B contains no printer's division for G.[47] In fact, however, in the photocopies preserved in the Beethoven-Archiv such entries are very clearly visible. There is a series of numbers over the first staff that agrees exactly with the page numbering in G. The instruments are ordered differently in G from the way they are in B. To help orient the engraver, an editor at the publishing firm numbered the staffs in B with red ink in the order in which they were to appear in the printed version. The other entries in B in red ink, as described by Schünemann, probably were also entered in connection with the publication of the printed score G. It seems that the corrections on the list of March 28, 1809, and perhaps also those of November 2 of the same year, were taken up and entered in red ink in B during its preparation as a printer's source for G. Nonetheless, the questionable passage in the third movement of the symphony, measures 238a and 239a, was not corrected. The printed score G would agree perfectly in this respect with its *Stichvorlage*, score-copy B: First-ending and second-ending measures are not indicated, and repeat signs are lacking. Beethoven's letters of August 21 and October 15, 1810 were obviously not heeded.

*   *   *   *   *

This investigation of the sources has yielded ambivalent results. The erroneous readings of B, F, and G are presumably rooted in the autograph, which, at the time B was prepared, was inadequately marked. The error went unnoticed by Beethoven at least until August, 1810, and then it was eliminated in such a way that the movement acquired the traditional three-part form that had already appeared in the sketches. Sources A (in its later state), C, D, and E show the five-part division that had been heard at the first performance on December 22, 1808 and that probably maintained its validity for some time thereafter. Its cancellation in favor of the three-part form took place only after much delay, and certainly did not belong to the spontaneous "little improvements" that Beethoven undertook in the wake of the first performance and sent to the publisher on March 28, 1809. The later contraction of the movement to its three-part form in D and E was probably not the result of a new and aesthetically motivated consideration of the work, but rather the result of an effort to reconcile two different textual versions, of which the first, the printed version F, could no longer be revoked.

Beethoven could certainly request the elimination of the two superflu-

---

[47]Schmieder, *op. cit.*, pp. 258–59.

ous measures 238a and 239a (not that his request was ever honored). But as to the introduction of repeat signs, the indication of first-ending and second-ending measures, or even the eradication of the repetition, as in C, D, and E—even he must have realized that technical considerations made these demands unrealistic and, as far as the dissemination of the printed parts F was concerned, no longer desirable. Not only would measures 3/4 and 239a/238b have had to receive double-bars and repeat signs, but first-ending and second-ending marks would also have had to be introduced into measures 238a/239a and 238b/239b. In addition, the number of measures of rest that were indicated in summary form in the resting parts would have had to be redivided and calculated anew. In this light, the return to the three-part form shown in the sketches and in the parts D and E represents a pragmatic coming-to-terms with the situation as it stood. His precise instructions to Breitkopf and Härtel at this time on the marking of the scherzo in the String Quartet Op. 74 are perhaps to be seen against this background.[48] Here, at least, where it was still possible to do so, the composer wished to ensure the realization of his intentions.

As the strongest argument against the three-part form, Gülke, strictly following Canisius's example, adduces the remark of Franz Oliva about the third Gesellschaft concert on April 9, 1820 in Beethoven's conversation books: "I forgot to tell you that the dilettantes shortened your Symphony yesterday—in the third movement they left out almost half; the fugato middle section was played only once, then came immediately the passage where the violins have pizzicato, and the transition into the finale; it made a very bad effect."[49] Perhaps Gülke is right in assuming that around 1820, manuscript materials with the five-part version were still circulating and being used in performance; perhaps, however, Oliva was merely making a subjective comparison to what seemed to him the exemplary performances of the impresario Ignaz Schuppanzigh, who had by now been away for years.[50] And possibly he was also recollecting even earlier conversations in which he had taken part years before. At the time that Beethoven ordered the cancellation of the two superfluous measures 238a and 239a (in the summer and autumn of 1810), Oliva, as successor to Gleichenstein and early predecessor of Schindler, had assumed the enervating role of tolerated admirer, unpaid secretary, and

[48]See Beethoven's letter to Breitkopf and Härtel of August 21, 1810 (Anderson no. 272).

[49]*Ludwig van Beethovens Konversationshefte,* ed. Karl-Heinz Köhler and Dagmar Beck, II (Leipzig, 1976), 53.

[50]One day before this same Gesellschaft concert of April 9, 1820, and in connection with it, Oliva reports: "The Symphony in C minor has been very well performed under Schuppanzigh several times—he understood it." See *Beethovens Konversationshefte,* II, 47.

tormented confidant of the "divino maestro." The correction of the faulty third movement of the symphony could not have taken place without a considerable degree of energetic discussion.

We do not know how Beethoven replied to Oliva's criticism of the concert in 1820. Yet we must assume that, for whatever reasons, he had finally accepted the shortening of the movement. The revision in parts D and E do not come from the composer's own hand, but were surely made with his knowledge, since in all probability a portion of these parts, if not all of them, was found among the personal papers of his estate (whereupon they were quickly dispersed). The striking parallels in the autograph manuscript—purchased at auction by the firm of Artaria and certainly not subject to any of the later entries made in parts D and E by their possessors, namely, the sewing-up of the appropriate pages (page 185 and all the pages in Mendelssohn 20)—support this hypothesis.

If we ask what is the "final version"—the "Fassung letzter Hand"—one must answer that it is the three-part version. The one that corresponds to Beethoven's artistic intentions, however, is in five parts.[51]

—Translated from the German by David L. Schwarzkopf and Lewis Lockwood

[51]In March, 1984, as this article was in press, the *Stichvorlage* for the first edition of the *Pastoral* Symphony, which was long believed to be lost, came to light. This new primary source may influence our views about the filiation and dating of the sources for Op. 67. It seems possible that a portion of the parts D, the Prague string parts, were copied from score B and therefore originated before the end of September, 1808.

Beethoven's Mass in C Major, Op. 86

J. Merrill Knapp

It has become commonplace for earnest students of music to seize upon some work of a major or minor composer and declare it to be "undeservedly neglected"—both in performance and in lasting value. While it is hardly my purpose to do this for Beethoven's Mass in C major, a certain amount of advocacy can be found in the foregoing consideration of the work. Every composer has pieces in his catalogue that do not show his best effort, and it is apt to be pedantry to exhume them merely for the sake of attracting notice. Beethoven himself, for instance, knew that *Wellington's Victory*, Op. 91 (The Battle Symphony) was hardly comparable to one of his symphonies; it was merely a *pièce d'occasion* for the purpose of bringing in revenue and attracting publicity. He did not take it very seriously.

But the C Major Mass is a different matter. It is one of only two settings of the Catholic Mass by one of the world's greatest composers, and Beethoven said in a letter to Breitkopf and Härtel: ". . . [the work] is especially close to my heart."[1] While some may doubt the full sincerity of this sentiment (Beethoven was trying to get the Mass published and the Leipzig group was reluctant), one cannot escape the conclusion that Beethoven had a high regard for this work, the first music he had written on the most familiar and solemn text in the Christian liturgy.

Op. 86 has always fallen in the shadow of the *Missa solemnis*, for obvious reasons. It is not one of Beethoven's gigantic creations, overshadowing everything around it, but is rather more conventional and traditional. It bears strong similarities to one of Haydn's last six masses, some of which Beethoven certainly knew (the *Heiligmesse* and the *Nelsonmesse* were listed in his *Nachlass* as Masses Nos. 1 and 3, respectively). Yet it is pure Beethoven on a high level. The composer made an early claim for it

---

[1]Anderson no. 169.

in a letter to Breitkopf and Härtel: "I think I have treated the text in a manner in which it has rarely been treated."[2]

It is surprising that there has not been more elaboration on these two comments. A search of the enormous Beethoven literature shows that very little has been written about this first mass. The observations have been cursory, and after a few sentences, comments in the general literature lead directly to the *Missa solemnis*.[3]

A review of familiar facts may be helpful to place the piece in perspective. Sometime in late 1806 or early 1807, Beethoven received a commission from Prince Nikolaus Esterházy (1765–1833), Haydn's second patron, to write a mass for the name day of his wife, Maria Josepha Hermenegild (1768–1845) in September, 1807. The procedure was already very familiar to Haydn, who had written his last six great masses for this particular occasion when he was recalled by the Prince to resume his duties (albeit mostly honorary) as Kapellmeister in 1795. Haydn, returning from London, faithfully fulfilled these commissions each year from 1796 to 1802, going to Eisenstadt and the Bergkirche from Vienna for the first performance. These were always held on the Sunday after September 8 (Maria Josepha's name day), unless that date itself fell on a Sunday. The Prince, who was evidently interested in little else but liturgical music, presumably handed this commission over to Hummel in the intervening years when Haydn was too elderly and frail to accomplish the task.[4] Yet Haydn undoubtedly had something to do with the fact that Beethoven, his former pupil, received the commission in 1806–07.

The first direct evidence of Beethoven's participation is a letter to the Prince of July 26, 1807 from Baden,[5] apologizing for his lateness in getting the music sent to Eisenstadt (he promised it would be there by August 20) and expressing his apprehension about submitting his work when it could be compared to Haydn's masterpieces. The Prince made a gracious reply on August 9, 1807.[6] The next evidence is a note from the Prince to

---

[2]Anderson no. 167.

[3]Standard biographies, *Jahrbücher*, specialized essays, publications of Congresses on Beethoven, etc. One exception is B. A. Wallner, "Beethovens C-Dur-Messe Op. 86 als kirchliches Werk," *Neues Beethoven-Jahrbuch* (Jahrgang 2, 1925), 119–36, some ideas from which are incorporated into this essay.

[4]Denis McCaldin ("The Choral Music," in *The Beethoven Companion*, ed. Denis Arnold and Nigel Fortune [London, 1971], p. 395) says Hummel wrote three of them before 1807. Joel Sachs, in the *New Grove* article "Hummel," says Hummel was appointed Konzertmeister at Eisenstadt in April, 1804 (in effect Kapellmeister, although Haydn continued to hold the title) and kept the position until 1811. Presumably, all of Hummel's sacred works were written for Eisenstadt.

[5]Anderson no. 150.

[6]Thayer-Deiters-Riemann III, p. 35. He said, in effect, that any comparison to

his Vice-Kapellmeister, Johann Nepomuk Fuchs (dated September 12, 1807),[7] stating that he had heard, to his displeasure, that only one out of five altos ("contraltisten") in the choir had appeared for Beethoven's rehearsal (perhaps the dress rehearsal?); Fuchs ordered all of them— singers and instrumentalists—to be there on the next day, Sunday the 13th, for the performance. If this note is taken literally, it is no wonder that the performance was unsuccessful as reported. Admittedly, Beethoven was always having trouble with his performing forces, and there may have been intrigue at Esterházy's court; but this evidence indicates the preparation was haphazard, to say the least.

Schindler takes over from here, and, as usual, his account has to be treated with great caution. At a reception held in the Prince's chambers after the performance, where it was customary for the work to be discussed, the Prince presumably said to the composer: "My dear Beethoven, what have you done again now?" ["Aber, lieber Beethoven, was haben Sie denn da wieder gemacht?"][8] This rather unencouraging and ambiguous question (Beethoven may have misconstrued it) was greeted by a laugh from Hummel, who was standing nearby. Beethoven became enraged, walked out, and left Eisenstadt that same day. However, a receipt for lodging indicates that Beethoven did not leave until the 16th,[9] so Schindler's account may be doubtful on several points (he softened the tale in the third and fourth editions of his book). Yet the event was probably not a great success,[10] and there is some evidence in later years that Beethoven remained bitter about the work's initial reception.

One of the first public notices for a partial performance of the Mass

Haydn's masses only raised the worth of Beethoven's works in his [the Prince's] eyes, and he looked forward warmly to receiving the score.

[7]C. F. Pohl, Grenzboten, November 15, 1868. Reprinted in Thayer-Deiters-Riemann III, p. 36. Gerald Schlag (foreword to Johann Nepomuk Hummel und Eisenstadt: Eine Ausstellung [Eisenstadt, 1978]) quotes a directive of June, 1804 by Prince Esterházy, making Fuchs responsible for the choir and church music; Luigi Tomasini, the chamber music; and Hummel, the rest of the Eisenstadt music (theater music, cantatas, etc.).

[8]Schindler (1860), pp. 166–67.

[9]Victor Papp, Beethoven es a Magyorak (Budapest, 1927), p. 71.

[10]Further corroboration of this comes from "The Diaries of Joseph Carl Rosenbaum, 1770–1829," ed. Else Radant, The Haydn Yearbook (Bryn Mawr, Pa., 1968), p. 138. The entry for September, 1807 reads: ". . . To Kar. in the morning . . . to Mass . . . with unsuccessful music by Bethoven [sic]." See also Schindler (1860), pp. 197–98. There also could be no doubt about the Prince's continuing reaction to the music. He wrote shortly afterwards to Countess Henriette von Zielinska: "Beethoven's Mass is unbearably ridiculous and detestable, and I am not convinced it can ever be performed properly. I am angry and mortified." (H. C. Robbins Landon, Haydn: Chronicle and Works: The Late Years, 1801–1809 [Bloomington, Indiana, 1977], p. 356.) Why the Prince reacted so strongly is difficult to say, as he was basically unmusical.

after Eisenstadt is found in the *Wiener Zeitung* of December 17, 1808, where it is announced that a Beethoven concert on December 22 at the Imperial and Royal Theater an der Wien is to include the Sixth Symphony, "Ah perfido," and two "hymns with a Latin text, composed in the style of church music with chorus and solos." These seem to have been the Gloria and Sanctus of the C Major Mass. Since the first edition, which appeared later, included the Kyrie with the Gloria as the first "hymn" and the Sanctus (with Benedictus) and Agnus Dei as the third "hymn," these sections may have been included in the concert. They were advertised as "hymns" because the church objected to the listing of specific liturgical titles in a public concert.

During 1808 and for a number of years afterward, Beethoven tried to get the Mass published by Breitkopf and Härtel in Leipzig. A score was finally printed only in October, 1812, and even then with no orchestral and vocal parts—an unusual procedure.[11] Beethoven's correspondence with the publishers throws an interesting light on his attitude toward the work and toward liturgical music in general. On June 8, 1808,[12] he asks them to consider the Fifth and Sixth Symphonies, the C Major Mass, and the Op. 69 cello sonata altogether for 700 gulden, along with his statement (cited above) about treating the Mass text in a different manner. Around July 8, he presses further:

> You must take the Mass, or else I can't give you the other works—for I pay attention not only to what is profitable but also to what brings honour and glory. You say that "there is no demand for church works." You are right if you are referring to works by composers of thoroughbass. But do have the Mass performed at a concert in Leipzig and see whether lovers of music will not immediately come forward desiring to possess it. Publish it by all means in a pianoforte arrangement with German words. Whatever you do with it, I guarantee its success.[13]

The topic of German words with the Latin text plays an important role in the correspondence. Dr. Christian Schreiber (a friend of Gottfried Härtel's) originally translated the Latin into German, but Beethoven was not wholly satisfied with the result. As late as January 16, 1811, he considered the translation of the Gloria "very suitable, but that of the Kyrie not

---

[11]Kinsky-Halm, pp. 237–42.

[12]Anderson no. 167. There is confusion as to whether Beethoven expected payment from the publisher for his Mass. Haydn was not paid for his because they were considered largely prestige items, meant for a special church occasion and not for a public concert. When Beethoven wrote about making a present of the Mass to Breitkopf and Härtel, it would seem that he had previously expected to be paid for it.

[13]Anderson no. 168.

so good." He went on to mention that several specific phrases were less than satisfactory and added:

> The general character of the Kyrie . . . is heartfelt resignation, deep sincerity of religious feeling, "Gott erbarme dich unser," yet without on that account being sad. Gentleness is the fundamental character of the whole work, and here the expression "Allgewaltiger" and so forth do not seem to convey the meaning of the whole work. Apart from "Eleison erbarme dich unser"—cheerfulness pervades this Mass. The Catholic goes to church on Sunday in his best clothes and in a joyful and festive mood. Besides the Kyrie Eleison is the introduction to the whole work. If such strong expressions were used here, few would be left for those portions where really strong expressions are required.[14]

Much later, in 1823, Benedict Scholz, Director of Music at Warmbrunn in Silesia, wrote a German translation of Op. 86 on his own initiative.[15] Beethoven was so pleased with it that he wanted Scholz to do the same for the *Missa solemnis*. But Scholz, unfortunately, died shortly thereafter, and the task was never accomplished. His translation of the Mass in C was quite free, certainly much less than literal.[16] Beethoven's insistence all those years on a German translation for a Latin text that must have been utterly familiar in a staunchly Catholic country seems odd. But he and the publishers undoubtedly had a wider distribution in mind, particularly in the Protestant North. While composing both the C Major Mass and the *Missa solemnis*, Beethoven was very particular about learning the exact meaning of the Latin text, and this surely meant resorting to German equivalents.

Just a week or two after his early July letter to Breitkopf and Härtel, Beethoven wrote again to the publishers from Heiligenstadt, presumably in response to their having balked at taking the Mass along with the symphonies and cello sonata for the price offered. He offered to make a present of it to them, even taking on the cost of copying it himself,

> . . . for I am absolutely convinced that once you have had it performed at your winter concerts in Leipzig, you will certainly provide it with a German text and publish it. Whatever its fate may be, it now belongs to you.
>
> The reasons why I particularly wanted to bind you and no one else to publish this Mass are 1) because notwithstanding the utterly frigid

---

[14]Anderson no. 294.

[15]Anderson, p. 1044, footnote.

[16]Anderson, p. 1193, footnote. See also Joseph Schmidt, "Die deutschen Texte zu Beethovens C-dur Messe," *Veröffentlichungen des Beethovenhauses in Bonn* (Bonn, 1928), V, 13–28.

attitude of our age to works of this kind, the Mass is especially close to my heart: and 2) because I thought that by means of your type-setting for printed notes you could produce it more easily than other German publishers who in general know nothing about scores.[17]

During 1809, the Mass was tied in by Beethoven with *Leonore-Fidelio* and *Christus am Ölberge* as a desirable package for Breitkopf and Härtel, but again nothing happened. By February 4, 1810, there seemed hope in that Beethoven talked about revising the organ part, which he said needed changes, and sending it to the publishers separately. He never did so, however.[18] Another uncertain item was the matter of the dedication. Beethoven evidently never seriously considered Prince Nikolaus, probably because of the Prince's reaction to the work at its premiere.[19] He wavered between Nicolaus Zmeskall and an unidentified lady, who may have been Bettina Brentano, and finally decided on Prince Kinsky. There was more uncertainty in 1811; but by the spring of 1812, Beethoven had received proofs of the Mass, so Breitkopf and Härtel had presumably decided finally to go ahead and print it.

When Beethoven sent back the corrected proofs to the publishers on July 17, 1812, his cover letter made some interesting comments about the music:

> At the beginning of the Gloria, I have altered C to ¢ time signature, thus altering the tempo; and that is the way the time was indicated at first. A bad performance at which the tempo was too fast induced me to do this. Well, as I had not seen the Mass for a long time, this point struck me at once and I saw that unfortunately a thing like that has to be left to chance—In the Sanctus a remark could be inserted somewhere stating that in the enharmonic variation the flats can be omitted and instead of them only sharps retained, that is to say: I could never hear this passage sung by our choirs as purely as it should be unless the organist quietly struck the chord of the seventh. It may be that you have better choirs at Leipzig—It would be a good thing at any rate to indicate somewhere that in this passage sharps could be used instead of flats, as indicated here (they would have to be added, of course, in the engraved copies exactly as they are here).[20]

Beethoven's remark about the tempo of the Gloria is self-explanatory;

---

[17]Anderson no. 169.

[18]The circumstances are summarized by Willy Hess in the *Revisionsbericht* for the Eulenberg edition of the Mass (London, 1964), pp. xvii–xviii.

[19]See letter of June 1, 1823 from Beethoven to Schindler (Anderson no. 1188).

[20]Anderson no. 375. Anderson reproduces (p. 379) the way Beethoven wanted this portion of the Sanctus to look.

but the request about the notation of the Sanctus helps to clear up an uncertainty that has persisted for years about measures 7–8 of the Sanctus.
Since the passage between measures 5 and 9 is unaccompanied, one can
see why Beethoven was concerned. But to have sharps instead of flats
looks very odd on paper:

Example 1. In writing to his publishers, Beethoven did not bother to put
in some of the sharps.

Even today, scores vary as to the way these measures are printed. For
instance, the Broude Bros. vocal score agrees with the first edition of
Breitkopf and Härtel in 1812, while the Eulenburg miniature score (ed.
Hess, 1964) uses flats.

Although Beethoven may not have been a practicing Catholic most of
his life, he was certainly brought up on the rites of the Church. Bonn was
Catholic, the seat of the elector of Cologne, and owed its allegiance to
Vienna. The court of the Electors Maximilian Friedrich (ruled 1761–84)
and Maximilian Franz (ruled 1784–1833), although influenced by ideas of
the Enlightenment, was at least nominally Catholic, and we know that
Beethoven in his early youth was assistant (1782) and then deputy court
organist (1784) at Bonn. He must thus have come to know liturgical music intimately and heard or performed many contemporary masses. That
he himself should compose one was therefore not a strange event. In Vienna as well, his lessons with Haydn, Schenk, Albrechtsberger, and För-
ster must have included some strict church music if his studies were
mainly counterpoint. They certainly included fugue writing.[21]

If there had to be a model for Beethoven in the C Major Mass, it was
obviously Haydn—and perhaps also Hummel[22] and Cherubini. Although considerable emphasis has been put on the differences between
the C Major Mass and its predecessors (one authority going so far as to
speak of "die für die damalige Zeit fast revolutionär anmutenden
Neuerungen, die er bereits in jener ersten Vertonung des Messetextes
durchführte" ["the innovations, which seem almost revolutionary for
that time, that he brought about already with this first setting of the Mass

[21]Alfred Mann, "Beethoven's Contrapuntal Studies with Haydn," *The Musical Quarterly*, LVI (1970), 711–26.
[22]Roger Fiske, *Beethoven's Missa Solemnis* (London, 1979), pp. 4–7.

text"]),[23] the fact remains that the essential structure of the work is traditional Haydn-Viennese, even though Prince Esterházy and others may have been surprised by the music.

There are the usual five large movements—Kyrie, Gloria, Credo, Sanctus, and Agnus Dei—if it is understood that the Sanctus includes the Benedictus text, which it should liturgically but which Haydn makes into a separate musical movement in all of his mature masses. In both Op. 86 and the *Missa solemnis*, Beethoven makes a similar musical separation between Sanctus and Benedictus, but does not indicate the separation in the score. The Benedictus of the *Missa solemnis* is preceded by a Praeludium, during which the bread and wine are presented.

The plan of the Op. 86 Kyrie is very similar to those of Haydn and others of the time, being, in a general sense, three sections according to the three parts of the text. This structure often bears a resemblance to sonata form, with little or no development or transition but with the "Christe eleison" in the dominant key; it is this way most of the time in Haydn, with or without new thematic ideas. Yet there is a definite return or "recapitulation" of the tonic with the second Kyrie. The only difference with Beethoven in the C Major Mass is that he goes to the mediant for the Christe—surely no great surprise, because it had been done often elsewhere in his music. Denis McCaldin feels that this wider range of tonality in Op. 86 (E major in the Kyrie; E♭ for "Et incarnatus est," A major for the Sanctus) was one of the reasons that the Esterházy court was perplexed by the Mass.[24] But Haydn, in the *Paukenmesse* (also basically in C major), had gone to A major for "Qui tollis," C minor for "Et incarnatus," and F major for the Sanctus. In the *Heiligmesse* (B♭), it was a B♭ minor and D♭ major for the Agnus Dei; and in the *Nelsonmesse* (D minor and D major), B♭ for "Qui tollis," G major for "Et incarnatus," B minor for part of "Et resurrexit," and G major for the Agnus Dei. Some of these keys may be more closely related to the main tonality of each mass than others; but surely the distinctions between Haydn and Beethoven in this respect are not that great.

In the Gloria, two Allegro sections surround a slower section in a dif-

---

[23]Willy Hess, "Beethovens Missa Solemnis," *Beethoven Studien* (Munich-Duisberg, 1972), p. 232. Also, Herman Kretschmar (*Führer durch den Konzertsaal*, II, Part I [Leipzig, 1888], p. 160) says: "Dass sich Beethoven mit dieser C-Dur Messe auf einen ganz andern Boden stellte, als der war, auf welchem die Messe seiner Zeit auch die Haydns und Mozarts, zu entstehen pflegten."

[24]McCaldin, *op. cit.*, pp. 387–410. Another objection apparently raised at the time was that the Mass did not contain a real fugue, which was the favorite art form of Prince Esterházy (see Schindler [1860], pp. 212–13). What a "real fugue" was supposed to be is difficult to say.

ferent key—all grouped according to text. The middle part starts with "Qui tollis," the last Allegro with "Quoniam"; the movement ends fugally with "Cum sancto spiritu in gloria Dei patris, amen," as was customary at the time. This is almost exactly the pattern followed by Haydn in his *Paukenmesse* and *Nelsonmesse*.

The Credo is also in three general sections, with the first, "Credo in unum Deum" (mostly C major), being Allegro con brio; the second, "Et incarnatus est," Adagio in E♭; and the third, "Et resurrexit tertia die," Allegro ma non troppo in C major. The movement ends Vivace with a fugue on "Et vitam venturi saeculi, amen." Haydn follows this pattern as well.

The Sanctus and Benedictus have their two main units, each ending with "Osanna in excelsis." Beethoven uses the same music (a fugato) for the repeat of the Osanna. The Sanctus is divided by text into "Sanctus dominus Deus Sabaoth" (Adagio) in A major and "Pleni sunt coeli" (Allegro) in D and A major. The Benedictus is a long, separate movement (Allegretto ma non troppo) in F major for solo quartet, chorus, and orchestra.

The responsory form of the Agnus Dei almost determines its structure: three calls to the Lamb of God, the first two ending with "miserere nobis," the last with "dona nobis pacem," which becomes a separate section. It was apparently the custom in the Viennese Mass for the first sections to be in a minor key and the last to end in the tonic major with a cheerful change to a brighter tempo (here, Allegro ma non troppo follows Poco Andante). Beethoven's return in the final measures to the music of the Kyrie, but now to the words "dona nobis pacem," has often been cited as an unusual touch of unity that he gives to the Mass. But again, the practice was fairly common; Haydn did so in one of his earliest masses (F major, c. 1750) and in the *Missa Sancti Nicolai* of 1772.

Having pointed out the similarities in general design between Haydn of the late masses and Beethoven in this first mass, one must immediately and firmly say that Haydn is Haydn and Beethoven is Beethoven. Their methods may be the same, but the musical texture is different. Perhaps this is why so many commentators have stressed, with exaggerated emphasis, the so-called pathbreaking quality of the C Major Mass.[25] It is Beethoven's individual musical language within a conventional frame-

[25]"Der Schritt von Haydns grossen Hochämtern zu Beethovens C-Dur-Messe ist grösser als der von dieser zu den Messen in As- und in Es-Dur von Schubert, die in vielem ohne diese Beethovensche Messe nicht denkbar sind." Elmar Seidel, "Die instrumentalbegleitete Kirchenmusik," in *Geschichte der katholischen Kirchenmusik*, ed. Karl Gustav Fellerer (Kassel, 1976), II, 237–52.

work that has struck their attention, and not the structure itself, which was rooted in the liturgy and in the past. But this point has not been made clear, perhaps because of the common danger of isolating a very great figure from his surroundings and contemporaries and forgetting what has preceded him.

What else did Beethoven learn from Haydn? The integrated treatment of solo voices with the chorus was certainly one attribute. These voices, regarded largely as a unit, sing mostly as a quartet rather than as a series of individual soloists performing an aria, as is the case in many of Mozart's masses. Another obvious trait was the thematic and motivic development that Haydn had already demonstrated in his London symphonies and masses. But while Beethoven's ideas were partly an extension of what Haydn had wrought, their far-reaching and individual quality belonged to Beethoven alone.

Beethoven must have seen how Haydn's contrapuntal and fugal writing were colored by symphonic thinking. The middle parts of Haydn's fugues may take on the character of a development, with the subject being fragmented. The final section often resembles a recapitulation, rather than maintaining a persistent contrapuntal texture (as was usually done earlier), and the fugue may end with a homophonic coda on "amen" or another single word.[26] Beethoven added to all this his own desire for more expressivity, paying greater attention to individual words and phrases, which had to be illustrated in the music by dynamic, harmonic, and orchestral means. He also demonstrated an innate humility and devotion that transcended the impersonal surface of portions of the liturgical text. Finally, his own mark of unity both within and between movements gave the work its true Beethoven stamp. A discussion of the work itself will show what is meant.[27]

*   *   *   *   *

The Mass is scored for solo quartet, chorus, full winds (two each of flutes, oboes, clarinets, and bassoons), two horns, two trumpets, timpani, strings, and organ. Beethoven struggled over the organ part and never completed it to his satisfaction. Nobody seems to know where the bass figures came from, since they do not exist in either the autogaph or the Eisenstadt copy.

Already in the Kyrie, Beethoven was determined to get to the heart of

[26]See Edward Olleson, "Church Music and Oratorio," *The New Oxford History of Music* (London, 1973), VII, 288–335 for a good summary of these points.

[27]References are to the Eulenburg miniature edition of the full score, ed. Willy Hess (London, 1964).

the opening prayer, with its terse Greek words. He expresses them musically in a quiet and devout manner, the Lord and Christ being mediators in this opening supplication for mercy. Yet the music is never stagnant. Between the autograph and the first edition, Beethoven had second thoughts about the exact tempo he wanted; his final wording, although almost superfluous and contradictory ("Andante con moto assai vivace quasi Allegretto ma non troppo"), at least shows his wish to achieve the proper pace. The opening "Kyrie eleison" flows up and down stepwise, the choral soprano and alto in thirds, the tenor and bass rooted in a C major foundation, and the strings in quiet eighth-note movement underlining the voices. The orchestra (with added winds) and the chorus reach a sudden forte climax, with a passing reference to E major, at the end of the phrase. After a few measures' interlude of mostly winds in thirds echoing the initial Kyrie phrase, the solo soprano, followed by the other soloists, sings the second thematic idea of the first group—a lyrical series of turns around steps of the scale, rising from C and tending always toward the mediant, which the chorus reinforces by its emphasis on V of iii (and III). Finally, at measure 37, E major is reached and stated firmly by all the solo, choral, and instrumental forces on "Christe eleison," initiating the second section of the movement.

Extension brings some variation of this phrase by the soloists, followed by typical Beethoven sforzandi and changing dynamics under the chorus. Measures 56-67 are a varied repeat of the ten preceding measures. Then the opening Kyrie is anticipated, first in the bassoons and then in the choral tenor and bass, doubled by violas. This serves as a retransition, with developmental touches of the "Christe" theme in the voices. Suddenly the climax comes on a double forte (measure 80), with the bass E of the previous measure having slid down to D, which becomes the fifth of V of C major—a striking, impressive, and characteristic Beethoven gesture. This brings back the opening and second Kyrie phrases in the tonic. As in a recapitulation, they remain there, despite some threats to stray tonally. A lovely coda rounds off the movement, establishing a mood of calm with a bit of the subdominant and with open octaves for the chorus, yet reminding us of the unease in asking for ultimate mercy by means of a sudden diminished chord and some fairly violent alternation of piano and forte. Final tranquility is attained with a serene choral octave on G, the orchestra establishing the tonic.

The opening of the Gloria is a song of praise and must illustrate a sense of triumph. So it is with this work, in which full orchestra and scalar strings give powerful impetus to a homophonic chorus in a rushing Allegro con brio. At measures 7–10 a motive is heard that Beethoven interweaves through all this opening section, in both voice and orchestra:

Example 2

It permeates the fabric in good symphonic style, appearing sometimes in the voices, sometimes in the orchestra, and even being developed in a continuous phrase on "glorificamus te." The transition from "glory to God on high" to "peace on earth to men of good will" (soft, low choral tessitura—a hushed effect) is brought about by first violins and cellos in a dainty, descending figure, which will also be used later to lead into "Gratias agimus." The scoring for "Et in terra pax" is a melting horn counterpoint, with pizzicato strings providing further contrasts. "Bonae voluntatis" alternates imitative entries for the chorus with unaccompanied block chords—first forte, then piano. A particularly striking effect (which many have noted) is the dynamic, tonal, and registral contrasts Beethoven creates for the chorus between "benedicimus te," "adoramus te," and "glorificamus te." The first statement is a forte V—I (C major) progression in high register; the second, a sudden, low, piano B♭ chord (♭VII); the third, a forte V⁶₅ in high position (see example 3). This is Beethoven with a vengeance, and may have been one of the passages that shocked the company in Eisenstadt.

Example 3

The "Gratias agimus" is introduced quasi-psalmodically by the solo tenor, with a string and wind countermelody that is related to the transition figure just heard. Tonally, the rest of the passage (solo and chorus) is V/IV like its predecessor, but it never resolves to F. "Deus omnipotens" is emphasized by an interruption of the countermelody by trumpet and timpani, evoking the Father Almighty. The same interruption occurs a few measures later with "Jesu Christe," but there is no trumpet and timpani this time—only broken string chords. A cadence on F major formally closes the section with the phrase "Filius patris," which was the conventional conclusion of this part of the Gloria.

The "Qui tollis" again enters the realm of entreaty and prayer. Beethoven changes to Andante mosso, 3/4 in F minor. The soloists are preponderant until the "Qui sedes." Syncopation in both the orchestral accompaniment and the choral response of "miserere nobis" gives a sense of supplication and hesitancy to the texture. The soloists join together a cappella on "suscipe deprecationem," stressing the verb "suscipe" by repeating it differently in each voice—tenor, bass, soprano, and alto—in succession. "Qui sedes" brings out the distinction between man and divinity by means of a forte and a full orchestral tutti in A♭, with a climax on "dexteram patris." Before the "miserere nobis" is finished, Beethoven recalls the Kyrie theme, first in the winds and then in the chorus, as if to link the two calls for mercy. The modulation to V/C major, in preparation for the last section, goes through a lovely and unexpected D^7 chord with pizzicato strings (measures 200–203) to lead us back.

The final section (Allegro ma non troppo, 4/4 in C major) has a ten-measure introduction before the chorus enters with "Quoniam," which reflects a broad, steadfast homage to the divinity. It is straightforward, rising C major, with more tonal fullness obtained by dividing the violas and cellos. In declamatory octaves, the chorus reiterates the majesty of the text and rises to its natural climax on "altissimus." Then Beethoven launches into the "Cum sancto spiritu" fugue that will conclude the Gloria. Besides the subject, the fugue has a strict countersubject. Riemann and Hess note the prevalence of the sixth scale degree (A, in C major) in the subject and link it to the opening Kyrie as well as other places in the Mass. But in the fugue, at least, the two answers to the main subject entries are tonal, and the accented E, which is analogous to the A of the opening subject, is heard as part of the C major triad.

Instead of continuing his contrapuntal track, Beethoven interrupts the fugue with a repetition of the "Quoniam" theme, this time in E minor with rapid string figuration. This is somewhat unusual, but the circle of fifths leads back to the C major area, and Beethoven resumes his fugal texture at measure 280, with a stretto effect as measures 297–314 proceed. Another dramatic stroke is introduced with a series of "amens" that travel around a flat circle of fifths; the bass roots descend by thirds to a G♭ chord, which resolves to V$^4_3$ of C by having the upper three voices rise and the bass drop, each by a half step:

Example 4

After this, the "Quoniam" returns with a dualism of thirds and sixths, leading to an "altissimus" again and then bits of the fugal subject. The coda (measures 342 ff.) is developmental, with orchestra, soloists, and chorus discoursing on fragments of the subject or calling forth the "amen" theme in dramatic piano and forte contrasts. It is a magnificent and telling conclusion to the movement.

Certain sections of the Credo are the most difficult texts in the Mass to compose, because they are fundamentally doctrinal in character and do not offer a ready musical framework. Moreover, the words are many. There is, however, the advantage of the narrative as it pertains to Christ's birth, passion, and death, giving a natural opportunity for individual word-painting and with it the drama of crucifixion and resurrection. In the beginning, Beethoven stresses the importance of belief by giving the one word "Credo" a dramatic rise in the first ten measures, from a low choral piano unison up to a thunderous shout. The word is repeated four times; accompanying it is a motivic figure that penetrates the whole first section (up to "Et incarnatus est") and is almost the orchestral equivalent of the verb, rooted around various triads:

Example 5

One God ("unum Deum") and the Father Almighty ("patrem omnipotentem") are represented by powerful choral affirmations with full orchestra, as is "factorem coeli et terrae," with its ascent to "coeli" and descent to "terrae." "Et invisibilium" has the same kind of contrast found in the Gloria, made here by a sudden reduction in the orchestration to nothing but pizzicato strings, with soft octaves for the chorus.

These choral octaves continue the ringing affirmation of belief in the text concerning the second part of the Trinity (the person of Jesus) with scattered but inclusive emphases on "ante omnia saecula," ending in a precipitous B♭ choral unison. This acts as a dominant leading to E♭, where a dramatic hush of tremolos and orchestral sforzandos illuminates "Deum de Deo" and "lumen de lumine." The successive but separate choral entries travel around the flat side of the tonality (F minor and A♭ in addition to E♭), but get back to high G octaves on "Deum verum de Deo vero." This wide-ranging tonal flow renders a mystical color to "genitum non factum" (unaccompanied) and "consubstantialem patri." The rhythm of "omnia" also thoroughly penetrates the choral texture, as if the idea of omnipotence cannot be asserted strongly enough. The section ends quietly, leading through C minor but concluding with V/♭III, which leads to the major change of tempo and key (Adagio in E♭) for Part II of the Credo ("Et incarnatus est").

At this juncture, the solo quartet assumes the lead, anticipated in a transitional passage by a clarinet on a sinking B♭⁷ triad that makes the listener draw breath and prepare for something new. The quartet acts both in male and female pairs and as a unit to give added expressivity to "and was made incarnate by the Holy Ghost from the Virgin Mary." In a declamatory fashion, the solo tenor announces the happy message of "et homo factus est." (This traditional procedure is also followed in the *Missa solemnis*.) But the following words, "Crucifixus etiam pro nobis," bring the chorus back abruptly, as if Christ's crucifixion has become the responsibility of all mankind. Here the scoring and texture change dramatically, as one would expect. An ominous, hammering rhythm in the violins and violas, with sharp syncopation and sforzandos in the winds, points up the jagged, dotted choral entries in B♭ minor and culminates in an extraordinary chromatic phrase on "sub Pontio Pilato," which is tossed aside contemptuously. But this is quickly succeeded by another change—leaps and chromatic slides for a description of "passus" ("suffered") with diminished sevenths in the orchestra and with the voices emitting cries of pain. The repetition of "et" before the calm of "sepultus est" (low pitch, with the basses on the very bottom of a sonorous E♭ chord) seems to have been a Viennese characteristic, holding up the music ("stuttering out," as McCaldin puts it)[28] before the final resolution.

An augmented sixth, bringing back G and C, quickly leads to Part III (Allegro ma non troppo) and "et resurrexit." The solo bass announces the Easter message, and the ascension and resurrection are taken upward by the chorus to a high A on "coelum." Rushing triplets in the strings move the music rapidly forward, with one significant interruption by horns, trumpets, and timpani for the Day of Judgment ("judicare"). The doctrinal statement of belief in the Holy Ghost and the Church which follows gives less musical opportunity, and Beethoven largely contents himself with clear choral and solo declamation and, in one place ("et unam sanctam catholicam et apostolicam ecclesiam"), some resemblance to a chant. "I look for the resurrection of the dead," however, gives forceful and telling recognition to both "resurrectionem" and "mortuorum," the latter sinking to a quiet low at the section's end.

The fugue on "Et vitam venturi saeculi, amen" has a straightforward, sturdy C major subject and countersubject for the choral entries, doubled by various strings and winds. Then Beethoven has a full, homophonic

---

[28]McCaldin, *op. cit.*, p. 397.

enunciation with the subject in the soprano and the other voices filling in the harmony, which veers toward V of A major. The solo alto gives out the subject in A; then the chorus takes over with imitative "amens" in rising thirds, which bear some resemblance to the upward sweep of the Kyrie theme. This is followed by a stretto of the subject in all choral voices and a series of "amens," ending in a fermata on a V^7/C chord. From here to the end is really a coda, with elements of the fugal subject in the solo voices. The chorus at first punctuates with staccato "amens" and then takes over entirely in a joyous series of the same to conclude the Credo. This final section is a splendid blend of counterpoint and symphonic development that masterfully unites the older tradition and the sonata style, making them fit beautifully together with no awkward joins.

The Sanctus (Adagio) begins with a delicate orchestral introduction of winds, supported by violas and cellos, in A major. (This movement, like the Christe, stands in a third relationship to the tonal center—this time, the submediant.) The chorus, a cappella, then has the famous enharmonic passage mentioned by Beethoven in his July 17, 1812 letter to Breitkopf and Härtel (see pages 204-5). This beautiful bit of writing is followed by a dramatic four-measure contrast in orchestral texture, with timpani, cellos, and double bass pushing out a violent thirty-second note triplet rhythm, the first violins sweeping upward and downward in arpeggios, and the winds, horns, second violins, violas, and chorus filling in. But a half step upward from A to B♭ brings back the unaccompanied chorus, which almost immediately resolves back down to A as V of D major. The Pleni is a brief but forceful and imitative Allegro, contrasting "coeli" at the top of the phrase with "terra" at the lower end. The section ends with a fugato on "Osanna in excelsis," which, with A becoming the third of F major, leads into the Benedictus. The repeat of the Osanna at the end of the movement is exact.

This Sanctus has been criticized as being too abrupt and brief; with its violently contrasting passages within a few measures of one another, it supposedly lacks breathing space. But performed properly, it gains stature, and the contrasts find their own niche, acting their parts with weight and solidity.

It is conceivable that the Benedictus is guilty of the opposite sin—excessive length in relation to the rest of the Mass. But it retains its own validity by drawing on the solo voices and achieving an organic combination of quartet, chorus, and orchestra that is one of the high points of the Mass. The spirit is that of devotion: "Blessed is he who cometh in the name of the Lord." The two large parts of the piece each begin with unaccompanied quartet, homophonically singing what is almost a hymn.

Winding throughout the Benedictus in the orchestra is also another motive that appears in many different guises:

Example 6

Although the quartet assumes a major role in this section, echoes from
the chorus give a double-choir effect of eight parts as the two intermingle
and then separate from time to time. The orchestral fabric has an independent quality of its own, developing the motivic figure yet still supporting the voices. There are two deceptive cadences which avoid a close
on C at the end of the first part of the Benedictus; it is finally reached at
measure 90, with the chorus quietly intoning "Benedictus" in octaves.
The second part goes toward the subdominant (B♭), but does not stay
there long. This passage is extended in double-choir and echo fashion,
which, although it is repetitive, never seems superfluous. Two solo entries on "qui venit in nomine domini," one by the alto at measure 67 and
the other by the tenor at measure 121, must be handled with care by the
conductor and not rushed; for they are individual statements, almost operatic in their effect, and stand out from the general ensemble. After a
dominant seventh fermata, the movement closes with a quiet coda, the
height of simplicity and hushed reverence—chorus entirely in octaves,
orchestra weaving the string motive. The fall from F down to E (V⁷/A)
brings back the Osanna and a return to the original key.

The Agnus Dei (Poco andante in C minor) has the orchestra initially
building up the tonality in repeated eighth notes (12/8 meter), but soon
crying out the prayer for mercy to the Lamb of God together with the
chorus on a diminished chord. "Qui tollis peccata mundi" contains continuous choral appoggiaturas; these, together with the "miserere nobis,"
create pleading and uncertainty, which the orchestra imitates. The clarinet again has an important role in two remarkable passages: one in measures 18–19, unaccompanied; the other, a transition to the "dona nobis
pacem" at the end of the section (measures 36–39), with the chorus softly
intoning "dona" in anticipation. The division between the first two appeals to the Lamb of God is made by a temporary stop on G minor (v/C
minor) at measure 22. The "granting of peace" is then taken up by quartet, chorus, and orchestra in C major, Allegro ma non troppo, for the
final part of the Mass.

Beethoven avoids any lull by placing syncopated emphases on "pacem" and making a sudden, stormy return to "Agnus Dei" shortly thereafter—an insertion which may not be liturgically correct (although he does the same thing in the *Missa solemnis*) but which introduces an exciting number of orchestral sforzandos before the peace of the ending. The chorus adds to the unease by darkly muttering "miserere nobis" in their lowest register in thirds and even seconds, accompanied by a few spotty orchestral notes. Soloists, chorus, and orchestra then gather momentum as they trade back and forth various parts of the "dona nobis pacem" that were heard at the outset of the Allegro. Suddenly, in the midst of this surge, Beethoven turns again to E major on "pacem" (measures 124–27), as if to remind us once more of the unified prayer for mercy begun in the Kyrie. There is a touch of it also in measures 141–44. The last seventeen measures revert magically to Andante con moto, tempo del Kyrie, as Beethoven brings the opening music of the Kyrie to the text of "dona nobis pacem"—a lovely, calming, concluding effect that rounds out the circle and brings peace.

This Mass, then, is mature, percipient Beethoven, bringing to bear on one of Christianity's most familiar texts the full force of his personality and creative genius. It is spiritually religious and not dogmatic or routine. It breathes a spirit of prayer and mystical being that comes from the inner Beethoven. Whereas it really belongs in a church for a celebration of the Mass, it also reaches outside to humanity at large.

Reconstructing Riddles: The Sources for Beethoven's *Missa Solemnis*

Robert Winter

On the fifth of June, 1822, as part of the tangled web of shadowy dealings concerning the disposition of his *Missa solemnis,* Beethoven wrote to the music publisher Carl Friedrich Peters in Leipzig: "Das *grösste* Werk [emphasis Beethoven's], welches ich bisher geschrieben, ist eine grosse Messe mit Chören und vier obligaten Singstimmen und grossem Orchester" ["The greatest work which I have composed thus far is a grand Mass with choruses, four obbligato voices, and a large orchestra"].[1] This is the sole recorded instance in the composer's lengthy career where he invoked the superlative in offering a direct evaluation of one of his own works. The nearest rival to this direct testimony is Karl Holz's second-hand report that, of the first four late quartets, Beethoven considered the one in C♯ minor (Op. 131) to be his "greatest."[2] It is true that Beethoven's declaration concerning the Mass was part of a hard sell in which he boasted to Peters that he had been offered "100 full weight Louis d'or" for the work—a questionable claim. It is also possible that Peters was only one of several publishers to fall into the trap of advancing Beethoven money against a work he was never to deliver. It might also be argued that "grösste" applied at least in part to the sheer magnitude of the performing forces required for the Mass, not to mention its inordinate length. And a recent reviewer has suggested that Beethoven's characterization may have been prompted by Nägeli's announcement in 1818 of the publication of Bach's B Minor Mass, described by the publisher as the "grösstes musikalisches Kunstwerk aller Zeiten und Völker" ["the greatest musical work of art for all times and all people"].[3] But even after these

---

[1] Emerich Kastner, ed., *Ludwig van Beethovens sämtliche Briefe,* rev. Julius Kapp (Leipzig, 1923), letter no. 1019; Anderson no. 1079.

[2] Quoted in Thayer-Forbes, p. 982.

[3] See the review by Marianne Helms of Maynard Solomon's *Beethoven* in *Beethoven-Jahrbuch,* Jhg. 1978/81, p. 387.

several reservations have been dutifully noted, the claim advanced by Beethoven to Peters stands out as a singular one within a masterpiece-riddled production that provided abundant opportunities for similar assertions.

It is hence all the more surprising that a work evaluated so highly by its composer (a view shared at least in part by posterity), and upon which he labored so mightily, has received such scant attention in the scholarly literature, whether from Beethoven scholars or from the chroniclers of sacred music. Apart from Theodor Adorno's idiosyncratic appreciation in *Prisma der gegenwärtigen Musik*,[4] only Warren Kirkendale's fresh look at the liturgical sources more than a decade ago has pushed beyond the nineteenth century's comprehension of this epic work.[5] To be sure, Martin Cooper's *Beethoven: The Last Decade* devotes considerable space to the Mass,[6] but Cooper's often penetrating insights are limited by his dependence on outdated scholarship. Indeed, it is no exaggeration to say that Beethoven's settings of the folksongs supplied by George Thomson have received as much attention from the scholarly community as has the *Missa solemnis*.

If there is a valid reason for this neglect beyond the enormous complexities of the finished work, then it surely lies within the even greater complexities of the primary sources for the Mass. It is to a description and preliminary assessment of these sources that the present study is dedicated. Given Gustav Nottebohm's relentless tracking of the sketches for even minor works of Beethoven, his modest nine-page article in *Zweite Beethoveniana* on "Skizzen zur zweiten Messe" is laconic even by Nottebohmian standards.[7] As his opening makes clear, Nottebohm was not deceived as to the state of preservation of the sources:

> Skizzen zur zweiten Messe sind vollständig nicht vorhanden, und die vorhandenen stehen theils in einigen Skizzenheften, theils auf einer ziemlich bedeutenden Anzahl meistens nicht zusammen gehörenden Blätter. Es wurde zu Geschichte des Werkes wenig gewonnen sein, wollte man die Arbeit, so weit sie vorliegt und so weit es geschehen kann, auf Schritt und Tritt folgen.[8]

> [The sketches for the second Mass are not complete, and those that sur-

---

[4]Theodor Adorno, "Verfremdetes Hauptwerk: zur Missa solemnis" in J. E. Berendt and J. Uhde, eds., *Prisma der gegenwärtigen Musik* (Heidelberg, 1959).

[5]Warren Kirkendale, "New Roads to Old Ideas in Beethoven's Missa Solemnis," *The Musical Quarterly*, LVI (1970), 665–701.

[6]Martin Cooper, *Beethoven: The Last Decade* (London, 1970), especially pp. 221–75.

[7]N II, pp. 148–56.

[8]N II, p. 148.

vive are found partly in a few sketchbooks, partly on a rather large number of separate and unrelated leaves. It would add little to the history of the piece if one wished to follow the work, to the extent that it survives and to the extent that this is possible, step by step.]

This is not the place to address the broader issues raised by studies of the creative/compositional process, formulated in musical terms most recently by Douglas Johnson and prompting a host of direct and indirect replies.[9] But if we regard "sketch biography" as a legitimate, open-ended enterprise, then it is clear that today we are in a vastly better position to improve upon Nottebohm's gloomy assessment of a century ago.

The great majority of Nottebohm's examples are drawn from three successively used sketchbooks for the years 1819–22: Artaria 195, 197, and 201, all three now in the Berlin SPK. These standard-format volumes[10] were of the type that Beethoven kept on his work desk at home. Consequently, most—though by no means all—of their entries are in ink. The "ziemlich bedeutenden Anzahl meistens nicht zusammengehörenden Blätter" cited by Nottebohm refers primarily to the sketch complex known today as Artaria 180 + 200, a heterogeneous collection of pocket and standard-format leaves encompassing all portions of the Mass except the Kyrie. Because it, too, was owned by Artaria, Nottebohm became familiar enough with the autograph (Aut. 1 and Artaria 202 in the SPK)[11] to recognize that in many places, it preserved a version quite different from that in both the handsome copy presented to the Archduke on March 19, 1823 and that published in printed form by Schott just after Beethoven's death.

The chain of sources available to Nottebohm through the good graces of August Artaria was full of missing links. Perhaps the most important of these, a major document known today as the Wittgenstein Sketch-

---

[9]Douglas Johnson, "Beethoven Scholars and Beethoven's Sketches," *19th-Century Music*, Vol. II, no. 1 (1978), pp. 3–17. Two responses and Johnson's rejoinder appear in Vol. II, no. 3. (1979), pp. 270–79. See also the Introduction (pp. xxi-xxiv) to Robert Winter, *Compositional Origins of Beethoven's Opus 131* (Ann Arbor, 1982).

[10]The terminology employed here is adopted from my study of Op. 131, cited above. Many of the sources to be discussed are treated in greater bibliographic detail in Douglas Johnson, Alan Tyson, and Robert Winter, *The Beethoven Sketchbooks: History and Reconstruction*, to be published by the University of California Press in 1984.

[11]Autograph 1 preserves the Kyrie and Artaria 202 the Credo, Sanctus, and Agnus Dei of the Mass. The Kyrie was separated from the remainder of the work when Artaria sold it to the collector Georg Pölchau in the fall of 1828. Neither the manner in which the Gloria became separated nor its present whereabouts are known. The Kyrie was published in 1965 in a sumptuously faithful facsimile by the Verlag Hans Schneider, and forms the basis for Joel Lester's "Revisions in the Autograph of the Missa Solemnis Kyrie," *Journal of the American Musicological Society*, XXIII (1970), 420–38.

book,[12] had escaped Domenico Artaria's grasp at the *Nachlass* auction. It passed through the hands of no fewer than four different owners in the first five-and-a-half years after Beethoven's death, including the youthful Felix Mendelssohn. Work in this book—the earliest preserved in standard format for the Mass—directly preceded that in Artaria 195 and provides a host of rich insights into its genesis. Scarcely less important are a series of ten pocket sketchbooks (several preserved only in fragmentary form) that were filled during Beethoven's well-documented walks through the Viennese countryside. Three of the fragments of sewn pocket books are preserved largely or in their entirety in Artaria 180 + 200, a circumstance of which Nottebohm may or may not have been aware.

In addition to those pocket leaves whose appearance suggests original inclusion in a sewn booklet, there are twenty other groups—fifteen of which are found within Artaria 180 + 200 itself—ranging in size from a quarter sheet to a full sheet that also contain sketches for the Mass. A good number of these closely associated leaves are found adjacent to each other (though rarely in the correct internal order) within Artaria 180 + 200; they may have remained in this configuration after usage by Beethoven in spite of their unstitched makeup, or their present contiguousness may reflect a preliminary ordering by Nottebohm. At all events, four groups of pocket bifolia, each derived from its own specific sheet, appear separated within the manuscript as it is presently ordered. Based on contents and watermark distribution, they may be reconstructed, at least conceptually.[13] Establishing the chronology, both relative and absolute, of these bundles is an exasperatingly complex task at best, one that will ultimately require exhaustive transcriptions of all the relevant material. And although it greatly complicates the tracing of the sequence of compositional events, any attempt to unravel these drafts must proceed from the assumption of parallel and near simultaneous usage of both pocket and standard formats.

In addition to this battery of sketches and the accompanying autograph, two other types of primary evidence retain particular importance for the evolution of the Mass. We have already mentioned the copy presented to the Archduke; there were also another dozen copies prepared under Beethoven's supervision. Ten of these were dispatched to the aris-

---

[12]*Beethoven. Ein Skizzenbuch zu den Diabelli-Variationen und zur Missa Solemnis.* Übertragung von Joseph Schmidt-Görg (Bonn, 1968 [Facsimile] and 1972 [Transcription]). See my review in *Journal of the American Musicological Society,* XXVIII (1975), 135–38.

[13]A brief listing and description of the unstitched pocket sources for the Mass can be found in Appendix A.

tocratic subscribers recruited by the composer at the hefty fee of fifty ducats each, including the Russian Czar, the King of Prussia, and the King of France. An eleventh copy, largely in the hand of the scribe identified by Alan Tyson as Copyist B, is preserved in three bound volumes in the Vienna GdM;[14] its original usage is not known. The last complete copy is the *Stichvorlage* sent to Schott in January of 1825, written, as Beethoven complained, "bei einem Kopisten, der kaum versteht, was er schreibt" ["by a copyist who scarcely understands what he writes"].[15] Finally, a copy of the Kyrie and Gloria was sent in April, 1825 to Ferdinand Ries in Bonn; it is found today in the Beethovenhaus.[16]

It is not difficult to see that a reliable scholarly edition of the Mass would require a collation of a representative share of these sources, including at least the autograph and several of the revised copies. It is thus astonishing that the most reliable edition to date, that prepared for Eulenburg by Willy Hess, drew upon only the autograph, the copy preserved today in the Sächsischen Landesbibliothek in Dresden, and the textually almost worthless first edition. Available for easy consultation by any scholar today are the *Stichvorlage,* still held by Schott in Mainz; the copy presented to the Archduke and the one prepared by Copyist B, both in the GdM; and the sumptuous volumes in the Bibliothèque Nationale presented to Louis XV of France, one of the royal subscribers.[17] If there is one work, then, that justifies the inordinate expense of a new *Gesamtausgabe,* it is surely the *Missa solemnis.*

Finally, in addition to the better-known correspondence involving the Mass, no history of its evolution is complete without a thorough combing of the conversation books. In spite of the publication, in 1972 and 1976, of the relevant volumes for the years covering the composition of this work,[18] no study has made sustained use of them. It is true that the lack of a *Werkverzeichnis* in the first volume complicates the task, but even at best no such index would merit our unconditional trust; many entries referring to the Mass would be irrelevant, and other important references that are made only allusively would go undetected by the indexer. More problematic testimony is provided by other accounts also claiming to be firsthand, most notably those in the various editions of Anton Schindler's *Biographie von Ludwig van Beethoven.*

[14]Catalogued as A 21.

[15]Kastner-Kapp letter no. 1271; Anderson no. 1346.

[16]Catalogued most recently as SBH 738 (formerly BH 88), in SBH.

[17]Catalogued as L. 1121.

[18]*Ludwig van Beethovens Konversationshefte,* ed. Karl-Heinz Köhler and Grita Herre, with the collaboration of Günter Brosche. Band I (1972) includes ten volumes covering the period from February, 1818 to March, 1820. Band II (1976) includes twelve volumes covering the period from April, 1820 to February, 1823.

In pursuing answers to the most basic questions concerning the evolution of this mammoth project, any or all of the sources outlined above may come into play. The seemingly simple question of when and how work commenced on the Mass provides a perfect illustration of their complex interrelationships. We may never establish with certainty the mix of external stimuli and internal urges that prompted the composition of the *Missa solemnis*. What is known is that Beethoven's patron and pupil, Archduke Rudolph, was elected a cardinal on the 24th of April, 1819; less than two months later, on June 4, he was elevated to Archbishop of Olmütz. Until now, the earliest direct reference to this event by Beethoven has been thought to be the oft-cited congratulatory letter to the Archduke, written from Mödling shortly after Rudolph's nomination as Archbishop. After proffering his best wishes and serving up a series of excuses for not having paid a visit to his prize pupil recently, Beethoven continues:

> The day on which a High Mass composed by me will be performed during the ceremonies solemnized for Your Imperial Highness will be the most glorious day of my life; and God will enlighten me so that my poor talents may contribute to the glorification of that solemn day.[19]

Although the intention is clear enough, Beethoven is not explicit about whether he has or has not begun the composition of a mass.

For almost a century and a half, it was believed that the closest direct witness to the events of this period was Anton Felix Schindler. He had moved to Vienna in 1813 to study law, and was said to have met Beethoven—who was reportedly impressed by Schindler's radical student politics—the following year. Although Schindler did not claim to have become Beethoven's constant companion until about 1820, he speaks in his *Biographie* as if he were close to the composer even earlier. In the familiar excerpt from the third edition, Schindler wrote that the Archduke's appointment was "bereits um die Mitte des Jahres 1818 eine bekannte Tatsache. . . . Im Spätherbst von 1818 sah ich diese Partitur [for the Mass] beginnen, nachdem soeben die Riesensonate in B-dur, Op. 106, beendigt war" ["already a known fact around the middle of 1818. . . . In the late fall of 1818 I saw him begin work on this score, just after the gigantic sonata in B♭, Op. 106, had been completed"].[20] In recent years, however, the veracity of Schindler's accounts has come under increasing suspicion, based upon the discovery that many of his own en-

---

[19]Anderson no. 948 (not in Kastner-Kapp). Although context reveals the letter to have been written from Mödling, it is itself undated.
[20]Schindler (1860), I, 269.

tries within the conversation books were added after the fact.[21] Indeed, the earliest verifiable written communication from Beethoven to Schindler dates from the fall of 1822, and it seems likely that close contact between the two dates only from this period.

This circumstance may go a long way toward explaining Schindler's alternative account of the genesis of the Mass in the seldom-cited first edition of his *Biographie;* as it is mentioned only briefly by Thayer, it merits quotation at some length here:

> Die Ernennung seines durchlauchtigsten Schulers . . . den er bis dahin zu einer bedeutenden Stufe der Ausbildung erhoben, und welcher der Einzige seiner Schüler war, den Beethoven gleichzeitig in der Harmonielehre unterrichtet hatte, die Ernennung dieses kunstreichen Prinzen zum Erzbischof von Olmütz brachte unsern Meister wieder jenem Zweig der Tonkunst zuruck, welcher der erhabenste und auch schwierigste ist, zu dem er sich neben der Sinphonie am meisten hingezogen fühlte, wie er dies oft betheurte.
>
> Er fasste nahmlich den Entschluss, zur Installation des Erzherzogs in sein Erzbisthum, die auf den 9. März 1820 festgesetzt war, eine grosse Messe zu schreiben. Er begann an diesem neuen Werke im Winter von 1818 auf 19 zu arbeiten, dessen erster Satz aber gleich in so breiten Dimensionen (gegen den ursprunglichen Plan des Autors) sich zu bewegen anfing, dass diese Bahn mit gewohnter Consequenz verfolgt, es gar nicht abzusehen war, in welcher Zeit diese Werk vollendet werden könne.[22]
>
> [The naming of his most prominent pupil . . . whom he had previously schooled to a high level, and who at the same time was Beethoven's only student in composition, the naming of this artistic prince as Archbishop of Olmütz brought our master back to that branch of composition which is the most noble and also the most difficult, and to which, along with the symphony, he felt most drawn, a view he frequently reiterated. He therefore resolved, for the installation of the Archduke as Archbishop, which was set for the 9th of March, 1820, to write a grand mass. In the winter of 1818/19 he began work on this composition, whose first movement immediately began to assume such

---

[21]The first to draw attention to the existence of these forgeries was Peter Stadlen (see his brief contribution in *Österreichische Musikzeitung,* XXXII [1977], 246 ff.); without acknowledging their debt to Stadlen, a considerably more comprehensive picture was assembled by Dagmar Beck and Grita Herre, first with "Einige Zweifel an der Überlieferung der Konversationshefte," *Bericht über den Internationalen Beethoven-Kongress Berlin 1977* (Leipzig, 1978), pp. 257–68 (discussion and illustrations on pp. 268–74); and then with "Anton Schindlers fingierte Eintragungen in den Konversationsheften" in Harry Goldschmidt, ed., *Zu Beethoven-Aufsätze und Annotationen* (Berlin, 1979), pp. 11–89.

[22]Schindler (1840), pp. 112–13.

vast proportions (as opposed to the author's original plan) that the usual result ensued, whereby it proved impossible to say what time frame might be required for the work's completion.]

In this rendering there is no mention at all of the Archduke's pending appointment having been "a known fact around the middle of 1818." Beethoven's intention to compose a "grand mass" for the installation service is registered, but the commencement of work falls in the "winter of 1818/19," more consistent (as Thayer observed)[23] with a superficial description of the contents of the Wittgenstein Sketchbook published by Max Unger in 1937.[24] Given the now-known likelihood that Schindler was not in very close touch with Beethoven during this period, and given the internal contradictions within Schindler's own accounts, we are better off today looking elsewhere for evidence about the genesis of the work.

Fortunately, several pieces of evidence that have not been considered previously do serve to establish the early chronology of the Mass with more certainty. The first is an entry by Beethoven in a conversation book. Aside from a small pocket booklet datable to February and March of 1818, the earliest preserved example of this species (necessitated by the composer's clinical deafness from 1818 on) is a sizable volume of more than a hundred leaves whose contents can be dated with considerable accuracy.[25] In an entry on folio 10[r] that must fall in the very first days of April, 1819, Beethoven writes: "preludiren des/Kyrie vom organisten/stark u. abnehmend/bis vor dem Kyrie/piano . . ." ["prelude to the/Kyrie by the organist/loud and then dropping out/until before the Kyrie/piano"].[26] This thought appears among a series of notices—primarily about books—that Beethoven copied periodically from the Viennese newspapers, and constitutes one of the typical musical memoranda to himself that dot the conversation books. The significance of the note is considerable, for it describes exactly what happens in the finished work. The organist undergirds the opening forte tutti, and is then specifically directed by Beethoven to drop out while the remainder of the introduction continues piano until the entry of the chorus. There seems, then, little reason to doubt that by the beginning of April Beethoven was beginning to occupy

[23]Thayer-Forbes, p. 720.

[24]Max Unger, "Die Beethoven-Handschriften der Familie W. in Wien," *Neues Beethoven-Jahrbuch*, VII (1937), pp. 167–68.

[25]See *Beethovens Konversationshefte*, Band I, p. 37.

[26]*Beethovens Konversationshefte*, Band I, p. 42 [fol. 10[r]]. Cooper cites this same passage from the Schünemann edition, but translates it incorrectly as "Preludium of the Kyrie to be played loud by the organist and then decrescendo until before the piano [before the] Kyrie." This leads him to connect it with mm. 18–20 of the finished score, where the organ is in fact silent.

his thoughts with the composition of a mass, and almost surely the one we know. On the other hand, it seems unlikely that very much work could have preceded an entry such as this.

In an equally intriguing entry of three pages later, a representative of the Archduke reports:

> Gestern früh um 5. Uhr/hat Sr K [aiserliche] H. [oheit] einen Anfall/von seiner Gewöhnlichen/Krankheit bekoñen, und/heute befinden Sie Sich/schon etwas besser. / Ich werde es Ihnen/zu wiessen machen wenn/Sie Komen können und Morgen werde ich/es Sr Hoheit sagen/ dass Sie heute hier/waren.[27]

> [Yesterday morning at 5 A.M. His Royal Highness suffered an attack of his usual illness, and today he is already feeling somewhat better. I will let you know when you may come, and tomorrow I will inform him that you were here today.]

What was the purpose of Beethoven's visit? Is it inconceivable that he had not only just begun work on the Mass, but was seeking to share his plan with its presumed dedicatee, only to be stymied by one of the Archduke's periodic attacks of epilepsy? Indeed, the letter from the summer does not mention the Mass as if it were the first time the Archduke had heard of it; if such were the case Beethoven would very likely have assigned the idea a more prominent position within the letter. Even though Rudolph's election to the cardinalate was not to take place formally until the latter part of the month, and even though his nomination as Archbishop followed yet another six weeks later, it seems probable that such a sequence of moves by an institution as conservative and tradition-bound as the Catholic church would have been plotted well in advance. Beethoven was certainly close enough to the Archduke's inner circle to have been apprised of these developments. In allowing himself about a year to complete the planned project, the composer doubtless believed he could finish the Mass before the installation ceremonies on March 9, 1820. His underestimating by more than 250% has been widely publicized; yet it represents only a somewhat more dramatic example in a lifetime of rich fantasy about projected completion dates.

A closer look at the primary musical sources for the Mass both confirms the circumstantial evidence in the conversation book concerning chronology and illustrates the unusual relationships in the Kyrie between sketch and autograph. In a thoughtful and thorough study, Joel Lester pointed up the pivotal importance assigned in the Kyrie autograph to the "cue staff."[28] It was Lewis Lockwood who, in one of the

---

[27]*Beethovens Konversationshefte*, Band I, p.42 [fol. 11^v].
[28]Full citation in note 6; see especially pp. 427 ff.

seminal essays launching the new wave of Beethoven studies, first pointed up the composer's idiosyncratic reliance on this technique, in which a principal voice underneath a larger score (either a chamber or an orchestral work) provides the thread of continuity that is then fleshed out in the individual parts above.[29] Lockwood's exploration of the sketches for what would have been Beethoven's Sixth Piano Concerto led him to view the score sketch (DSB, Artaria 184) as a complex, nonlinear link between one-line continuity drafts and a finished score.[30] I have found equally dramatic examples of the cue staff among the plentiful score sketches for the late string quartets.[31]

In speculating about the relationship between the material on the cue staff in Autograph 1 and sketches outside of the autograph, Lester suggests at four different points that work encompassing stages both before the cue staff and between the cue staff and the final version was carried out in a separate sketchbook. For example: "Possibly the original cue staff was copied rapidly at one time from a sketchbook source, which accounts for its continuous appearance over many pages."[32] Or: "Probably the earlier cue staff version was crossed out and then Beethoven returned to a sketchbook to work out what is now [in the autograph]."[33] The sketch sources themselves suggest an interpretation that is somewhat different.

In his account of the sketches for the Mass in the Wittgenstein Sketchbook, Max Unger noted that "mit diesem Bande tauchen nicht nur die frühesten Entwürfe zu den Diabelli-Variationen auf, sondern auch die ersten zum Kyrie der zweiten Messe. . . . Sie sind aber von der gedruckten Gestalt sehr weit entfernt" ["in this volume surface not only the earliest sketches for the Diabelli Variations, but also the first for the Kyrie of the second Mass. . . . They are, however, very far removed from the printed version"].[34] But these sketches reveal a great deal more than Unger's scanty description suggests. First, there is the most obvious and puzzling feature—their scarcity. Work on the Kyrie consumes less than two dozen fragmentary lines on four pages: folios 9^v, 10^r, 11^r, and 43^r (the last of these deserves special consideration later). Even granted the considerably larger size and complexity of the Gloria, the almost forty pages

---

[29]Lewis Lockwood, "On Beethoven's Sketches and Autographs: Some Problems of Definition and Interpretation," *Acta Musicologica*, XLII (1970), 32–47 (see especially pp. 44–47).

[30]Lewis Lockwood, "Beethoven's Unfinished Piano Concerto of 1815: Sources and Problems," *The Musical Quarterly*, LVI (1970), 624–46.

[31]See Winter, *Compositional Origins of Beethoven's Op.131*, especially Chapters 7 and 8.

[32]Lester, *op. cit.*, p. 433.

[33]*Ibid.*, p. 432.

[34]Max Unger, *op. cit.*, pp. 161, 168.

of sketches that it receives are by comparison far more extensive than those for the Kyrie.

It may seem tempting, then, to suggest that the majority of Kyrie sketches have been lost. But scrutiny of the sketches themselves does not support such an interpretation. On folio 9ᵛ, their mere decipherment is made more difficult by Beethoven's use of three imperfect quills, compounded by Schindler's clumsy reinforcement of fainter passages. Schmidt-Görg's overly literal or incomplete transcriptions (how can one decipher a line without making a decision as to what clef it is in?) must be modified substantially, both for internal consistency and for the relationships between the sketches and the autograph to emerge. Many of the entries on folio 9ᵛ-11ʳ were doubtless made before the autograph was begun. Although Schmidt-Görg assigns the brief sketch on the second half of staff 1 to the Kyrie, both its triple meter and phrase structure blend more naturally into the landscape of the Diabelli Variations:

Example 1. Wittgenstein, folio 9ᵛ, st. 1 right

The first unambiguously texted entry is found three staffs later. Insofar as its original form can be deciphered, it seems to represent an early stab at the basic declamation of "Kyrie" (cf. measures 21 ff.):

Example 2. Wittgenstein, folio 9ᵛ, st. 4-5

The tentativeness and discontinuity of the draft (even more pronounced in the original) mark it as the kind of sketch one would expect to find during the initial stages of composition. In spite of a family resemblance to the finished version, this is doubtless what Unger meant by "sehr weit entfernt."

A little farther down on the same page, however, a two-staff entry that Unger failed to notice relates directly to the Kyrie as we know it:

Example 3. Wittgenstein, folio 9ᵛ, st. 10/11 middle

As the only explicit instrumental directive among these sketches, the oboe line is easily associated with measures 49-53 of the finished work. Indeed, it is surely no accident that these very bars proved a stumbling block in the autograph itself. The passage in question is one that had grown out of the germinal idea in bars 4-7, appearing in more elaborate, fleshed-out form in measures 12-17, and again as the scaffolding for "eleison" in measures 33-37. At its fourth appearance, as example 4a shows, Beethoven's initial instinct was to begin a repeat similar to that in measures 13 ff., with the first violin carrying the embellishment:

Example 4(a). Autograph 1, folio 5ᵛ, mm. 48-49

In the next stage he rearranged both parts, assigning a more simplified role to the violin and setting up the primacy of the oboe line:

Example 4(b). Second layer

What follows in the oboe part includes portions of at least six different versions of measures 49-53 (examples 4c-4h). The internal ordering is speculative at some points, although the succession from cue staff to main score in the unused bars, and then from cue staff to main score in the final version, offers the virtue of simplicity:

Example 4(c). Autograph 1, folios 5ᵛ-6ʳ, mm. 49 ff.; cue staff under unused bars

Example 4(d). Unused bars, first layer

Example 4(e). Unused bars, second layer

Example 4(f). Cue staff under final version

Example 4(g). Final version, first layer

Example 4(h). Final version, second layer

It is very likely that the pencil used for measure 50 of example 4c (including the tie) and that used for the last three quarter notes in the revision of measure 51 in example 4f were made on the same pass through the cue staff.

The crucial question might appear to be how folio 9 in Wittgenstein (example 3) relates to the parallel sketches and revisions within the autograph itself. Since the tie across each barline is nowhere present in the sketchbook (notwithstanding Schmidt-Görg's silent addition in each of the first two bars), it could be argued that all of the revisions within the autograph took place after the sketchbook entry. On the other hand, the pitches in the sketchbook version are closest to those in example 4b, the ultimate reading. The sketch entry may also have directly preceded example 4f, the only other instance in which the text is also underlaid. But in the end it is not crucial exactly where the Wittgenstein draft fits in; what is crucial is that such an entry could not have been made before the Kyrie was well under way.

In Wittgenstein, then, we have on the same page both very early notations for the Kyrie (those for the Christe on staff 12 bear even less resemblance to the final version) and at least one entry that relates directly to a specific passage worked out within the autograph. Since there is no reason to believe that the sketchbook has suffered structural damage either immediately before the earliest or after the latest Kyrie sketches, the reasonable inference is that the majority of work on this movement took place outside of the standard-format sketchbook. It is precisely Beethoven's generous reliance upon the cue staff throughout the heavily corrected portions of the autograph that lends support to the notion that Wittgenstein was utilized only peripherally in the drafting of the Kyrie.

A fragmentary but highly valuable morsel of evidence supplies a solid wedge of support for this interpretation. Although there are no surviving pocket sketches directly contemporary with folios 9^v–11^r in Wittgenstein, there is a pocket source whose entries are closely linked to several pages further on in the standard-format book. The two pocket leaves that remain from the earliest pocket sketchbook for the Mass (SBH 668) contain numerous notations for the Kyrie, Gloria, and Credo. The identifications in Schmidt[35] were doubtless facilitated by voluble inscriptions for the Kyrie ("Ky[rie] eleison, elei[son]"), for the Gloria ("omnipotens/orgel/posaun im pedal" on folio 1^r—exactly the point in the final version where Beethoven introduces the trombones for the first time [see measures 185 ff.]), and especially for the Credo ("credo andächtig/piano credo in unum/geheimnis/voll/et incarnatus/in g moll/et resurrexit" on folio 1^v; "kann durchaus/wiederholt 2mal credo credo/das incarnatus solo/der chor dazwischen/credo credo" on folio 2^r [see plates XVI–XVIII]). A few preliminary jottings for the Credo appear in Wittgenstein on folios 10^r, 11^r, and 12^r. But the one readily recognizable musical idea in SBH 668 is the motto theme of the Gloria (the only text to appear is "deo" at the bottom of folio 2^v [see plate XIX], but parallel entries in Wittgenstein confirm the association with the opening of the Gloria); under the lone Kyrie entry it makes its first appearance:

[35]SBH, p. 299.

Example 5. SBH 668, folio 1ʳ

The haste with which these entries were made—perhaps without their composer's breaking stride—precludes an unambiguous transcription. It is unclear, for example, whether staffs 5/6 continue directly to staffs 7/8, or whether the entry at the beginning of staff 8 (in a darker pencil; cf. plate XVI) belongs to the sketch (I have elected not to include it). But the A major interpretation of staffs 7/8 bears an uncanny resemblance to an entry on the same staffs of folio 14ʳ in Wittgenstein, where the opening three bars provide a dominant-chord upbeat to the following D major statement in octaves:

Example 6. Wittgenstein, folio 14ʳ

In addition, the tenor clef that presumably inaugurates the vocal portion of staff 7/8 in example 5 has its analogue in the very first appearance of the Gloria motto in Wittgenstein:

Example 7. Wittgenstein, folio 13ᵛ

From the disposition of this entire set of entries in the standard-format book, it is probable that Beethoven actually began on the bottom four staffs (13/16) with the alto and then the soprano before deciding to squeeze in the tenor and bass entries in front of them—perhaps taking his cue from the pocket volume. In fact, a second entry on folio 2ᵛ of SBH 668 is even more closely related to example 7:

Example 8. SBH 668, folio 2^v

Together, these four examples demonstrate that the entries in the pocket fragment were made about the same time that Beethoven was working on folios 13^v–14^r of the standard-format book. Hence of special interest is the brief entry in the pocket source for the Kyrie, sandwiched between the first Credo inscription and the Gloria head motive:

Example 9. SBH 668, folio 1^r

If we follow the suggestion of the supplied accidentals and read the texted portion in the soprano clef, then this brief excerpt matches well with both the pitches and the text of measures 156–62. (The viola or alto passage on staff 6 probably refers to the "eleison" motive.) What a single sketch can teach us about this particular passage is inconclusive, but from its mere presence we may infer several points. First, it is unlikely that Beethoven would have made this isolated entry before he had drafted the movement up to this point. In other words, during the half dozen pages of preliminary sketches for the Mass between folios 9^v and 14^r, he very probably drafted about three quarters of the Kyrie, most of it in score. Second, the fact that the autograph betrays no signs of compositional struggle at this juncture (see folios 17^v–18^r) reinforces Lester's hypothesis that such clean pages were replacements for earlier, heavily corrected ones. Third, the existence of this pocket sketch lends further credence to the supposition that there is no large cache of Kyrie sketches missing from sketchbooks (aside, of course, from what else may have been in SBH 668). Finally, the pocket entry offers more confirmatory evidence to that already assembled in Wittgenstein: Continuity sketching for the Kyrie took place not in the customary sketchbooks, but on cue staffs within the autograph itself. Lester's surmise that the cue staff was copied from earlier drafts in sketchbooks is certainly plausible, but in the case of the Kyrie it does not seem to have been true. In essence, Beethoven's confident vision of the Kyrie (and perhaps his zeal) led him to the decision—reckless, as it turned out—to proceed directly to the full score. Although Schindler's propensity for exaggeration and falsification is amply documented, the tortuous book of genesis transmitted in the Kyrie autograph supports the account offered in the first edition of his *Biographie*.

A primary motivation for this microscopic scrutiny of the Kyrie sketches was to determine whether the contents of the surviving sketchbooks support a general date of the spring of 1819 (more specifically, around the beginning of April) for Beethoven's commencement of work on the *Missa solemnis*. We have now established with some certainty that the Kyrie sketches in Wittgenstein are all that Beethoven made in standard format. Except for an undatable sketch for Op. 107, no. 3 on folio 2^r of Wittgenstein, all of the sketches before folio 9^v, as well as some or all of those on folios 9^v–11^r, belong to the other major work begun in this period, the Diabelli Variations, Op. 120. In spite of the wealth of composers who responded to Diabelli's call, we still do not know precisely when the appeal was first issued. What is apparently the earliest dated variation, that by Carl Czerny, is inscribed "7 May 1819"; there is no guarantee that this was the first variation submitted, and word of Diabelli's plan may have leaked to Beethoven even sooner. Even if the evidence of Wittgenstein may suggest a slightly later starting date of sometime around May for commencement of work on the Mass, it does not in the main undercut the evidence within the conversation book. At all events, their combined testimony suggests with considerable authority that the project could not have been started before April. The importance Beethoven attached to the Mass is demonstrated by his willingness to abandon—for more than three years, as it turned out—the Diabelli project after some nineteen variations had already been drafted.

Having established a context for the beginning of the Mass, the larger and even more complex issue is how work on the undertaking proceeded. In the remaining pages we can only point to a few of the high spots and suggest some directions for further exploration. Beginning with Nottebohm, writers have repeatedly noted the long period of gestation required for the completion of many of Beethoven's most celebrated works. It was Nottebohm whose sleuthing established that the earliest sketches that can be associated with the Fifth Symphony date back to the spring of 1804, four full years before the work's completion. Both Thayer and Nottebohm turned up evidence for perhaps the most spectacular example in Beethoven's œuvre, the Ninth Symphony, particularly its choral finale. According to a letter in early 1793 from Beethoven's Bonn friend Bartolomäus Fischenich to Charlotte von Schiller, Beethoven was already contemplating a strophe-by-strophe setting of the celebrated ode

"An die Freude." It was Nottebohm who pointed up the brief entry for excerpts from the ode in a sketchbook from 1798, Grasnick 1. His account of the now-lost Boldrini Sketchbook from 1818 included a sizable number of entries, largely for the first movement, with a few tentative ideas for other movements. Together with the more extensive sketches from 1823, then, it would appear that the gestation period of the Ninth Symphony encompassed a full three decades. But popular accounts generally fail to note either the intensity or continuousness of the sketching. A letter from 1793 and a few random entries in a sketchbook of five years later do not add up to intensive work, aside from there being as yet no connection with a symphony. The Boldrini sketches present little more than the opening bars of the first movement—Tovey's "mysteriously attractive humming sounds." Only when the composer returned to these sounds in the spring of 1823 did he focus his entire compositional energies on this still infant work, completing all but the final details in a ten-month burst of manic activity.

Close scrutiny of the sources for virtually all of Beethoven's major instrumental and choral works yields the same kind of results. In one important respect, the sheer bulk of the sketches has fostered the view of slow, laborious, and hence continuous struggle. But the mere existence of a vast body of material does not, in and of itself, say anything about the tempo and rhythm, so to speak, of creative activity. That Beethoven compulsively committed to paper ideas that most composers discarded before taking up the pen has only the most oblique connection with titanic struggle over a protracted period of time.

If there is one work that ought to reinforce the stereotype of slow and laborious struggle, it is surely the *Missa solemnis,* whose gestation spans not one but four standard-format books and almost a dozen pocket volumes—a situation unparalleled in the rest of Beethoven's output. No less an authority than Kinsky-Halm reckoned its "gesamte Entstehungszeit" at "4¼ Jahre." But assuming that work commenced in April of 1819, exactly how much of the next four-and-a-quarter years were actually devoted to its completion?

Making this determination requires dating a sizable number of late sketches, a tenuous affair at best. Biographical landmarks become relatively scarce after 1818, and the marked slowdown in the number of new works leaves fewer compositional traces as well. Even the indispensable aid donated by the conversation books and sketches in multiple formats rarely lends itself to a clear verdict. Take, for example, the seemingly straightforward question of when—and the more elusive one of why— Beethoven first interrupted work on the Mass to begin the Piano Sonata in E major, Op. 109:

Concordance	Wittgen-stein	SBH 665	Conversation Book[36]
Credo, "sub pontio Pilato"	fol. 34ᵛ	p. 2	
Credo, "et sepultus"	fol. 34ᵛ, st. 15/16	p. 3	I, 161 (c. Dec. 20,1819)
Closely related musical entries	fol. 36ᵛ, st. 7, 10	p. 4, st. 1–4	
First appearance of Credo head motive	fol. 37ʳ, st. 5/6	p. 4, st. 8	
Sanctus	fol. 41ʳ, st. 1 ff.	p. 20, st. 5 ff.	
Credo, opening with various tonic upbeats	fol. 43ᵛ, 44, Leaf I (Grasnick 20b, fol. 2)	pp. 21, 22, 28	I, 376 (c. March 24, 1820)
Gloria, Presto cf. mm. 525 ff.	fol. 43ᵛ, st. 1/2	p. 31, st. 1/2 ff. (a more worked-out version)	
Credo, "descendit"	fol. 42ᵛ; Leaf M (Grasnick 20b, fol. 6)	p. 20, st. 4	I, 385 (March 26–27, 1820)
Song, WoO 150, brief sketch unlike final version	Leaf I		Autograph dated March 4, 1820
"Sanct Petrus" Scherz, Hess 256		p. 32	I, 187, text only (early Jan., 1820) I, 245, refer-ence to WoO 175 (early Feb., 1820) Anderson no. 1067, WoO 175 (un-dated)

36The conversation book citations are from the Köhler-Herre edition; I,161 means

Outbursts against Johanna van Beethoven	Leaf J (Grasnick 20b, fol. 3)	I, 311 (March 6, 1820)
Op. 109/I	Leaves J-M pp. 39-41, 43 (Grasnick 20b, fols. 3-6)	II, 56, opening incipit (April 11-13, 1820)
	(Leaf K has conversation book incipit)	
"Hofmann" canon WoO 180	Leaf D (SBH 672)	I, 392, text only (March 29, 1820)
"Geh' Bauer" pun	p. 43	II, 52 (April 10, 1820)

There is, as we can see, rather close sequential correspondence between the entries in the larger, standard-format volume (Wittgenstein) and the pocket volume used out-of-doors (SBH 665; the Gloria entry in SBH 665 is clearly somewhat later than that in Wittgenstein). The problems arise in attempting to match these with the scattered references in the conversation books, or with other biographical evidence. If one argues that Beethoven would have drafted the "Sanct Petrus" Scherz shortly after entering an initial version of the text in a conversation book, then it would appear he could have commenced work on Op. 109 as early as January. If one looks instead to the song sketch, then—assuming Leaf I is correctly reinstated into Wittgenstein at this point—he probably began the sonata in March. But if one finds most persuasive the musical concordances of late March between the Credo entries in Wittgenstein, SBH 665, and the conversation books, as well as the incipit from early April, then the sonata could not have been started before that month. After the claims of each evidentiary strand are weighed, the following conclusions suggest themselves in this instance:

1) The critical sketch is that for WoO 150. Assuming that the short entry found on Leaf I in Wittgenstein (one unlike the final version) preceded the writing-out of the brief autograph, then the work to this point in the standard-format book could not have been completed any later than the first few days in March. Against the argument that Leaf I was not originally part of Wittgenstein is its place in the sequence of leaves from Grasnick 20b, one that partially fills a demonstrable void at this point in the sketchbook. In addition, the two entries for the opening of

Band I, p. 161, and so forth. It must be said that the transcriptions of musical entries are among the few faulty aspects of these generally reliable volumes.

the Credo on Leaf I, each preceded by a tonic upbeat similar to those found on folios 43–44, provide strong confirmatory evidence of the original adjacency of these leaves.

2) Hence the two Credo entries from late March in the conversation books must have been made three to four weeks following their earliest appearance in the sketchbooks.

3) Conversely to 1), the sketch for Hess 256 on page 32 of SBH 665 does not provide a solid chronological anchor. To begin with, the text of the pocket sketch curiously reverses that of the January conversation book:

Conversation book: "Sankt Petrus ist/kein Fels,/Auf ihn kann man/ nicht bauen."[37]

Sketchbook: "Sanct Petrus ist ein Fels[,] Auf/diesen kann man bauen[.]"

In the February entry Hofrat Karl Peters writes: "Die 2 schönen Canon/sind gewiss schon ausge/löscht."[38] He is surely referring to the two brief riddle canons, WoO 175, that Beethoven enclosed in Anderson letter no. 1067. Although Kastner-Kapp (pp. 547–48) placed the letter in 1820, Anderson assigned it, without comment, to 1821 ("1881" is actually printed, but 1821 is surely meant). The conversation book entries suggest that the canons were composed and dispatched around January of 1820. But musically these have only the opening incipits in common with the three-part, largely homophonic Scherz found in the pocket volume, and there is no reason to assume that both were conceived at the same time. An equally convincing stimulus for returning to "Sanct Petrus" was provided by the appeals court decision of April 8, 1820, which reversed an earlier verdict and now granted Beethoven and Peters exclusive coguardianship of Beethoven's nephew. At all events, there is no need to date the pocket draft much before April.

4) A similar situation prevails for the complete draft of the "Hofmann" canon, WoO 180. Although Beethoven's first reference to this somewhat lame pun ("Hoffmann, Hoffmann, sei ja kein Hofmann") surfaces as early as around March 12 in the conversation books, the words that are actually set on Leaf D of SBH 665 do not appear until March 29. It is not very likely that the composer drafted the music before deciding upon its text.

5) The Op. 109 sketches in the standard-format and pocket sources are not directly parallel. Those from Grasnick 20b show the movement at its moment of conception; no more than the first eight bars reach anything like their final form. The pocket volume, on the other hand, contains spe-

---

[37] *Beethovens Konversationshefte*, Band I, p. 187 [fol. 12ᵛ].
[38] *Beethovens Konversationshefte*, Band I, p. 245 [fol. 34ᵛ].

cific work for the development (including measures 18–19 and 25–41), the end of the recapitulation (measures 63 ff. *passim*), and the coda (including measures 77–85). This squares well with the concordances already discussed, and suggests that the movement was begun during the early part of March (in Wittgenstein), and that its completion (in SBH 665 and perhaps elsewhere) stretched on into April. It had probably reached an advanced stage by about April 24, when Beethoven's friend Oliva noted, half questioning, in a conversation book: "und benutzen Sie das kleine neue Stück zu einer Sonate fur den Schlesinger etwa" ["and you will use the little new piece in a sonata for Schlesinger"].[39] Since a "Sonate" is not mentioned among the surviving sketches, nor further movements indicated, it is possible that Beethoven initially planned only a single movement, altering his plans after taking up negotiations about new sonatas with Adolf Martin Schlesinger.[40]

We can only speculate as to why Beethoven interrupted the considerable momentum of the Credo to take up new projects. The piano piece was not the only one contemplated; the leaves from Grasnick 20b also resurrect the germinal symphony last addressed in the Boldrini Sketchbook of 1818, adding several ideas for further movements. The renewed interest in the symphony may have related to talk of a planned "Akademie" in a conversation book entry of March 11.[41] It is also possible that Beethoven was experiencing a higher than usual level of anxiety as the prolonged, exhausting litigation over the guardianship of his nephew Karl drew to a head; the composer received a favorable verdict on April 8, but it was at the cost of much of his honor and self-respect. Finally, the Archduke's installation on March 9 may have freed Beethoven psychologically from a single-minded commitment to the Mass project.

This same kind of detailed reasoning *cum* speculation is demanded frequently when considering the multilayered evolution of the Mass. By balancing the categories of evidence discussed above, we can reconstruct a reasonably accurate picture of Beethoven's creative activity between April, 1819 and mid-1823. The dates offered below refer to the main sketching on a given work or movement (canons are not included), with the most tenuous boundaries marked "circa"; none of them can be off by more than a month or so:

---

[39] *Beethovens Konversationshefte*, Band II, p. 87 [fol. 49ʳ].

[40] For the most recent background to Beethoven's dealings with Schlesinger, see Alan Tyson, "New Beethoven Letters and Documents," in Alan Tyson, ed., *Beethoven Studies 2* (London, 1977), pp. 24–26. Since Schlesinger's letter of April 11, 1820 is lost, we cannot say for sure whether he specifically requested new sonatas from the composer.

[41] *Beethovens Konversationshefte*, Band I, p. 322 [fols. 3ᵛ–4ᵛ].

Date	Work: Movement
April–c. May, 1819	*Missa solemnis*, Op. 123: Kyrie
c. June–December, 1819	Op. 123: Gloria
c. January–early March, 1820	Op. 123: Credo (through drafting of "Et vitam" fugue subject); early Sanctus
March–April, 1820	Piano Sonata in E major, Op. 109: first movement
c. late April–c. July, 1820	Op. 123: Credo, especially completion of "et vitam" fugue
c. August–October, 1820	Op. 109: second and third movements
c. November 1820–February, 1821	Op. 123: Benedictus (and more Sanctus?)
January 1, 1821	Bagatelles, Op. 119, nos. 7–11 (date of autograph)
c. March–July, 1821	Op. 123: Agnus Dei and Dona
August–December, 1821	Piano Sonata in A♭ major, Op. 110 (with first version of finale)
December, 1821–c. late March (early April?), 1822	Piano Sonata in C minor, Op. 111
early January, 1822	Op. 110: definitive version of finale
c. April–August, 1822	Op. 123: more Dona and basic completion of autograph score (beginning of copying?)
September, 1822	WoO 98; Op. 124
October–November, 1822	Op. 123: final revisions in autograph
November, 1822	Bagatelles, Op. 119, nos. 1–6 (date of autograph)
December, 1822	Ariette, "Der Kuss," Op. 128: reworking
April, 1823	"Lobkowitz" Cantata, WoO 106
November, 1822–mid-1823	Op. 123: preparation of copies, (with addition of trombone and organ parts); completion of Op. 120 in April, 1823, followed by continuous work on the Ninth Symphony

A few of these items require brief comment. As already noted in the Concordance Table, early ideas for the Sanctus appear near the end of Wittgenstein, as well as in SBH 107 (with the opening motive commencing in both instances a whole tone lower). The movement was almost certainly left in a fragmentary state at this juncture and finished at a later occasion. The most likely time slot for its completion is the end of 1820 or the beginning of 1821, when Beethoven is known to have been working on the Benedictus, and when we can hypothesize a gap in the desk sketchbook then in use, Artaria 195.

Further, it is difficult to pinpoint the date by which Op. 111 was completed. If we take seriously Beethoven's claim of April 9 in a letter to Adolf Martin Schlesinger that he will be dispatching a second copy of the finale of Op. 111 by the next day's post (Anderson no. 1074), then we might presume that he had completed the first version by early March. But Beethoven was prone to dissemble in such matters, and almost a month later he wrote again to Schlesinger (Anderson no. 1075), expressing the anxious hope that the replacement movement had now arrived. In evaluating this evidence it is useful to keep in mind that the composition of Op. 110 occupied Beethoven for a good five months. Both of the last two sonatas necessitated second autographs for their finales (and Op. 111 is no less complex for having only two movements). Their composer had already engaged in a colorful series of wishful promises to dispatch both of them soon, dating back to September of 1820.

There is also the potentially misleading but not entirely irrelevant circumstance that the sketches for Op. 111 in Artaria 201 occupy more than three-quarters of the eighty pages that we can assign with near certainty to the first nine months of 1822; even if Beethoven had reached page 21 by the 13th of January, he still had to complete a very resistant *Urschrift* of the first movement, draft the intricate finale (no other movement of a piano sonata is sketched so extensively), write out the autographs of both movements, supervise a copy to be sent to Schlesinger, revise the variations, and, finally, supervise a second copy of this movement to be dispatched to Berlin. In light of all the circumstantial evidence that inveighs against an uncritical acceptance of Beethoven's claim in the April 9 letter, I am inclined to believe that work on the various phases of Op. 111 occupied the composer more or less continuously until at least late March of 1822, and it would not be at all surprising if the final completion of the project extended until mid-April (he was, of course, compiling corrections to Schlesinger's edition as late as the early summer of 1823), whereafter Beethoven finally returned to uninterrupted work on the Mass.

This same kind of skepticism must be exercised when attempting to fix the date by which the main composition of the Mass was complete. In the letter of June 5, 1822 quoted at the outset of this essay, Beethoven refers to the work as if it were finished. The same tone is adopted in a letter of a month later to Ferdinand Ries (Anderson no. 1084). In fact, as early as mid-May the composer informed Franz Brentano in Frankfurt that he was "having the score copied over again" (Anderson no. 1076). But there is very likely some of his habitual over-optimism involved here as well. At least one major revision to the autograph of the Credo, and another smaller one involving the end of the Gloria, turns up as late as October or November (see the following discussion of autograph revisions). Unless Beethoven was engaged in the wasteful (and expensive) practice of making changes to a work after he had farmed it out for copying, much—if not most—of this activity took place after October. Only a detailed investigation of the structural properties of a significant number of the supervised copies could fix the full extent of Beethoven's exaggerations.

What the sketches do sustain is the notion that by the end of August the major creative work on the Mass was complete, for about this time Beethoven accepted a commission to add two pieces to those already composed for "The Ruins of Athens" a decade earlier, as part of the musical celebrations for the opening of the Josephstadt Theater. There are no further entries after this for the Dona, the last major section to be composed. From this point the problems that remained were not those of invention, but of refinement. The subsequent trickle of smaller works that begins in November of 1822 with the autograph of the first six of the Op. 119 bagatelles provides further evidence that the project was now largely complete.

Between April, 1819 and August, 1822, there were three large-scale interruptions of work on the Mass. The first, Op. 109, halted progress at a crucial juncture in the Credo, although Beethoven was not able to complete the sonata until he had returned to absorb the considerable momentum of the fugue on "et vitam venturi." A less dramatic but considerably lengthier interruption of nine months ensued at the end of 1821, during which the two final piano sonatas were produced. (A more colorful—and fictitious—account of the genesis of the last three sonatas can be found in Thomas Mann's *Doktor Faustus.*) There is virtually no interplay between sonata and Mass sketches within the desk-sized books, and the modest amount found among the pocket sources does not necessarily reflect the actual chronology. In the main, it is fair to say that work on the Mass ground periodically to a temporary but emphatic halt. No other work of Beethoven's presents such a stop-and-go evolution.

The actual elapsed time spent in the basic composition of the *Missa solemnis,* then, covers a period of some twenty-nine months between April of 1819 and August of 1822. This is, to be sure, a considerable amount of time, but for a work of nearly two thousand measures, involving more than two dozen separate orchestral and vocal parts, it is scarcely excessive. Nor should we be surprised that an additional eight or nine months were required to complete the arduous task of preparing and correcting more than a dozen manuscript copies. Hence it would seem that while Beethoven was prone to exaggerate the speed with which he could compose, we are equally prone to exaggerate the chronological dimensions of the struggle. Beethoven—as many a writer or scholar will ruefully acknowledge—was only engaging in the time-honored custom of setting a delivery date that presumed the most ideal of working conditions. In the end his chronic procrastination (crossing the thin line into conscious deception an uncomfortable number of times) seems to have exercised only a beneficial effect upon the artwork itself.

This picture of the bedrock compositional layer tells only half the story. The sources make clear that Beethoven alternated between the initial drafting of movements in the sketchbooks and the ongoing effort to create a finished autograph of portions previously sketched. Although, as we have already noted, the autograph of the Gloria is lost, happily the almost 280 pages required for the Credo, Sanctus, and Agnus Dei do survive. Their appearance is fundamentally different from that of the Kyrie autograph. Although Artaria 202 still leans most of the time toward the category of a composing score or *Urschrift*, there is virtually no reliance on a cue staff for guidance. The presence of long continuity segments within the sketchbooks themselves attests to this basic shift in strategy. By the time he reached the Credo autograph (and probably already within the Gloria), Beethoven realized that more advance preparation and planning was necessary before he could embark upon a full score.

We can gain valuable insights into the parallel progress made in the autograph by locating the passages within the sketchbooks and conversation books that relate specifically to its revisions.[42] In addition to the entries in Wittgenstein and SBH 668 already discussed, a single entry on folio 43^r of the standard-format book almost certainly pertains to measures 29–31 in the autograph of the Kyrie:

Example 10. Wittgenstein, folio 43^r

---

[42]The first scholar to call attention to Beethoven's habit of entering corrections in an autograph within a sketchbook was Lewis Lockwood in his discussion of the A major

Although folio 3^v in Autograph 1 shows heavy corrections at this spot in the winds, these simply concern the distribution of the $\frac{7}{2}$ spelling specified in the sketch. Folio 3^v probably represents a correction to the previous leaf in the autograph, which was the first to be excised. This Kyrie revision occurs directly following a pencil draft for the conclusion of the Gloria (beginning on page 20 of Artaria 180; not included in the Schmidt-Görg transcription), suggesting that Beethoven was simultaneously engaged in drafting the Credo, finishing the Gloria, and making a final pass through the autograph of the Kyrie.

Both of these standard-format entries were presumably made toward the end of February, 1820, and it is probably not a coincidence that the Kyrie and Gloria were each reaching their final form just before Beethoven took his first break from continuous work on the Mass. This picture is reinforced by three other bits of evidence relating to the Gloria. The first is a conversation-book entry from mid-December, 1819 for measures 272–74 ("miserere").[43] The second is a similar entry from late January, 1820 for the bass part of measures 507–12.[44] Both of these seemingly random jottings were doubtless linked to corrections made in the now lost Gloria autograph. Finally, these are congruent with the less developed sketches for the final Presto (measures 525 ff.) found in both Wittgenstein and SBH 665 (see the previous Concordance Table).

A similar combing-through of the remainder of the Mass sources reveals several more such interrelationships between sketch and autograph. The most spectacular of these are the multiple drafts for the "judicare" of the Credo, many—though by no means all—of which are quoted by Nottebohm in *Zweite Beethoveniana*, p. 155. Although Nottebohm makes no mention of it, a quick glance at the autograph (cf. Artaria 202, folios 28–29) confirms the direct link between it and all of these versions. Falling as they do toward the end of Artaria 201 (see pages 109 and 121) and on a loose leaf also containing sketches for no. 6 of the Op. 119 bagatelles (see Paris, Bibliothèque Nationale, Ms. 58, no. 4), these revisions from c. November, 1822 are probably among the last significant internal changes made by the composer. Considerably less extensive but no less arresting is the brief entry on staffs 4/5 of page 110 in Artaria 201, which at last presents the ultimate version of the end of the Gloria—a problem

cello sonata, Op. 69; see Lockwood, "On Beethoven's Sketches and Autographs," pp. 38–40.

[43]*Beethovens Konversationshefte*, Band I, p. 145 [inside front cover].

[44]*Beethovens Konversationshefte*, Band I, p. 227 [inside front cover]. Because of their placement within the respective volumes it is possible that both this and the previous entry were made somewhat outside of the strict chronological sequence; there is, however, no reason to think they were done substantially outside of the time frame encompassed by the individual volumes.

first addressed by Beethoven in Wittgenstein almost two and a half years earlier. The solution reached by the composer, with its avoidance of the final downbeat in the chorus, literally hurls a metrically unfettered shout of praise out into the universe.

A work embodying as many evolutionary layers as the *Missa solemnis* is not likely to yield up its secrets easily. Although the Mass in C of a decade earlier served in some respects as a prototype (particularly in its symphonic cast), the *Missa solemnis* posed compositional problems that were unique in Beethoven's four-and-a-half decades as a composer. Only once before had he been deprived of the sonata aesthetic in a large-scale work in a major genre, and—as is amply documented—the creation of *Leonore/Fidelio* had given him fits. By 1819 he had demonstrated his unparalleled mastery of every instrumental genre within the Viennese classical style. In the hands of his contemporaries the sacred tradition at best recycled tired formulae, more often descending to a level indistinguishable from operatic pastiche. From the frequency with which Beethoven's friends and acquaintances inquired in the conversation books of 1819 and 1820 about progress on the Mass, we can surmise that its composer attacked the seemingly insoluble problems with an intensity and resolve remarkable even for him. As this preliminary survey has sought to illustrate, few of Beethoven's works have left behind so graphic an account of their genesis as this extraordinary *pièce d'occasion*. If we have proposed solutions to a few of its most basic riddles, far more remain to be posed and answered within its remarkably rich repository of primary sources.

Appendix A

Unstitched Pocket Sketches for the Missa Solemnis

No fewer than twenty loose bundles of pocket sketches have survived for the *Missa solemnis*. A half dozen of these consist of either a single pocket bifolium or a larger unit that was never torn into separate bifolia. Another ten are found on adjacent leaves within the sketch complex Artaria 180 + 200. Finally, four bundles must be reconstructed from separate locations within this same manuscript. All three categories are included below in the order of their contents (except for no. 4, presumably used in some proximity to no. 3). Although a general chronology results, an accurate internal chronology—especially in the case of the abundant sketches for the "et vitam venturi" fugue—must await detailed transcription and study of these documents.

The size of the bundle is given in portions of a standard-format gathered sheet. For example, a ³/₄ sheet contains three standard-format leaves = three pocket bifolia = six pocket leaves. The information supplied concerning paper types is limited to the number of staffs, the total span in millimeters (TS), and the principal sketchbook that employs the identical paper type. (For our purposes, "paper type" includes both the sheet watermark and the staff ruling.) Readers interested in pursuing this dimension further can find complete details in our forthcoming *The Beethoven Sketchbooks*, by Douglas Johnson, Alan Tyson, and Robert Winter. Where a paper type is not used in a sketchbook, a brief description of the watermark is appended. Since Artaria 180 + 200 is numbered as a series of standard-format leaves, L and R are used to distinguish the left and right sides of a pocket bifolium. The modern numbering, whereby Artaria 200 is an extension of the 1–102 pagination of Artaria 180, is used. The succession of pages given is the suggested order from beginning to end within the reconstructed bundle (the sign / indicates the bibliographic center), and is based upon features such as watermark succession, the bias of the central fold, the presence of writing across this fold, and musical and notational connections within the proposed bundle. Where a pocket bifolium is suspected to be missing, this is indicated within the bundle by upper-case letters (A?, B?, etc.).

1. Artaria 180; pp. 29R, 30L/30R, 29L. A ¹/₄ sheet for the Gloria; 12 staffs, TS = 186 + to 187 mm. KIESLING watermark similar to that on paper used to sketch the finale of Op. 106 (cf. SV 43, 143, 385, and a sheet in the Scheide Library, Princeton [not in SV]). Another single pocket leaf bearing a related KIESLING watermark and identical rastrology (London, British Library, Add. Ms. 29997, fol. 10) includes sketches for a canon, "Cacatum non est pictum," as well as for the fugue of the Gloria. However, its irregularly torn inner margin conveys the appearance of having been removed from a sewn bundle (doubtless to obtain the canon, as is the case with SBH 672).

2. Artaria 180, pp. 110R, 109L, A?, 108R, 107L, 106R, 105L/105R, 106L, 107R, 108L, A?, 109R, 110L. A ³/₄ sheet for the Credo; 12 staffs, TS = 186 to 186- mm. Paper type iden-

tical to that in the pocket sketchbooks A 44 and A 45 (GdM), used to draft the last two movements of Op. 106.

3. Artaria 180, pp. 43R, 44L, 45R, 46L/46R, 45L, 44R, 43L plus Artaria 205, bundle 6c. These two ½ sheets probably belonged to the same original sheet, although this can no longer be shown conclusively. Sketches for the Credo; 20 staffs, TS = 353 to 355 mm. Anomalous paper type found otherwise only in Artaria 153, pp. 97–100 (DSB) and in the following entry. Features a large shield in quadrants 1 and 2 and a crown with the letters IRM underneath in quadrants 3 and 4.

4. Paris, Bibliothèque Nationale, Ms. 58, No. 1. A full sheet used in folded but uncut fashion. Includes sketches for an "agnus," presumably intended for Op. 123; same paper type as 3.

5. Artaria 180, pp. 49R, 50L, A?, 52R, 51L, 54R, 53L/53R, 54L, 51R, 52L, A?, 50R, 49L. A ¾ sheet for the Credo, "et vitam"; same paper type as 1.

6. Artaria 180, pp. 40R, 39L, 38R, 37L, A?, 41R, 42L/42R, 41L, A?, 37R, 38L, 39R, 40L. A ¾ sheet for the Credo, "et vitam"; 12 staffs, TS = 186+ to 187- mm. Same paper type as the fragment of a stitched pocket volume, Artaria 180, pp. 23–26, 31–32 + SBH 669.

7. Artaria 180, pp. 57R, 58L, 56R, 55L, 91R, 92L, 93R, 94L/94R, including "et vitam"; 16 staffs, TS = 194 to 195- mm. Same paper type as the Wittgenstein Sketchbook.

8. Artaria 180 + 200, pp. 99R, 100L, 103R, 104L, 101R, 102L, 97R, 98L/98R, 97L, 102R, 101L, 104R, 103L, 100R, 99L. A full sheet for the Credo ("et vitam") and Benedictus; same paper type as 7.

9. Artaria 180, pp. 66R, 65L, 64R, 63L, 59R, 60L, 61R, 62L/ 62R, 61L, 60R, 59L, 63R, 64L, 65R, 66L. A full sheet for the Credo; 16 staffs, TS = 196- to 196+ mm. Same as one of two related paper types in Artaria 195, the standard-format book of 1820 for the Mass.

10. Artaria 180, pp. A?, 89R, 90L, B?, 95R, 96L/96R, 95L, B?, 90R, 89L, A? A ½ sheet for the Credo; same paper type as 9.

11. DSB, Aut. 55, part 2. A ⅝ sheet, uncut but used in pocket format for the Credo; 12 staffs, TS = 187 mm. Same paper type as SBH 665, 666, and 667, the series of three pocket sketchbooks for the Credo and Benedictus.

12. Artaria 180, pp. 48R, 47L/47R, 48L. A ¼ sheet for the Credo, "et vitam"; same paper type as 11.

13. SBH 670. A ¼ sheet for the Credo, "et vitam"; same paper type as 11.

14. DSB, Artaria 205, bundle 6b. A ¼ sheet for the Agnus Dei; same paper type as 11.

15. Artaria 180, pp. 81R, 82L/82R, 81L. A ¼ sheet for the Dona; 16 staffs, TS = 196- to 196+ mm. KIESLING watermark similar to that found on pp. 17–20, 25–28 of Artaria 196 (SPK), the autograph of Op. 110.

16. Artaria 180, pp. 80R, 79L, 83R, 84L, 14R, 13L, 11R, 12L/12R, 11L, 13R, 14L, 84R, 83L, 79R, 80L. A full sheet for the Dona; same paper type as 15.

17. Artaria 180, pp. 15R, 16L, 17R, 18L, 78R, 77L, 76R, 75L/75R, 76L, 77R, 78L, 18R, 17L, 16R, 15L. A full sheet for the Dona; same paper type as 15.

18. SBH 671. A ¼ sheet for the Dona; 16 staffs, TS = 196+ to 196.5 mm. Watermark shows three widely spaced horizontal moons; matches no other known types.

19. Artaria 180, pp. 4R, 3L, 6R, 5L, 8R, 7L, 10R, 9L/9R, 10L, 7R, 8L, 5R, 6L, 3R, 4L. A full sheet for the Dona; 16 staffs, TS = 194+ to 195- mm. Same paper type as all but the outer sheet of Artaria 201, the standard-format book of 1822 for the Mass.

20. Artaria 180, pp. 67R, 68L, 69R, 70L, A?, 71R, 72L/72R, 71L, A?, 70R, 69L, 68R, 67L. A ¾ sheet for the Dona; 16 staffs, TS = 196- to 196+ mm. Same paper type (though from a brownish rather than a greenish batch) as the Engelmann Sketchbook from the spring of 1823.

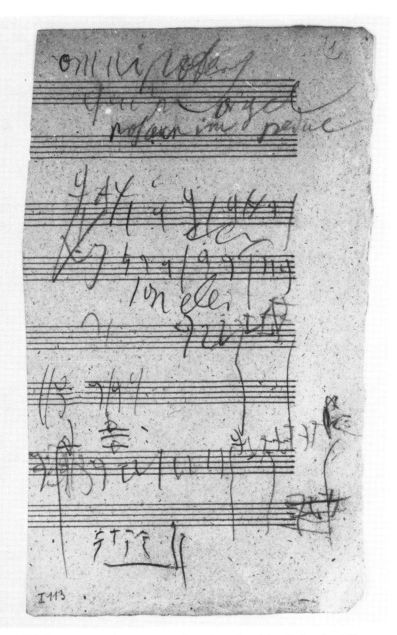

Plate XVI. Fragment of a presumed pocket sketchbook for the *Missa solemnis* (Bonn, Beethovenhaus, SBH 668 [BH110]), folio 1ʳ

Plate XVII. SBH 668, folio 1ᵛ

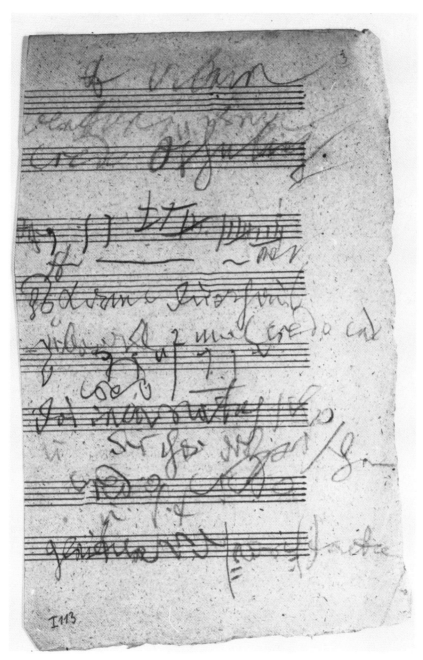

Plate XVIII. SBH 668, folio 2^r

Plate XIX. SBH 668, folio 2ᵛ

Index of Beethoven's Works

General Index